*Partnerning with*

# Earth

*The Incarnation of a Soul*

A Lorian Association Textbook by
## David Spangler

# Partnering with Earth
## *The Incarnation of a Soul*

ISBN-13: 978-0-936878-60-7

Spangler/David
Partnering with Earth/David Spangler

First Edition August 2013

Published by:
LORIAN PRESS
2204 E Grand Ave
Everett, WA 98201

**LORIAN PRESS** is a private, for profit business which publishes works approved by the Lorian Association. Current titles by David Spangler and others can be found on the Lorian website www.lorian.org.

**THE LORIAN ASSOCIATION** is a not-for-profit educational organization. Its work is to help people bring the joy, healing, and blessing of their personal spirituality into their everyday lives. This spirituality unfolds out of their unique lives and relationships to Spirit, by whatever name or in whatever form that Spirit is recognized.

For more information, go to www.lorian.org or email info@lorian.org

# Contents

This textbook derives from the transcript of an online class called *Down to Earth* presented by the Lorian Association in 2012. The content has been shaped in part by the unique nature of the online classroom environment and by each of the participants. It has minimal editing to preserve the flavor of the original class.

# INTRODUCTION

My objective for this book is that at the end, you will have an understanding of the Self—your self—as seen through the lens of Incarnational Spirituality. Further, I hope that this will give you an expanded and empowered view of yourself, of who you are as an incarnate person. To do this, we will be looking both at a set of ideas and at the application of those ideas in your everyday life. This book has a philosophical and cosmological component, but its ultimate intent is a practical one. The benefits of Incarnational Spirituality come from being lived, not simply thought about or believed in.

Let me begin by telling a story.

When I was seventeen, I had a vision that in various ways has guided my work ever since. It came spontaneously, triggered by a question that a friend asked me about what I saw myself doing in the future, a perfectly appropriate question as I was just about to enter college. The vision itself was fairly simple: a generic figure glowing with Light that changed into a chalice or grail and back again. With it came a message that said in essence that this was an image of the light and spirituality inherent in the incarnate state. In other words, it wasn't a vision of some subtle being or transpersonal state but one of the potential of being incarnated as a physical person.

At the time, there was nothing I could do with this vision other than register it as something interesting. But three years later, I had left college, moved to Los Angeles from Phoenix, and started a career as a spiritual teacher—something I could not imagine and did not imagine myself doing when I was seventeen. I wanted to be a molecular biologist!

In Los Angeles I began working with a non-physical being whom I called John, who became my partner, colleague and mentor for the next 27 years. (The details of this story and more are in my book, *Apprenticed to Spirit.*) He originally introduced himself as someone interested in the blending and integration of the soul and personality—the transpersonal and personal sides of ourselves—and in the days before I moved to Scotland and became a co-director of the Findhorn Community, that integration was the focus of our work.

In particular, John said it was necessary to move beyond what he called the "problem of the transpersonal." This "problem" had four parts. It created a false dichotomy between different vital aspects of ourselves, generating internal conflict. It privileged the transpersonal in inappropriate ways over the personal so that integration between the two became more difficult. It created a "crack" or "fault line" in our personal energy field that made contact and partnership with higher energy beings more challenging and potentially dangerous than it needed to be. And finally, the times in which we are living need attention on the incarnate levels. In effect, the flow of life had shifted on a planetary level from being focused on the "higher," transpersonal dimensions to being focused on the physical and "incarnate" realms. As one subtle being put it to me many years later, "the problem with humanity is that you're not incarnated enough."

It wasn't that the transpersonal levels were wrong or dangerous in themselves, only that a balance needed to be restored, one that honored the physical world and physical incarnation—and the personal self—as much as it honored the transpersonal, the non-physical, and the infinite. Wholeness, integration, and coherency were the keywords.

The point of this story is that right from the beginning of my work, I had an interest in the nature of the self as a whole being. The seeds of what many years later has become Incarnational Spirituality were planted then. Likewise this book has its roots in my vision as a seventeen year-old and in my early work with John.

This idea of wholeness is a thread that will run throughout our work together in this book. Later I'll define more fully what I mean by it. For now I simply want to alert us to its presence as a theme. I'll be talking about what I call holopoiesis, the natural impulse within us to manifest wholeness. This, too, will be a consistent theme.

My approach in this book will not be psychological. I have no training in psychology and have only an educated layman's knowledge of the field based on my own reading. Nor is my approach philosophical. Again, I have no training or background in philosophy. Instead, I approach this phenomenon of the self as a seer, a kind of "esoteric naturalist," someone who observes the working of subtle energies and subtle beings. This book is really a sharing of my "field notes."

I do not regard this material as cast in concrete or as "revelations" from "on high." It is a perspective based on my explorations as one person. I try to make my observations as accurate and clear as possible, but the nature of the subtle worlds is such that someone else exploring the same terrain might experience and see something different or come up with different interpretations. And the exploration is ongoing. There is nothing final about what I'm presenting in this book. Think of it as a set of hypotheses growing out of a continuing process of investigation and observation.

We'll begin with an overview of the incarnational process itself, what I call "incarnation in three acts." This is the means by which the soul manages to be "Partnering with Earth."

The incarnational process gives us a context for exploring the following ideas:

Soul and Identity
The Chalice and Holding
The Incarnational System
Self-Light
Emergent Self
The Generative Self

These ideas will guide and shape our discussions over the bulk of the book.

# CHAPTER ONE, INCARNATION:
# A PLAY IN THREE ACTS

## GAIA: EARTH AS ORGANISM

In 1979, the British scientist James Lovelock published *Gaia: A New Look at Life on Earth*. In this book he reintroduced the modern world to the idea that the planet as a whole was a living organism, which he named "Gaia," drawing on Greek mythology. I happened to know Lovelock and his collaborator on the Gaia Hypothesis, Lynn Margulis, who during her lifetime was one of the world's most prominent microbiologists and who was responsible for showing in the laboratory that synthesis and cooperation were more important in the course of evolution than competition. I was privileged to be with them on several occasions when they debated together the degree to which Gaia was truly an organism; James was willing to go further in that direction, it seemed to me, than was Lynn who was more hard-headed as a scientist.

What did astonish James was the extent to which his work and the Gaia Hypothesis were taken up and promoted by people involved in various spiritual pursuits. He felt he had been addressing the community of scientists—who had a hard time at first accepting his proposals—and discovered instead that the ones who most listened to him were religious and New Age people. This wasn't surprising, though. The idea that the earth is a living being is an ancient one, perhaps one of our most ancient spiritual ideas. Modern western culture is one of the very few societies in history that hasn't had some concept of the earth as being alive. When Lovelock offered what appeared to many as scientific proof of this ancient perception, it's not surprising that the idea took off and became enshrined in recent spiritual history.

While the Gaia Hypothesis has garnered enough supporting evidence over the years since 1979 to now rank as the Gaia Theory (i.e. it's no longer hypothetical), earth as organism is a far cry from the motherly, loving, overlighting, powerful spiritual being that the name Gaia suggests. It is seen simply as a possibly sentient but definitely dynamic system of homeostasis, or more precisely of homeorhesis. The difference is between a system that merely returns to a particular state again and again and one that returns to a "trajectory" of states that change over time, a dynamic arc of unfoldment and development. But there is no will involved, no directing consciousness governing the process.

The Gaia Theory is a welcome step forward for our highly materialistic culture, a step that opens the door to a broader understanding and perception of life. But it's still just a small step. The Gaia of the Gaia Theory is conceived of as an organism roughly equivalent in sentiency to a single-celled microbe, operating mainly through its homeostatic and homeorhetic automatic response systems. It is not seen as a truly conscious or purpose-driven entity.

Our own body has such regulatory systems as well which serve to keep us within a particular temperature range and which adjust various other chemical and hormonal balances within our bodies. But we experience ourselves as much more than just the sum total of their operation. We experience will, purpose, the capacity to imagine and to think, the felt sense of an identity. We experience a self that is more than the simple total of bodily processes.

Subtle perception suggests that this is true for Gaia as well. Yes, the simple regulatory processes described in the Gaia Theory do exist, but much more is there as well. Gaia is a living soul, a planetary spirit, holding in itself resources of will and purpose that foster the evolution of life and consciousness within and upon its planetary body. The nature of this spirit and its level of consciousness may be beyond our capacity to fully understand, but on the other hand, it is a sentient field within which we participate. In some ways, as part of the earth, we also are a part of Gaia.

Our book is an exploration into the nature of self as seen from an incarnational perspective. This exploration must begin with Gaia for that is where the processes of incarnation—the very nature of incarnation as we know it—begin. After all, as physical persons, we are incarnated into the body and energy field of this great Being. Our selves participate in the Self of Gaia, something we'll explore in more detail as we go along in this book.

To understand this, we need to appreciate that Gaia as an organism exists in its own cosmic environment. We live in the midst of mountains and plains, rivers and oceans, deserts and jungles, but Gaia lives in the midst of suns and stars. It is traveling through space at approximately 575,000 MPH. This is just on the physical level. Looking into the non-physical realms, we find our world in a web of dynamic relationships with many types of stellar, solar, and planetary consciousnesses.

As a consequence Gaia lives in what I can think of as an "energy-rich environment," one that is filled with life, ideas, inspiration, creativity, and other qualities, and in this environment our world is a growing, evolving Being, taking in what it can and giving out to the cosmos what it has to contribute.

## CIRCULATION

In Figure 1 we see Gaia interacting with its cosmic environment. It is drawing in subtle energies from the stars and subtle energies from the sun (really, from the great Lives and spiritual Presences that embody the stars, of which our sun is one as the star closest to the earth).

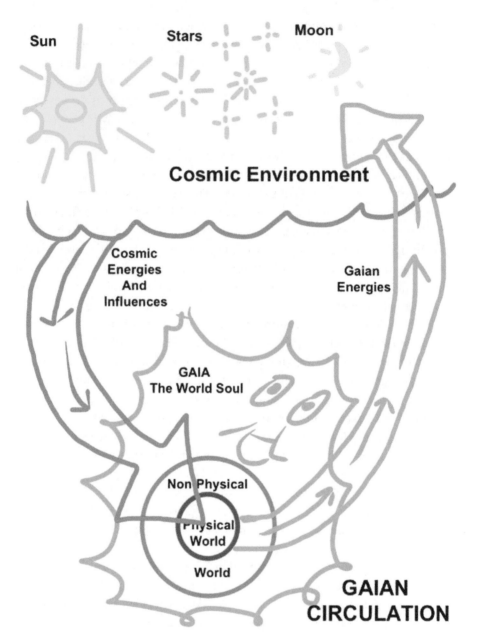

Sun          Stars          Moon

**Cosmic Environment**

Cosmic
Energies
And
Influences

Gaian
Energies

GAIA
The World Soul

Non Physical

Physical
World

World

**GAIAN
CIRCULATION**

FIGURE 1

These subtle energies are received by the overall life-field of the Earth, of Gaia, but they must then be "digested" and assimilated, becoming part of the subtle field that is part of Gaia and then part of the physical world. Subtle life energies and qualities that may begin in the loving presence of a Stellar Being eventually become part of the life of a blade of grass, a molecule of carbon, an atom within that molecule. There is a process of integration that is analogous to the process of digestion and assimilation in our own bodies.

Many years ago, I was out for a walk in the woods. As I walked along, there suddenly arose from out of the ground about fifteen feet or so in front of me, a green star, like a miniature sun. It wasn't too bright to look at, but it definitely radiated, and what it was radiating was a green light that I felt as a quality of life. As this thing hovered pulsing in the air in front of me, I heard words that said, "The earth is also a star, a star of life."

This may be an aspect of Gaia we don't think of, the way in which our world is generative and gives subtle energies and qualities back into its own cosmic environment.

So Gaia is part of a system of circulation of life and other qualities and energies moving through the cosmos, breathing in and breathing out. At a planetary level, this circulation is one of the causes of the phenomenon of incarnation.

There is a fascinating movie put out by NASA showing the flow of air traffic patterns over the USA over a 24 hour period. This movie is an interesting analog to the flow of subtle forces flowing into and out from the earth, moving in all directions. At one point in the movie, you see in the upper right corner a huge influx of lines (airplanes) moving in from Europe to the USA. Think of this as a flow of stellar energies moving in to the life-field of the planet.

Of course, no picture can depict the true nature of this circulation as Gaia breathes in from and breathes out into the universe.

I have had occasion to travel in the company of spiritual allies to what I think of as the "edge" of the world, a place where Gaia is sending its radiance out into the cosmos and receiving cosmic energies in return. It looks nothing like the movie of air traffic patterns, and yet, there is a similarity. There is a sense of many currents flowing into the world, looking like streams of luminescence swirling into the sky (and as I write this, I realize that there is also a similarity to witnessing the aurora borealis or northern lights). This is only how my earthly mind interprets the impressions I'm receiving in such a place, but there is still a sense of great beauty and activity as planetary, solar and stellar energies mix and blend and pass each other, enriching the earth, enriching the earth's immediate subtle environment within the solar system and beyond.

The question is, how are these solar and stellar energies assimilated into the planetary organism that is Gaia? How do they circulate within the body of the earth?

It's in answering this question that we touch on one of the mysteries behind incarnation.

When we think of incarnation, we think of a single individual taking on physical life for the purpose of growth or service, paying off karma or fulfilling a mission, learning or even adventure. There are many reasons a soul may come to this world, but we think of them within an individual context; that is, they are individual, personal reasons or reasons held by a group of which this soul is a part.

But when we take a Gaian point of view, when we see incarnation from a planetary perspective, then it takes on another dimension altogether. It becomes part of the circulatory flow of subtle energies and life qualities moving from the cosmos and into and through the layers of the earth or moving from the earth back into the cosmos. Incarnation becomes an instrument of planetary breath and circulation.

Let's go back to the image of all the air traffic moving towards and over North America (it's even more impressive if you watch the movie). Each of the dots or lines represents a single aircraft and most of them are passenger jets carrying a number of people, usually over a hundred. Looking at all these flights, think of how many thousands of human beings are in the air at any one time circling the globe. There is a virtual cloud of humanity around the earth made up of individual persons riding in individual planes.

There are millions of people moving into and out of incarnation each year (there are no exact figures, but the approximate totals are about 12 million people being born each year and 6 million dying). As I write this at 11 pm Pacific Standard Time, according to Worldometers, 348,000 people have been born and 150,000 people have died so far today. Each person is a unique incarnational story, a unique, individual manifestation of sacredness, but taken all together, like the image of the airplanes over North America, you have an incarnational cloud of life and energy moving into the physical realm from higher layers of energy within the subtle body of Gaia and moving out from the physical realm back into those higher layers. In short, you have a pattern and process of circulation that has a planetary significance as well as individual ones.

Whatever the personal reasons you or I or any person may incarnate, and whatever happens to us when we die and move back into the subtle realms, from a planetary perspective humanity (of which we are a part) is a collective carrier and transformer of subtle energies and qualities between the layers of the world. We are part of the process of circulation, part of the process of assimilation and integration of cosmic energies moving into the earth and part of the process of radiance that brings the living energies of Gaia out from the world and into the surrounding solar and stellar subtle environments.

As individuals we may or may not feel this or be aware of this. Any one person may or may not be involved in his or her life in this process of assimilation and integration or this process of emergence and radiance. I'm not talking at an individual level here. But humanity collectively is a bridge between the layers of Gaia. As we humans move in and out of incarnation, we create the bridges through which cosmic energies become part of the realm of materiality and the developments and unfoldments of the material realm become part of the higher levels of Gaia and ultimate radiate back into the cosmos. We are an integral part of the process of planetary circulation.

So, from one perspective, incarnation is the description of a "metabolic function" within the body of Gaia. Earth has a physical domain, an energetic field (like an aura), and a subtle domain, and incarnation allows for the circulation of subtle energies throughout these layers.

When we incarnate, one of the impulses behind it—a very impersonal and planetary impulse at that—is this flow of circulation. Whatever our personal reasons for taking up physical life may be and becoming a physical self, we ride to and from the physical world on currents powered by the metabolic processes of the earth (or Gaia) as a whole.

But there's more to the picture than just circulation.

### ENERGIES? WHAT ENERGIES?

Before we go further, I want to pause a moment and discuss nomenclature with you. Throughout this text I'll be talking about "subtle energies" (or just "energies"). Indeed, the heart of the book is to look at the self as a "subtle energy phenomenon." But what does this mean? Just what are these energies? What am I talking about here?

We're all familiar with physical energies, such as the energy of heat or of electricity. Subtle energies are not like those. You can't heat your food or light up your house with subtle energies—or at least we haven't discovered how to do that yet!

In physics, "energy" is a measure of the capacity to do work. This is what we mean when we say we are feeling energetic; we have a sense of being able to act and accomplish. We apply this notion of energy to more than our physical capacities as well. We talk about our mental energy, which may measure how much studying we can do or how alert we are to solving problems; or we talk about emotional energy, by which we often mean our capacity to deal with problems and relationships and with other people and their issues (or for that matter, with our own emotional ups and downs).

The meaning of "subtle energies" is not so far from our understanding of mental and emotional energies. Like the latter, it indicates a non-physical capacity, but a capacity to do what?

At the most fundamental level, subtle energies represent a capacity to be.

I might describe the most basic subtle or spiritual energies as the universe's capacity to exist. And while I don't think of heat or electricity as sentient, subtle energies are. Sentiency is not quite the same as consciousness, but it is a capacity to be aware and to respond. In my experience, all subtle energies are sentient, though they do not all possess what I would recognize as consciousness.

Indeed, our capacity to think, to feel, and to experience consciousness is directly founded on the basic sentiency of subtle energies. They are energies of life, and at the most basic level, they foster life. They foster the capacity to be and to become, to grow, to unfold, and to develop more complex patterns of awareness and consciousness.

I might describe subtle energies (of which there are many different kinds, though all reflect the basic sentiency and capacity for life that I just mentioned) as movement or flow within the presence of the Sacred. But the fact is that what I call "subtle energies" might more precisely be thought of as being "energy-like." Calling them "energies" is a kind of analogy based on our physical experience of energies. There are subtle energies that manifest in the subtle environment closest to the material world that do so in a manner comparable to physical energies. For instance, chi or ki, the subtle energy that we all possess within our bodies and which we are most familiar with in the martial arts, can be measured in the laboratory and has discernible and quantifiable physical effects. The Chinese in particular have been doing considerable research work in this area.

But when I begin talking about the "energies of the soul" or the "cosmic energies" or "Gaian energies," I'm talking about a phenomenon that is very real, that produces changes and effects, particularly within the various non-physical regions around the earth, but that is also very different from the kind of energies we are familiar with physically, including chi.

The fact is, I don't have a good word to use for this phenomenon in its various forms. It is more than anything we experience simply as "energy." But the fact that it does flow (or alters its state between one thing and another, thus creating a differential), that it does affect capacity, and that it does initiate change and sets activity into motion, all lead me to think of it as "energy-like" and thus leads me to use an "energy language" to talk about it. I do so knowing how easy it is for our minds to slip into interpreting this kind of language in everyday, physical terms until it might seem we're talking about some kind of spiritual electricity.

We're not.

OK, so we have this image of the world engaging with its own cosmic environment, its consciousness engaging on a level of life and awareness far beyond our own. As part of this engagement, it receives subtle energies from the cosmos through which it moves, from stellar and solar sources. It turn it gives back the fruits of its own inner life. This whole process might look something like this:

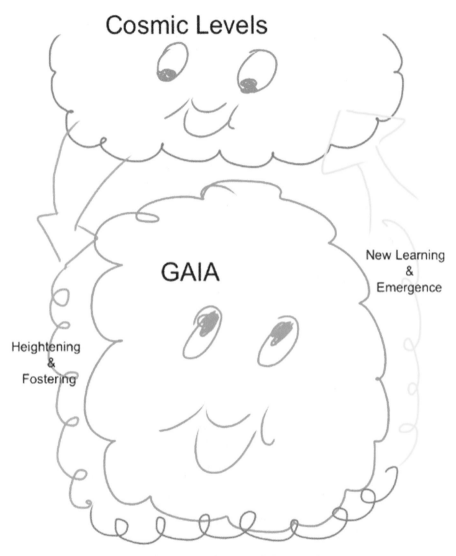

CIRCULATION & METABOLISM OF COSMIC ENERGIES

FIGURE 2

Essentially, Gaia takes in cosmic energies (or presence or spirit or whatever other term you might like to use here), processes them and uses them to heighten and foster its own life. This processing takes the form of embodiment, integration and expression; in other words, Gaia translates the heightening and fostering impact and intent of the cosmic forces into some form of doing within its own life. It translates them into action from which new information, new learning, and even new capacities may emerge. Gaia is enriched, its own life deepened, and out of that deepening, it has more to give back to the cosmos.

At least this is the general picture. But how does all this happen? It's not as if there are transmissions wires that run "cosmic electricity" into the ground to power the earth. We're talking about the stimulation and heightening of consciousness here. How does it take place?

How do cosmic forces and energies engage with the world, working their way down through the levels of planetary spirit and form and even into the very atomic levels on which physical matter rests?

The answer is through consciousness itself. Consciousness is the bridge:

But now the question arises, whose consciousness is the bridge?

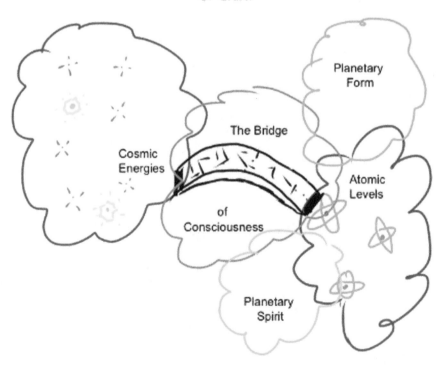

WHAT CARRIES COSMIC ENERGIES INTO ALL LEVELS
OF GAIA?

FIGURE 3

The simple answer is that it's Gaia's consciousness. And as far as I understand it, this is true. But it's not the whole picture, for while Gaia as the World Soul has its own unique identity, there is a collective Gaian consciousness as well in which we all participate.

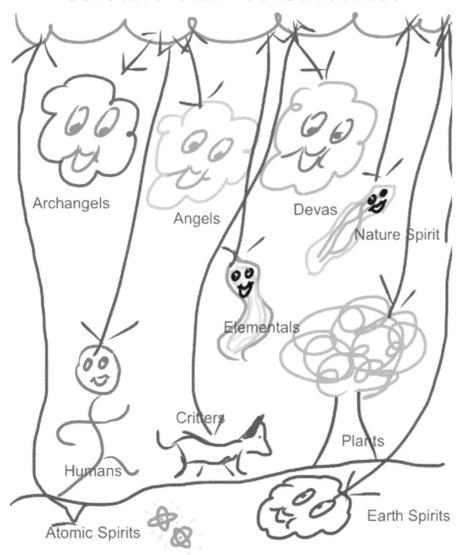

Collective Gaian Consciousness

Archangels

Angels

Devas

Nature Spirit

Elementals

Critters

Plants

Humans

Atomic Spirits

Earth Spirits

FIGURE 4

This little drawing just represents some of the participants in and contributors to the collective Gaian consciousness. There are archangels, angels, Devas, nature spirits, elementals, earth (or mineral) spirits, "atomic spirits" (the life within the molecular and atomic levels of existence), plants, animals ("critters") and of course, ourselves, humanity—both incarnate and dis-incarnate.

As the arrows indicate, there is a two-way flow here between each being and type of being and the life-field of Gaia itself. These lines and arrows are most definitely NOT puppet strings but lines of relationship.

When I eat an omelet, it's not in a form my cells can absorb. I could lay the omelet on my arm or on my stomach, and all that would happen is that I'd get greasy skin. My body cells would remain untouched, unfed, and unchanged. In order for my cells to be nourished by the energy contained in the omelet, it has to be broken down into a form to which they can relate. That's what the digestive process is all about, beginning with the teeth and ending in the small intestine.

Something analogous occurs with these "higher" spiritual and cosmic energies. In their "raw" or pure form, not many lifeforms or consciousnesses on earth can even perceive them, much less absorb them in a nurturing way. So they are received by beings whose consciousnesses CAN absorb and hold these cosmic energies—generally planetary spirits such as archangels and certain kinds of Devas. These beings in turn assimilate and transform these cosmic energies into a form that other beings can then perceive, receive, hold and absorb. The "energies" are passed on to the angels and lesser Devas, and then onto nature spirits, elementals, and so on. As they move towards and into the physical realm, these energies become accessible to plants, animals and human beings.

In this way, we are all involved in the metabolic processes that receive, hold, and absorb cosmic energies into the earth.

BUT....

What I've just written is only partly true. Anytime we use a physical analogy (like digestion) to describe a non-physical process, we leave something out. The process of assimilating cosmic energies and returning planetary energies to the cosmos isn't quite as linear as this description might convey, nor is it as hierarchical.

Yes, higher beings do step down, transform and pass on spiritual energies, putting them in a form that less advanced or complex lives and consciousnesses can perceive and receive. But that's not the whole picture, and the reason is that consciousness is not stratified like steps on a ladder. Many beings possess the ability to experience across a wide spectrum of states of consciousness, much like a radio that can receive many stations along the bandwidth and not just one or two.

Humanity has just such a capacity.

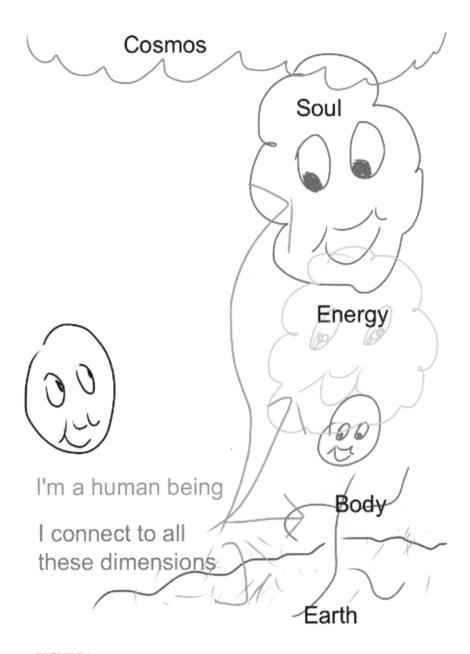

FIGURE 5

We may not always do so, but we have the capacity to attune to a wide range of subtle and spiritual conditions, presences, energies, and so forth. Our bodies give us access to the earth, our subtle bodies give us access to the subtle energy environment, our souls give us access to the wider domains of the subtle and spiritual realms, including to the cosmic levels.

We are not the only species that can do this, by the way. As I understand it, some trees can do this and some animals as well, and many subtle beings have a very wide range of attunement and engagement as well. Nevertheless, it is one of humanity's particular gifts to Gaia that we can operate within a wide range of attunement and participation. We incarnate in a way that makes this possible, allowing us—if we choose to do so—to take part in the Gaia's "metabolic processes" as a truly profound act of service and partnering. This is a particular focus of Incarnational Spirituality.

Here's a nice picture by Deva Berg from the *Soul's Oracle* card deck that

also illustrates this community of planetary consciousness that can together attune to the cosmos.

It's not just a matter of attunement, though. Also needed is the capacity to "hold" the frequency, intensity, and content of the cosmic energies or for that matter, of any kind of subtle energy. An archangel and I might both be able to attune to such energies as they enter the sphere of the earth, but the former will be able to take on and hold a much greater amount and intensity of these energies than I can do.

It's as if we both can get to the well of cosmic energies, but I arrive with just a small bottle with which to carry something home while the angel arrives with a whopping great multi-gallon jug.

The idea of holding is important. It's not enough to have access to certain spiritual and subtle energies. A lifeform—whether it's Gaia or you or me or a caterpillar—has to be able to hold the energies (the stimulating forces, if you will) that it receives.

Imagine that you're thirsty and I have a pitcher of water. If I pour the water on your hands, most of it will be lost; you are unable to hold it. If you have a glass, you are able to hold the water and drink it.

Gaia needs to be able to hold the cosmic energies that come to it. Holding is part of the process of circulation, assimilation, integration, and emergence.

FIGURE 6

Holding is an important aspect of incarnation. We seek to go from weakness to strength as we seek to be able to hold the spiritual and subtle energies of the earth of which we are a part.

When we see a strong person holding a weight. We understand his power to hold to be a function of his strength. But we need to look deeper. It's not simply that he has strong muscles (or that a less muscular person has weak ones). His strength is not a muscle power alone. It's a function of the relationship between muscle, bone, and tendons. And his ability to hold heavy weights is also a function of the surface on which he is standing. For example, how firm and solid or soft and yielding is it? Furthermore, his strength is also a function of gravity. The scrawny man would have no trouble lifting the weights if he were on the moon where gravity is one-sixth what it would be on earth. So firm, healthy, well-developed muscles are one part of the picture, but not the whole picture.

Holding is a manifestation of a relationship. Think of a group of firemen holding a net. They can hold much more working together in this way in relationship than any of them could on his or her own.

Again, I'm using physical metaphors here, and that is always misleading when discussing non-physical realities. Subtle energies are not like weights that we lift or bodies that we catch. But they do possess qualities and characteristics that are metaphorically like weight and mass. I call them vectors, and they carry an impact which the energy system (i.e. organism or consciousness) that receives them has to absorb and handle.

Furthermore these physical metaphors portray holding as relatively passive. Yes, the men are doing work to hoist and hold the weights, but the weights themselves are passive. I might say that these physical metaphors portray lifting more than holding.

Holding isn't simply a matter of containing and lifting; holding is a condition that allows other processes—processes of assimilation, integration, and emergence—to take place. A pot holds the ingredients of a stew together so that the processes of cooking can take place and turn those ingredients into the stew-and it would do no good for that pot to dissolve or crack when heat is applied or when the stew reaches a certain temperature. We'll talk more about this when we explore the incarnational system later in the book.

What is not captured in these physical metaphors (well, perhaps a tiny bit with the firemen) is that holding as I use the term is all about creating an energetic field. It is the field that holds, and the field is generated by relationships.

This is why a purely linear or hierarchical description of the influx and processing of cosmic energies is not sufficient. It's not like a bucket brigade in which higher levels with bigger buckets pass stepped down energies to lower levels with smaller buckets which in turn pass them down to still lower levels with tiny buckets. Instead, there is a continuum of activity and relationship along with the fostering and heightening energies pass as they are assimilated and turned into expression and connection—into more relationships, really—and then transformed into new learning, discovery, expanded capacities, and emergent qualities, as illustrated in the picture in FIGURE 2.

Which brings me to the "Paper Towel Theory of Consciousness and Incarnation" or "Why are there individual selves?"

Here's an experiment you can do at home.

You will need a sheet of ordinary paper such as you might type on or use in your computer printer. You will need a sheet of paper toweling. And you'll need a glass of water and a counter top.

Pour some water onto the counter top as if you had spilled it. Now trying soaking it up with the sheet of computer or typing paper. The paper will get wet, but how much of the spilled water does it absorb and get up from the counter?

Now repeat this by pouring some more water onto the counter top. This time soak it up with the paper towel.

Which paper was more absorbent? Which paper soaked up the most water?

The times I've done this experiment the paper towel beats the sheet of plain computer paper hands down when it comes to absorbing the water. And the reason is not hard to find: the paper towel, even though it may have the same overall dimensions as the sheet of plain paper, has more surface area with which to absorb the water. This is because it has all the little bumps and ridges on it.

# The Paper Towel Theory of Consciousness & Individuality

The One

A Single Surface Area

Multiple Surface Areas--More "Absorbant"

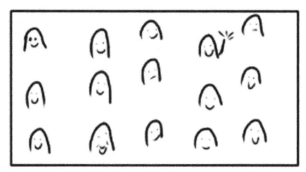

Individuating Oneness -- The One + Many

FIGURE 7

In esoteric literature, the earth is sometimes referred to as a "sacred planet." Given the amount of violence and suffering that makes up the evening news and the morning newspapers everyday, a person might be forgiven in wondering what's so sacred about it? It can seem like a pretty tough and unpleasant place to be at times.

When I've asked this question of my inner colleagues, the answer has been that the rich diversity of form and consciousness and life that makes up the earth in both its physical and non-physical aspects creates a density of interaction and relationship; like a paper towel, the earth has a lot of surface area of consciousness. It can both absorb subtle energies because of this but more importantly, it generates a richness of relationships that can in turn create multiple fields for holding and assimilation, expression and emergence (again, a kind of "paper towel effect").

In short, our world is relationally dense. We live in a paper towel world.

This doesn't mean, however, that the fields we generate will automatically lead to coherency and integration. It's obvious from human behavior that we have a ways to go yet before we've learned how to be in the world in a truly harmonious and holistic way. But we're learning—sometimes the hard way. And that is one of the objectives of incarnation.

A paper towel world offers many advantages as well as challenges. The main challenge is in maintaining holopoiesis, the act of fostering and supporting wholeness between all the individual units, the "bumps and ridges." Wholeness in this context is best understood as a metabolic condition: it's the manifestation of harmonious and mutually beneficial connections and relationships between all the parts of a system. This system could be a person, and the wholeness is the metabolic harmony between his or her cells, tissues, and organs (a state we think of as health). It could be a planet, where the wholeness is between all the creatures and ecological processes that are its constituents. Because the moment you separate a unity into a diverse multiplicity, you risk conflict between the individual units unless there is some impulse or process that draws them together to work together while still preserving the individuality that you want. That impulse is what I call holopoiesis, and in my experience, its primary (though not its only) manifestation is as the quality we call love.

The advantages lie in the ability of differences to interact to create new learning, new possibilities, and emergent, unexpected qualities.

We experience this all the time in our lives. I have an idea, you have an idea, our mutual friend has an idea, and when we put them all together, something magical happens and a new idea that combines the best of our contributions, perhaps in surprising and unexpected ways, emerges. We learn from each other's differences. We are even born from the coming together of genetic differences from our two parents.

Differences create
New learning!

EMERGENCE HAPPENS!

FIGURE 8

So the "paper towel" world, filled with different individual life forms, provides greater "surface area" for absorbing subtle energies, creates connections and relationships that generate fields for holding and other activities, and generates emergence in the form of new learning, new capabilities, and new forms of expression, which in turn can give birth to new qualities and subtle energies.

In this context, it is the quality or impulse of Self that takes the flat surface of the plain paper—the singular "surface" of oneness—and creates the bumps and ridges of individuality, differentiation, and diversity that turn it into a paper towel.

So, let me sum up this part of this chapter's text. It forms the "set" or even the theater within which incarnation's three acts take place.

The earth is a living organism, one that, like all lifeforms, interacts with its environment and in the process grows and evolves. The environment for this planetary consciousness is one that we would call "cosmic," "stellar," and "solar," words that have particular meanings to us from our perspective but which may mean something quite different to the awareness of Gaia, the World Consciousness.

From this environment, Gaia draws in nourishment and stimulation; my less-than-perfect term for this is "cosmic energies." The earth breathes in these subtle forces, metabolizes them through processes akin to circulation, and returns its own energy contributions back to the cosmos.

The "metabolic" processes take place primarily in a continuum of consciousnesses, of which humanity is a part. Cosmic and planetary energies fundamentally act to stimulate consciousness, enhancing the capacities to from boundaries, maintain identity, form connections, and create space for emergence to take place. They act in holopoietic ways, manifesting in myriad ways the coalescing, empowering presence of love.

In this process, humanity occupies a particularly strategic role due to our abilities to hold and express individuality (thus enhancing the "paper towel effect"), span several levels of both physical and non-physical reality with our consciousness, and form connections and partnerships across a wide spectrum of planetary life, including both physical and non-physical aspects.

One of the principle ways we do this is through incarnation which spans the gap between the physical world and the realm of the soul (and all the subtle realms in-between), helping to create the bridge shown in FIGURE 3, and enables us to create a particularly strong kind of "bump" in the paper towel in the form of our personal, incarnate self. It also provides a mechanism for our own learning, growth and development.

Through incarnation, we become instruments of holopoeisis, planetary growth, and cosmic emergence.

Plus we get to hang out at malls.... :-))

**THE THREE ACTS OF INCARNATION**

FIGURE 9

We customarily think of incarnation as beginning with birth and ending with death. From my point of view, this is only the "middle act" of what is really a three-act drama. By focusing only on the part from womb to tomb, we end up with a skewed and limited picture of who we are and of the nature of incarnation itself.

Given that we have limited time in this book, I don't want to spend too much of it on the process of incarnation itself. I want us to focus on the phenomenon of the self, specifically our individual, personal self. But this self exists in the context of this incarnational process which in turn is part of the larger Gaian context I just wrote about.

So an incarnation ultimately begins and ends with the soul, a complex field of consciousness operating in its own native environment. I'll have more to say about the soul in next chapter's text. For now we'll simply think of it as that mysterious spiritual, non-physical source from which our incarnate life begins.

An incarnation begins when the soul commits to an intention to engage with physical life. It ends when the fruits of that intention are fully "harvested" and assimilated by the soul. This can be a lengthy process in earthly terms, much longer than the few decades the personality lives on earth. Indeed, this "middle act" may—and usually is—the shortest part of the whole incarnation.

Note the similarity between this FIGURE 9 and FIGURE 2 shown earlier.

The incarnational process is a fractal of the process by which the world takes on and assimilates higher or more complex energies stemming from cosmic sources. In effect, the soul is for each of us a cosmic source relative to our everyday consciousness.

When the soul commits to a physical life, it begins a process of forming a vessel that will carry that intent forward. This is not the physical body—that worthy doesn't enter the picture until much later at the beginning of "Act II." The soul forms a field of intent which it then weaves into connection and relationship with the various forces and elements of the earth and of humanity (in both their non-physical and forms. In effect, the soul forms the web or container that will hold the energy of its intent, and it does so in relationship with others.

This "intent" or "field of intent" is not quite the same as a mental thought or an emotional desire; it's not identical to what we usually experience as an "intent" in our daily lives, though it's analogous to it. Put another way, it's not something that occurs only in the mind of the soul the way we might make a decision or formulate a plan. If it has any analogy to a physical process, it would be to the budding of a plant or the budding of a single-celled organism by which it produces a fractal of itself.

However, this "soul bud" doesn't separate from its parent. It remains continually "attached" or embedded in the overall presence of the soul. But there are boundaries that form around it to differentiate it from other aspects and patterns of the soul, and it does have specific soul energy allocated and dedicated to it.

NOT THIS     BUT     THIS

FIGURE 10

Actually, the metaphor I use most often for this process is that of writing a book, let's say in this instance a novel. When I get the idea for a story and decide to turn it into a piece of deathless literature (or so I may wish!), there's a part of me that attaches to this idea. In fact, I am working on a novel right now called *Aftermath*, so I can use it as an example. I'm actually working on three books simultaneously right now (no wonder my hands get sore!). There's the part of me that has conceived of these books and intends to write them. This part of me, which is analogous to the soul, is my whole self—David—and it contains the knowledge of writing that can produce the books. But each of these books is different and requires a different approach and style; one is fiction, the other two are non-fiction. Each has its own individuality and personality, its own boundaries. And there is part of me attached to each book, a part that carries the vision for the book and is actually actively involved in producing it. This part of me shares the same boundaries and individuality as the specific book project. When working on *Aftermath*, I don't access the same intents and trains of thought and specific applications of the skill of writing as when I'm writing a text book on subtle activism (or for that matter, this book).

In other words, there is a *Partnering with Earth* David, a *Subtle Activism* textbook David, and an *Aftermath* David, each of whom is different and each of whom is also part of "Big D," the David that is my whole self and that is more than just a writer. These other David's don't separate themselves from me as Big D, yet they represent distinct individuations. I become in the moment a different David when working on Aftermath than when writing this book text. Yet, I'm the same David.

As incarnate personalities, we are not separate from our souls. We may be a bump on the paper towel that is the soul, but we're still attached to and part of that paper towel.

This means that the process of incarnation is really one of differentiation, not of "journeying" as such. Aftermath David doesn't "travel" away from Big David even though he lives in a different, more constrained world—the world of the novel—than does Big David or Whole David and thus is different from Whole David.

There are two metaphors that are commonly and frequently used to describe incarnation. One is that the soul enters a body (and a personality) the way a driver enters a car. The other is that incarnation is a journey away from the soul, away from our "true self" and our "true home," a journey into an alien land from which we will one day return.

All metaphors, including the ones I'm using here, distort the reality somewhat; they only give a partial view. They are suggestive, not literal.

But the two metaphors of "car and driver" and "journeying" are particularly misleading when it comes to understanding incarnation and the relationship of soul and personality. It's not that they're wholly false, only that they fail to convey the indivisibility of the soul and the intimacy of the relationship between soul, body, and personality. They both suggest a separation that is not there, at least not in my understanding. They can be useful in describing some aspects earthly life, but they miss the mark when it comes to giving us a proper insight into the nature of incarnation.

Consequently, Incarnational Spirituality goes beyond both these metaphors, affirming that we are more than a driver in a car (or worse, the car being driven by something else) and we are not really on a journey away from "home" or put more precisely, in a condition of separation from the soul.

IS also changes another image long held and taught in spiritual circles of both the East and the West. This is the idea that the personal self, the Ego, the personality—whatever we call it—is an obstruction to the soul, an illusion, or a flawed and fallen instrument. Instead, Incarnational Spirituality affirms that the personal self not only exists but that it is an integral and important part of the spiritual unfoldment and incarnational process of the soul (remember the bumps on the paper towel).

In this context, Incarnational Spirituality is a spirituality of the incarnate, personal self and its capacities as a participant within the life of Gaia.

[A SIDE NOTE:

Earlier I wrote that Incarnational Spirituality changes the traditional approach from one of seeing the personality or ego and attunement and attention to worldly things from being an obstacle to spiritual growth to being an integral part of the spiritual practice. I want to elaborate on this just a moment before going on to the three acts.

It's not that the older perspectives were wrong, though I do believe that over the centuries they went further than they needed to and overly-privileged the transpersonal over the earthly and the personal. Rather it's that Gaia and humanity have both been evolving, or at least changing. Just as the clothes I wore when I was 12 won't fit me now (heck, the clothes I wore last year won't fit me now!), so spiritual practices and teachings that were appropriate and meaningful at one stage of human experience are not as appropriate now.

Perhaps the biggest shift that I'm aware of is a shift in the flow of subtle energy from the transpersonal to the personal or from spirit to matter and with it a need for spiritual practice to focus on the incarnate side of things. In a human being, this would be akin to a person who has been a disciplined meditator and who has spent hours and hours in contemplation and contact with the inner worlds realizing that he has neglected his body and is now spending those same hours in a gym building up his physical resources. The contemplation and meditation haven't stopped, but they been reassigned a different priority, so to speak, and allocated fewer hours compared to the time spent on building the body.

With Gaia, it's not quite as simple as that, of course. There are many forces at work and currents flowing through the planetary subtle fields, so it's tricky to generalize. There will always be exceptions. But the main generalization I can make is that nothing is static and that there are no absolute or ultimate approaches to spirit. The guidance given to human beings by the wise ones of millennia ago or even centuries ago was appropriate to the time and the conditions. Now conditions have changed or are changing, both physically and in the subtle worlds, so different approaches are needed.

Incarnational Spirituality grows out of this change.

END OF SIDE NOTE]

# CHAPTER TWO, PROLOGUE: THE SOUL
*or Where Incarnations Go to Begin*

Soul is an ambiguous term. It's used in many different ways in our culture, from a measure of a person's passion for and attunement to a particular activity ("He played the trumpet with soul!") to the spiritual part of us to an eternal personality. In my own case, I use "soul" to mean the Self's instrument of incarnation and evolution in relationship to the earth.

Beginning with an experience I had when I was seven years old, I've had an ongoing engagement with the level of consciousness and life I think of as my soul, and it's been an object of exploration and investigation. Over the years a rather complex picture has emerged of the soul, and I'm far from fully comprehending it. It seems at times to me that we have several souls or one soul that has a variety of interactive but distinct parts; in other words, it's a dynamic system in its own right.

In FIGURE 11, I offer a visual (and highly simplistic and symbolic) representation of the different aspects (or types) of soul that I've encountered in my explorations. This is a work-in-progress, but this is my best understanding to date. It forms a cast of characters all of whom take part in all the acts of our incarnational play.

OK, the first thing I want to say about this picture is that the relationship between these levels of soul isn't as vertical and apparently hierarchical as this picture suggests. All these levels are embedded in each other and flow into each other to some extent. I could have drawn this as a cluster of concentric circles. But frankly, given the limits of my artistic skills and the need to make the information as visually accessible as possible, this is the best way for me to do it. Just don't take it too literally!

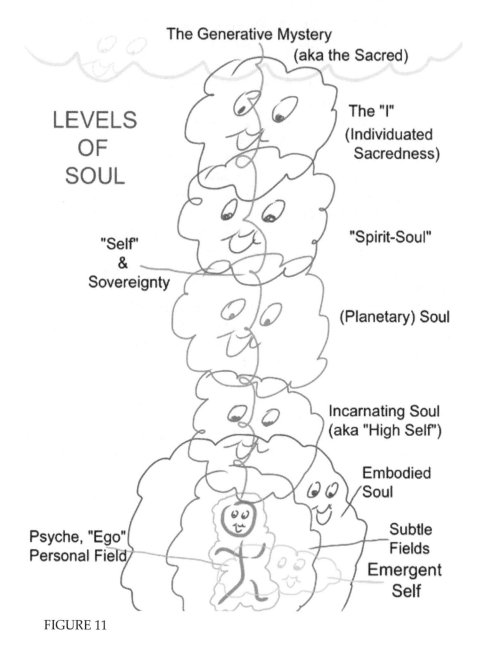

The Generative Mystery
(aka the Sacred)

LEVELS
OF
SOUL

The "I"
(Individuated
Sacredness)

"Self"
&
Sovereignty

"Spirit-Soul"

(Planetary) Soul

Incarnating Soul
(aka "High Self")

Embodied
Soul

Psyche, "Ego"
Personal Field

Subtle
Fields

Emergent
Self

FIGURE 11

However, each of these levels do represent distinct fields of presence and energy to me, with discernible boundaries. Each is a "chalice" specifically designed to hold certain kinds and frequencies of subtle energies and information.

One way to think of this is to imagine the soul as a single, complex entity, and each of these levels I portray here in effect as organs within this entity, just as we have organs in our body. We experience ourselves as being one single body, a somatic unity, yet we are also aware of the distinctness and specific functioning of our organs such as heart and lungs and stomach. I am encouraged in this perception by something my mentor, John, once said when he referred to the personality as "an organ of the soul." I'll write more on this later—after all, it's really the theme of this book!

Let's begin at the top. In a real way, the Sacred (which I often call the Generative Mystery) is the source of all our incarnations because it is itself the ultimate source of the incarnational impulse and its various processes. And it is the source of the phenomenon of Self, which I also consider a Sacred idea or impulse. The Self is the function that creates the individuating bumps on the cosmic paper towel.

In this drawing, you will see a line descending vertically through all the levels of Soul which is labeled "Self & Sovereignty." This is to suggest that Self is not a thing, nor is it a particular layer or level; it is a function of individuation that runs through all the levels and makes them possible. It is what connects them to the Sacred (among other things) and holds them in existence. In the specific context of our individual physical incarnations I call this connective power our "Sovereignty" because it suggests to me our capacity for self-governance and the ability to stand in the presence of our Selfhood, our connection to Sacredness. We might think of it as the "spine" of the soul, the "spine" of incarnation.

As the Generative Mystery (GM) expresses the function of Self, it creates individuations of itself (bumps on the paper). This is the primal level of differentiation and individualized beingness, and I call it our "I." The "I" is much more to me than just the soul. It is our sacred identity, the expression of the first of the four Principles of incarnation as described in An Introduction to Incarnational Spirituality (the other three are Boundary, Connection, and Emergence). This "I" is our root-Self or what I sometimes call our "Ur-Self" (so named after Ur, in archeology considered the first human city ever constructed and thus the model for all cities that emerged thereafter).

The "I" is present, just as Sacredness is present, in all the levels of soul. It is present in our everyday lives as our felt sense of being an individual self. It behaves a bit like a function as well—something that enables the expression of identity and selfhood—but it is also a level of consciousness that, in my estimation, is the part of us most attuned to and part of cosmic levels of being.

So we have The Sacred which gives birth to Self as a function which gives birth to our "I" which is our individuated (and individuating) Sacredness.

The "Spirit-Soul" is an umbrella term for me. As I mentioned, when I attune to my own soul, I may actually end up contacting several different "kinds" or levels of soul. One is recognizably a level of consciousness specifically in relationship with Gaia and in a way shaped by that relationship. It's what in the diagram I call the "(planetary) Soul," and I'll have more to say about it in a moment.

But there is a threshold there, and if I peer beyond it, I'm aware of a whole other level of consciousness that itself may possess several layers or levels and which is concerned with much more than just planetary existence. I think of this as the cosmic level of soul, and the term I usually use for it is "Spirit."

This composite level of "Spirit-Soul" represents all the levels and layers of beingness and consciousness that lie between the "I" and the level I usually think of as my soul or "planetary soul." I have no ideas how many of these levels there are; they are almost all beyond my pay grade or my ability to attune to them. I'm aware of them in much the same way I can see the distant mountain range of the Olympics when I'm out driving where I live.

Humanity as a whole as a collective field of consciousness and energy did not originate on this world. I don't mean that we came here in flying saucers or any such thing; only that there is part of each of us that is older than humanity's existence on this planet. We came to this world, so I am told, from other spiritual dimensions to take part in the grand experiment and unfoldment of Gaia's own incarnation. That part of us that predates earthly humanity is this Spirit-Soul. It is that part of us that most easily and readily attunes to and absorbs what I've been calling cosmic energies.

The way in which most of us have contact with this level of being is through qualities that it embodies, such as love. That is, I think we experience this level primarily as a function which stimulates certain holopoietic qualities and impulses within us. But it's part of our greater Beingness and is in a sense the Soul of our soul itself.

I include it in this diagram not because it plays a direct role in the three acts of physical incarnation but out of a sense of wanting to offer as whole a picture as I can. And though it is by our standards a very rarefied and transpersonal level of being and consciousness indeed, it is certainly available to be contacted, and people do contact it (though I think that in many cases when they do, it is so overwhelmingly awesome and so apparently vast by comparison to earthly consciousness that they think they are in contact with God ... and for most practical purposes, they are!).

When we think of humanity, we think of our own species with a hominid body. A human being has a torso with a head, two arms and two feet. But Humanity is also what I think of as a Sacred Idea, a kind of function that has taken a particular form on our world but could take other forms on other worlds. Some years ago, my mentor and partner John had me journey to a place that, to my mind at least, was at the edge of the world. To get to it, I went to a place on the subtle realms that I think of as The Library. This is a place of knowledge and learning, and to my mind's eye, it almost always looks like a graceful, truly beautiful building based on classic Greek architecture with columns and porticoes. The substance from which it is made appears to me as a luminous marble, glowing white but not unpleasantly so. The stone itself is alive, and while it appears most often to me as a building, I know that in reality it is the substance and life-field of a great Being whom I think of as the Librarian.

Anyway, on this particular occasion, I was directed to a room that was open at one end. Extending out from it was a walkway, wide enough for two people to walk side by side. When I stepped out onto it, I realized that aside from the building at my back, all around me was empty space, filled with stars. It sounds daunting but in fact it felt warm and inviting, even loving, as if all the stars were a vast community of beings (which, in fact, they are) and I was stepping into their midst. I had no sense of fear in walking out on this walkway.

The walkway led to what was like an island, a small chunk of real estate, and in the middle of it was a fairly large well. Around this well was a circular platform with another walkway with a railing. You could lean forward on the railing and peer into the well, and what I saw when I did so were more stars. But the Well was also filled with a presence, as if it were a point of contact with some vast cosmic Being that filled the cosmos around me.

Standing on this circular platform, I became aware of other walkways like the one I had crossed over on extending out in all directions, and I knew intuitively that they led to other worlds. It was like this was some kind of inner meeting place. As I stood there looking about, I became aware of a figure approaching the well from another direction. As it close enough that I could make it out, it hailed me. This being looked for all the world like a giant snail—not exactly a terrestrial snail but close enough to bring that correspondence to mind. It had a round hump on its back much like a shell—though I don't know if that's what it was—and it traveled on a rippling "foot" or length of muscle much like a snail does. It didn't have a snail's head, though; its body raised up above the "shell" and towards the top was a face of sorts with eyes, but clustered all around this face was a fringe of small tentacles which I assumed weren't its "hair" but were used for sensing, gripping, manipulation, and who knew what else. It may not sound like it from my description, but it was a graceful, beautiful being.

It wore what appeared to my eyes as a kind of harness over its fleshy part, the part that arose from the "shell," and hanging on this harness were what looked like patches or ornaments. Seeing these, I had an intuition that they were badges of office or identifiers of some kind, much like a martial artist might wear a white belt or a black belt.

As I said, as this being drew closer, it hailed me, and I felt a warmth and loving hospitality radiating out from it. It didn't say anything, didn't use words; in fact, I'm not even sure it had a mouth or at least what I would recognize as a mouth, though as I say, it did have eyes that were human-like. But it communicated telepathically and empathically. It said that it was a junior priest on its world—at least, that's how I interpreted and translated the images and feelings I received—and coming to this Well was part of its training, a kind of test of its ability. It asked me if that were true for me, too. I had this amazing sense of the two of us as two students or apprentices meeting at this Well and comparing notes about our training. There were no great cosmic revelations from this being, only a kind of friendly camaraderie and a curiosity about who I was and how I was being trained. I think it was this quality to the meeting that convinced me of its reality and made me sure this wasn't just some figment of my imagination. I hate to use the word "banal" to describe our meeting, but really it was like a couple of college kids meeting at a bar. Very ordinary in an extraordinary way. I wouldn't have been surprised if he'd produced a six-pack of Bud Lite!

I definitely had the sense that for this being, meeting members of other species from other worlds was commonplace. It didn't seem at all amazed at meeting me at this Well, though I was amazed myself. And as I say, it conveyed a lovely sense of warmth and friendliness.

The reason I'm sharing all this, though, is that as I communicated with this being, what struck me most was its humanity. If I closed my eyes and just felt its presence, I could easily have been with another human being. Aside from its form, it did not feel alien to me. I felt—and I'm sure it felt as well—as though on a spiritual level we were both part of the same collective field of being. We were both humans, though I was a hominid human and it was a molluscan human. I felt as if I were in the presence of kin. (Heck, I felt closer to this snail-person than I have to some human beings I've met! Ha!)

My understanding is that Humanity is a cosmic entity (speaking collectively), a particular configuration of consciousness and spirit that incarnates on many worlds, taking different forms as required by the environmental conditions of those worlds. And it's what I call our "Spirit" or "Spirit-Soul" that is part of this larger, cosmic field of Humanity.

However, when this cosmic Human field engaged with Gaia and became part of this world, then a particular manifestation of this Spirit took form, one in alignment and resonance with the life-field and energy field of this world. This manifestation is what I call the Soul or more precisely the Planetary Soul, suggesting it is unique and adapted to the requirements of this world. Thus, the snail-being and I appeared to me to share the same Spiritual collective—our

Spirits were part of the same Human Spirit—but we would each have had quite different Planetary Souls.

One way I think about the relationship of the (Planetary) Soul and the Spirit-Soul is that as Spirit Soul we incarnate into the field of the Earth once, and out of that incarnation, the (Planetary) soul is born. That soul, in turn, becomes the instrument for the "I"'s evolution in relationship to this world (never mind other worlds), and it evolves—in part at least—through engagement with the physical level over multiple lifetimes.

I—and we—want to be careful about language here. It's easy to get confused with all the different "souls" running around. The fact is that I'm still talking about one single Being here, one that has different facets or "wavelengths" along the spectrum of its existence. That singularity of beingness is what's represented by the "I."

It's possible to visualize these relationships as something like a set of nested Russian dolls, with one aspect nested and embedded within another. This is accurate as far as it goes, but it doesn't go far enough because the relationship between the differently sized Russian dolls is a spacial one while the relationship between the different "souls" or aspects of Self or "I" is not. It's something else, something multidimensional in which the "dolls" are not only nested in each other but participating in each other. They are simultaneously separate manifestations, yet they are intimately one and blended as well. The "little dolls"—like the personality or the "incarnate soul"—are not lesser than the "larger dolls" like the "I" or the Spirit-Soul. The relationship has hierarchical aspects but it bypasses hierarchy as well. Each "doll" is appropriate to its own level of functioning. They can stand as equals in each other's presence.

Let me repeat this, as this is a most important point: the incarnate person—made up of a set of relationships and connections I call the incarnational system that blends soul and personality, humanity and nature and so much else—is every bit as complex and beautiful a creation on its own level as the Soul or the Spirit-Soul are on theirs. They are just different, and in their difference are appropriate to the dimensional structure—the world—in which they are operating. Our Spirit-Soul or our Planetary Soul may be operating in more dimensions and in a vastly more complex and spacious environment than our personalities, but they are not better than our incarnate self. They are not more sacred. They are as sacred. They are not closer to the Divine by virtue of being non-physical, transcendent or transpersonal than our personality. They are as close to the Divine as we are here on earth. Yes, there are huge energetic differences between these two manifestations of the "I," and some of the problems we encounter in incarnation are a result of this energy differential. But these other levels are not our parents, our elder brothers or sisters, or our superiors. They are our partners. They are part of us and we of them. They offer what our level of consciousness cannot provide for itself, but by the same token, we as incarnate consciousness experience and offer what they cannot. Each part of us is an element in a whole system, and its this wholeness that most clearly and powerfully manifests sacredness.

So as I continue, please keep this in mind. I am drawing cartoons here, but hopefully they suggest the relationships involved. And hopefully I can keep all this clear enough that you won't get confused.

The Planetary Soul is what I usually simply call the soul, and I will continue to do so. By the way, I usually just refer to the "Spirit-Soul" as our Spirit, but this can be confusing too since we often use the word "spirit" in a more generic way to mean the animating life force or the universal presence of God rather than a particular state of being within the overall field of the "I."

As I understand it, the soul comes into being as a result of the engagement of the "I" with the energy field of Gaia, the World Soul. In effect, the soul (well, most souls, anyway) is born within and out of the energy field and life-field of the World Soul. In this way, we are both "cosmic" and "planetary." The exact mechanism for this birth may not be the same for all souls, and not all beings incarnating into the field of the Earth go through it or produce a planetary soul. But as a rule of thumb, this is what happens for most of us.

The soul is the "I" wrapped in a "shell" or boundary made up of planetary vibrations and wavelengths that allows the "I" (or, if you wish, its Spirit or the Spirit-Soul) to connect and engage with the unique vibrations of this world. A temporary "body" can certainly be constructed if the Spirit-Soul doesn't intend to stay long or get too involved with planetary energies, but most of us are here for the long haul (several thousands if not hundreds of thousands of years, chronologically speaking).

Note that the soul is not the only expression of the "I." The latter is quite capable of manifesting other vehicles for engaging with other worlds as well, so it's not like we're bound to the earth for hundreds of thousands of years. But our soul—the planetary soul—once created is maintained for however long—and it can be for thousands and thousands of years—the individuality remains involved with the earth.

The soul grows and develops as any organism does. It does so on its own level in relationship with other souls, with other dimensions, with other realities to which the soul has access, and with other parts of itself, the parts within its Spirit and "I." But it also grows through engaging with the physical plane and its unique conditions, becoming part of the great circulation of subtle energies from cosmos to planet and back again.

In other words, it can grow through the process of incarnation, experiencing multiple lives upon the physical world and within the incarnate realms.

When I set out to write a book, it's as if I incarnate into the project. The book has an identity, it has boundaries, it is connected, and it emerges. I am part of each of these four elements, and the part of me that gives its attention and life to this project, "incarnates" within it and is a specific—and so some degree, a separate—part of me. And yet it's not as if I've chopped off the arm that will write the book or lost some part of me. I am still David. But I am also simultaneously "Book-David."

Furthermore, this book is not just a plan in my mind. The act of writing requires me to live into it. I become the book; its content emerges out of who and what I am. The book is part of my life, infused with my life, emerging within my life.

However, there are many parts of my life that don't enter into the book and that can't enter into it. I can't, for instance, be writing the book and cooking dinner at the same time. "Book-David" is not the same as "Father-David" or "Husband-David" or "Boardgame-Playing David" or any of the other Davids that represent the different aspects of my whole life. I can't pour all of me into a single book. Book-David is a fractal of Whole David but it isn't the wholeness or completeness or "everythingness" of David.

This is the image I have of the soul and the way it incarnates. In effect, the soul sets apart a part of itself and dedicates a certain amount of its energy and attention to this part. It establishes the identity of this part, it sets up boundaries, and within those boundaries it sets into motion the processes that will result in connection and engagement with the incarnate realm. It creates a "mini-soul" to oversee and participate in this incarnation. I call this the "Incarnating Soul" or the "Incarnate Soul." It is the part of the whole, planetary soul that is dedicated to this unique, particular incarnation. It is a fractal—or if you wish, a hologram—of the Soul as a whole, just as the soul is fractal or hologram of the "Spirit-Soul" and the "I." It remains part of the soul—it doesn't literally separate—but yet it does separate in a sense because it individuates in a particular way. The boundaries between the Incarnate Soul and the soul are real, even though they may be very permeable. The boundaries between a particular "Book-David" and the rest of me—the Whole David—are very real, too, but they are not like walls; they are structures of attention and intention and are also permeable.

The Incarnate Soul is the part of the soul that enters into and becomes part of a particular incarnation. It is possible for a soul to generate more than one Incarnate Soul, that is, to have more than one incarnation going at once, just as I can write more than one book at once. But each such incarnation—just as each such book—is wholly its own unique identity. It is a complete person.

At least initially, the Incarnate Soul cannot enter fully into the physical aspect (or for that matter, the mental and emotional aspects) of the incarnate state. Part of it remains in the subtle worlds as an overlighting presence, and this is what many traditions call the "High Self." The part of it that does enter into physical incarnation I call "embodied soul," and it is the essence of the sense of self and of the personality that we all experience as our everyday selves. As the diagram suggests, out of this embodied soul and the information that it contains, the subtle fields, the psyche or ego, the personal subtle field, and the body all emerge. All reflect this embodied soul and thus all reflect the Incarnate Soul or High Self. The embodied soul is the life, energy, consciousness, and processes of soul intimately engaged with the life, energy, sentiency, and processes of the world and of incarnation. It's where the rubber meets the road. And out of this meeting, something emerges. On the one hand, this is what I call our "Self-Light" and on the other hand, it's also what I call our Emergent Self.

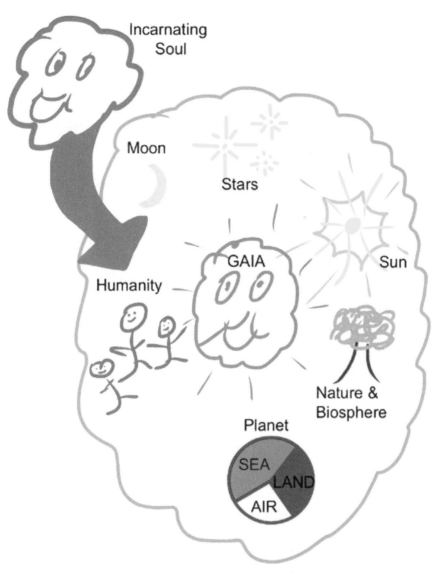

## THE GAIAN FIELD

FIGURE 12

As the soul begins its process of incarnation and starts to shape a part of itself into what will become the field of the Incarnational Soul, it has to take into account the energetic environment with which it is about to engage. Overall this environment is the Gaian Field, the living, sentient presence of the World Soul.

Energetically, this environment is made up of and permeated with emanations, information and influences coming from a number of sources, all of which are contributing to Gaia's own planetary incarnation. In the picture I select out some of the most prominent of these sources. There may well be others, and these sources do not all have equal impact, though that depends as well on what "layer" or "level" of Gaia's overall field you are engaging with. For instance, stellar influences are more prominent in the higher reaches of this field where as the influence of the biosphere and of the land is obviously much stronger on the physical level itself. But for the incarnating soul, it needs to be able to connect with all of these sources; if it were a radio, it would need to have enough bandwidth to receive information from all of them.

Speaking generally, the stellar influences, i.e. the subtle energies flowing into the planetary system from stars within the galaxy, affect the structure and energy of the Incarnational Soul itself as it embodies as a subtle entity within the Gaian Field and affect as well its connections to the various fields and bodies that make it up, as illustrated in the picture. Generally speaking, stellar forces affect the ability of any system to reach beyond itself into larger arenas of being and not collapse into a closed system. Stellar forces foster and nourish what might be called the mind of the Incarnational Soul.

Solar forces empower the flow of life-energies and vitality and also nourish the development of the subtle fields associated with the mind.

Lunar forces affect the flow of subtle energies in rhythmic ways. Think of the sun as a faucet pouring water into a tub, but think of the moon as a hand that gently moves that water back and forth in rhythmic waves. Lunar influences affect both physical tides and tides of subtle energies; they strengthen and empower difference, not so much by forming boundaries but by instilling change and rhythm. They nourish the subtle fields associated with emotion and feeling as well as with rhythmic vitality.

To use a musical analogy, the sun provides the sound, the moon provides the beat, and Gaia itself turns sound and beat into melody.

In effect, for the incarnating soul, the stellar, solar and lunar forces provide the tools for shaping planetary energies into human subtle bodies that distinguish humanity from the rest of the animal kingdom.

The other planetary sources of influence—nature, the biosphere, and the planet itself, made up of land, sea and air—shape and provide substance for the physical body. The collective field of Humanity provides history, context, and fine tuning for the mental and emotional subtle bodies as well as a species matrix for the physical form. All of these sources are permeated with Gaia's presence, love, and energy. And not shown in the picture, there are other influences that come from Gaia's own connection to the subtle worlds which may or may not play a role in human incarnation.

The incoming soul needs to form connections with all of these sources, and these connections become the basic structure of the Incarnational System.

In the Presence Exercise, we focus on the connections between the field of Humanity and the overall field of the World, in particular nature, the soul and other transpersonal forces, and the personalizing forces that arise from the body and from the planet itself. However, one could set up the Presence Exercise using a different set of four points. Based on the Gaian Field, one could use Moon, Sun, Stars, and Planet as the four points. You can certainly experiment with this and see what happens.

The bottom line is that the incarnating soul is entering an information-rich, dynamic, fluid sea of energy, information and influence, and it needs to make connections with this sea in ways that permit it to swim and navigate, not sink and disappear. That is what incarnation is all about.

And with this our Prologue is finished. On to Act I.

# CHAPTER THREE, ACT I: PRE-BIRTH

Now we continue with the "Play in Three Acts," an overview of the cosmology of Incarnation on which we will base our continued exploration of the self.

### ACT ONE: PRE-BIRTH

Coming into incarnation is a process akin to putting a human on the moon. It's a complex process that no one does on his or her own; we each have our own "Houston Control" to help us out. It is a process that has spiritual, planetary, species, psychological, energetic, and physical aspects—and that's before we emerge from our mother's womb!

If we believe that life begins at birth or that we did not exist before we were conceived, we miss out on the whole first act of incarnation, and we fail to recognize many of the forces and elements that have already gone into creating our incarnate self. Although what I think of as our "body-mind" begins in the womb, we really do not come into physical life as a blank slate. We are already "embodied" in subtle fields and "bodies" which provide the initial matrix around with the emergent self of body and psyche will organize and emerge. In a sense, before we are physically born on earth, we are already conceived and born as an incarnate individuality in the subtle worlds. We have already done an immense amount of organizational work with the help of "Houston Control," the various beings, human and otherwise, who assist souls in the incarnational process.

Consider, for example, that a particular incarnation may require the involvement of other souls and individualities who themselves are not yet physically born. "Contracts" are set up with those who will be parents and siblings, and these individuals may not yet have incarnated, so they are setting up similar appropriate contracts and relationships with other souls for themselves. Planning for a given life, particularly if the soul is highly developed and skilled in the incarnational process and has specific intents to pursue requiring specific conditions and a specific kind of body, can start two or three lifetimes removed or even more. That is to say, the planning for your life and the organizing of the forces that will shape your incarnate personality might begin before your grandparents are born, much less your parents. For you to get to point D may require two generations of grandparents and parents getting to points A, B, and C first. And your planning has to harmonize and fit with their own incarnations which in turn need to harmonize and fit with a host of others since they are not being born simply to aid you in your incarnation... well, you can see the complexity of it. Getting to the moon is actually child's play compared to what goes into organizing and preparing for the average incarnation.

This is the process I want to trace, as best I can. It's what constitutes Act One of our incarnation. I want to stress that what I'm sharing here is a generic perspective. Every soul has its own unique path into incarnation, though for the most part these paths cross over the same general terrain.

Let me say right at the outset, as I know the question will come up. Who we are as individual, incarnate, physical selves is a blend of advance planning in the subtle worlds prior to birth and experiences, opportunities, and conditions that arise spontaneously as we live our lives. A life is like a play that is partly improvised and partly scripted; how much improvisation and how much scripting may be there depends on the individual soul.

The course of our lives is not predestined or pre-ordained; we genuinely have free will in making choices and taking actions in our lives. But there are also structures that we ourselves, with help, have laid down in advance: cues and signs that signal when our life is to move in a particular way. We have the ability to override those cues, to "jump the tracks," so to speak, but for the most part, these "tracks" or cues or structures put us into a particular terrain but don't necessarily tell us where to put our feet with each step or how to cross that terrain.

We are emergent selves, as I hope to make clear as we go along.

Here's a personal example. Here are two structures I set up in my life, two patterns that were laid down in advance before I was born (mostly by me but in consultation with others who were also involved—my mentor John, who stayed in the subtle worlds, being one of those others). One was to become a spiritual teacher—or as I prefer to think of myself, a kind of "naturalist" of the subtle worlds. Another was to become a co-director of the Findhorn community.

As I've said elsewhere numerous times, my plan in life had been to be a scientist, specifically a molecular biologist. But in 1964, I began running into a number of cues—mostly in the form of people whom I met and inner experiences I began having—that made me feel this wasn't the road for me to follow. But I resisted. I had a path outlined before me; I wasn't that interested in changing it. But the cues got stronger until finally I realized that what I was was a spiritual explorer, not a traditional scientist.

Now I could have chosen to ignore all these cues, though admittedly it would have been hard, and once I moved into alignment with this new path, there were different ways I could have implemented being a spiritual teacher. And it certainly wasn't as if I suddenly knew what being a spiritual teacher was all about. I had to learn, but the learning was facilitated because I knew I was on the right track.

Going to Findhorn was a similar event. I had a successful teaching and lecturing career going in California. I had no need or desire to go live in another country in an intentional community. But when I first heard the word "Findhorn," it was one of those cues I know I'd laid down as a soul in the pre-birth state. The idea of Findhorn fascinated me and called to me, even though I had no idea what it really was. Even when I went to England and left London for a five-day visit of Findhorn, I had no sense that it was a place for me to stay. I had plans to go on and travel in Europe and then return to America.

But meeting Peter and Eileen and Dorothy, I had instant recognition that I knew these people and that we had work to do together. I recognized the energy that surrounded Findhorn as yet another cue. I could have chosen not to stay, but if I had, I wouldn't have met my wife Julie, I wouldn't have met all the others who became my Lorian colleagues, and a huge part of my work would have gone undone. (And I should say, it never even occurred to me I shouldn't stay at Findhorn—at that point in my life, I was very sensitive to these "pre-birth cues.")

However, how I did my work at Findhorn and how I engaged in my relationship with Julie and with others of the Lorians was not pre-ordained at all. That was up to me and to them, allowing for emergence and new learning between us.

There is always some planning that goes into almost all incarnations; how much is entirely a matter of the souls involved, what they wish to accomplish, how developed and skillful they are at incarnation, and other factors I'll describe later. This planning accomplishes two purposes.

One is just what you think it might be: the soul has an intent and plans what it will need and who it will need in order to fulfill that intent. Sometimes souls create a lot of plans, and sometimes very little, wanting the experience of a truly unexpected and improvisational life. In fact, a soul may simply want physical experience and is not too discriminating about what that experience is—it's just getting used to the vibes of the physical world; so it plans very little.

The second reason relates to one of the challenges of incarnation, which I'll describe shortly. Some kind of structure is needed to enable the energy field or life-field or consciousness of the soul to even engage with the physical world. Think of the soul as a vast amount of water. It needs to have some kind of container to hold what it pours out into the physical world; some holding structure is needed.

But these structures, no matter how planned, simply get the soul into physical embodiment. What happens then in the Second Act will be subject to unpredictable and unexpected forces acting in the incarnate world as human beings exercise their free will. Emergence happens.

And with this foreword, we begin Act One by looking at the challenges of incarnation. What does the soul face in coming down to earth?

## CHALLENGES TO INCARNATION

The soul faces three main challenges when incarnating, two of which are generic and structural and one of which is personal.

The personal one is simply the challenge of working out how to fulfill its intent. What kind of life does it want? What does it wish to accomplish? What, so to speak, is it's flight plan and what does it plan to do at its destination when it arrives? Working out these details includes determining who parents will be; what, if any, siblings will it have and who will they be; where in the world will it be born; what will be its nationality, its ethnicity, its culture; what will be its gender and what will be the overall condition of its body and genetic heritage? What lessons does the soul wish to learn? What does it wish to accomplish? What service does it want to render or contributions does it wish to make? What karma or past habits must it deal with? Who will be its companions? Will it have a spouse, and if so, who? Will they have children, and if so, who? The answer to these questions will go a long way to designing and shaping the soul's individual incarnational system.

I'll speak more to this particular challenge in a bit, but since it's personal, it's unique to each soul.

The two generic challenges I might call the challenge of differential and the challenge of integration.

## THE CHALLENGE OF DIFFERENTIAL

There are different ways of describing this challenge, but they all come down to this: how does a "high energy" field collapse itself into a comparatively lower energy environment? In effect, the soul exists in a higher dimensional realm and emanates a more complex and energetic field compared to the physical body and the body-mind. Metaphorically, it exists "up slope" from us. Incarnation is like running down hill, an idea we'll come back to later when we talk about Self-Light.

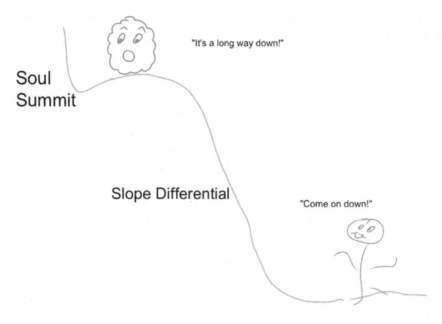

Soul
Summit

Slope Differential

The Incarnational Plain

FIGURE 13

Life depends on differentials, whether they're chemical, electrical, biological, energetic, or atmospheric. Differentials create flow and in many biological instances determine the shape of that life takes, as, for instance, when the concentration of sugar solution is higher on one end of a petri dish than on the other, a differential that causes a colony of microorganisms (who aren't dumb!) to spread out towards the sweeter side.

Subtle energy differentials was one of the first lessons that John offered me, and they are something I've lived with and dealt with nearly everyday for the past forty years in dealing with non-physical beings. It's one of the main dynamics for me in thinking about incarnation and the way that our self unfolds and manifests.

Here's how I describe this in Chapter Two of *An Introduction to Incarnational Spirituality*:

Let me tell a story from the history of physics.

For centuries, people have known of the three states of matter: solid, liquid and gas. But in 1879, Sir William Crookes, working in his private laboratory in London with early vacuum tubes, identified what came to be known as a fourth state. He named the gas-like phenomenon he observed "radiant matter" because of the way it glowed, but modern science calls it plasma. As it turned out, plasma was found to be the most common form of matter in the universe because all stars are made of it. We see plasma at work when we look at the glowing mass of our sun.

Plasmas exist over an extremely wide range of temperatures, including those one would find at the core of the sun. This created a problem. Scientists wanted to investigate such plasmas, but they were so hot that no physical container could hold them without vaporizing. The challenge was how to contain such plasmas so they could be studied.

The answer was that these very hot plasmas had to be held by something that was insubstantial, something that could not melt. This turned out to be a "magnetic bottle," a field phenomenon created by the interaction of specially designed magnets. The field these magnets generated between them created the boundaries that could contain the plasmas.

The magnetic bottle that can contain super-hot plasmas isn't a "thing." It's a dynamic magnetic process emerging from a set of relationships. It has no substance of its own but it's quite real and substantial nonetheless due to the relationships that enable it to remain in existence. The plasma is contained in a field of relationships.

There is an incarnational challenge that is metaphorically similar to the challenge the scientists faced in trying to hold and contain very hot plasmas. This challenge can be stated thusly: how can a multi-dimensional consciousness and life form become part of a three-dimensional world? How can a wave become part of a world of particles?

Put in more spiritual terms, how can the soul, a relatively unbounded and multi-dimensional state of being and sentiency, be held in a bounded and three-dimensional body and accompanying subtle energy field appropriate to existence on this earth?

The soul is very much more than simply the non-physical side of our personalities; it is more than just the part of us that survives after physical death. The soul exists in a very high energy state that extends into more dimensions of being than simply the three dimensions we're familiar with. I call it a "Higher Order Being." By comparison to the physical, incarnate world, the soul— your soul, my soul, and the souls of all beings—is "hot." Metaphorically, it's like plasma.

The answer to this incarnational challenge is analogous to the answer to the plasma problem. The part of the soul that incarnates is held in a field, a kind of "incarnational bottle" that is in principle akin to a magnetic bottle in that it is a container generated by relationships.

The creation of this "magnetic bottle" of incarnation—which I call the incarnational system—is the main story of Act I.

As you may know, when I do a book or give a lecture—whether online or face-to-face—it's almost always in collaboration with non-physical colleagues. I attune to a shared field of mind and thought and imagery, one that is co-created by my 'NPCs' in partnership with me.

What this feels like is stepping into a larger mental room that is filled with information, perhaps a bit like stepping into a pool of water. My task is to sift through this field of information and extract what I need. This of necessity involves an act of interpretation on my part.

Usually, my inner colleagues simply help me hold and regulate this field—they're not telling me anything or giving me information; there's no "channeling" going on. But they do monitor what I'm doing and saying, and if I start to go awry, they can (and do) step in and intervene. This doesn't mean the process is infallible—far from it—but it does have some quality control built in.

After I wrote the material above—and in particular after I wrote the last sentence about the incarnational system being the "magnetic bottle"—I felt one of these interventions. My colleagues weren't telling me this was an incorrect statement, but they were suggesting I review what I was saying and writing because I was missing something. What I'd said was right as far as it went, but it didn't go far enough.

So I've spent the past day reviewing this, not willing to write more text until I was clear what I was missing; it isn't always obvious to me. My inner colleagues only rarely give me direct information about what is wrong or what is missing; they'd rather I discovered it for myself as then it sinks in and becomes part of me. (Rather like my father who, when I would ask him how to spell a word, would hand me a dictionary and tell me to look it up. This used to frustrate me, but now, I'm grateful for the training...Thanks, Dad!) So I had to hit a pause button on writing the text while I reviewed what I was seeing and saying. And now I have a sense of what I was missing and am ready to proceed.

By the way, I share all this not to surround the information I'm writing with any kind of glamour but because part of my larger task is to share a vision of partnership with the subtle worlds and with NPBs and to give a sense of what that is like for me, hopefully conveying a sense of such partnership as a possibility for you in your life.

## THE TWO INCARNATIONS

### THE INCARNATE REALM

When we think of incarnating, we naturally think of entering the physical world. Being in a physical body is the usual definition of incarnation (after all, the word itself comes from roots meaning to "enter flesh"). However, what I mean by the incarnate realm is more than just the physical world. It also includes the subtle environment that surrounds and to some extent emanates from physical matter. This environment is itself layered, possessing different wavelengths or frequencies of consciousness and expression. In traditional esoteric teachings, these might be named the "etheric," the "mental plane," the "emotional plane," "the astral plane," and so forth. They are the realms in which the psyche exists and functions and also in which our incarnate subtle bodies operate.

Although this subtle environment is invisible and is made up of subtle energies, I don't think of it as part of the subtle worlds themselves. This may seem like a nit-picking or a meaningless differentiation, but in fact, I experience a distinct crossing of a threshold in moving from this subtle environment into the subtle worlds or vice versa. There is a qualitative shift of being and "dimensionality," a change of inner structure or architecture that occurs when crossing this threshold. Put in an older esoteric language, there are places in and around the world you can go in your etheric or astral subtle body but to venture very far into the subtle worlds, these subtle bodies will not suffice. They are part of the incarnate realm.

The incarnate realm is, for me, the energy field surrounding the planet earth—it is part of Gaia's subtle body, if you wish. This energy field is intimately tied to the physical world. When a soul incarnates, it needs to take on not just a physical body but an incarnational field that includes the physical body as well as subtle aspects that connect to and draw from the subtle environment. Incarnation, therefore, takes place not simply in the physical realm but in this larger Gaian dimension that includes the physical but includes subtle layers of being as well; it takes place in the incarnate realm as a whole.

In effect, the soul incarnates twice: first into the subtle field of Gaia and then into the physical plane. The subtle incarnation provides the matrix for the development of the physical body and the subsequent body-mind. With this in mind, I would say that Act I of incarnation involves not simply the creation of the incarnational system but the formation of a subtle field that becomes the incarnation into the subtle environment of the earth.

### THE SUBTLE INCARNATION

Before looking at Act I as a whole, let me be more specific about the subtle side of our embodiment within the incarnate realm.

Here's a picture:

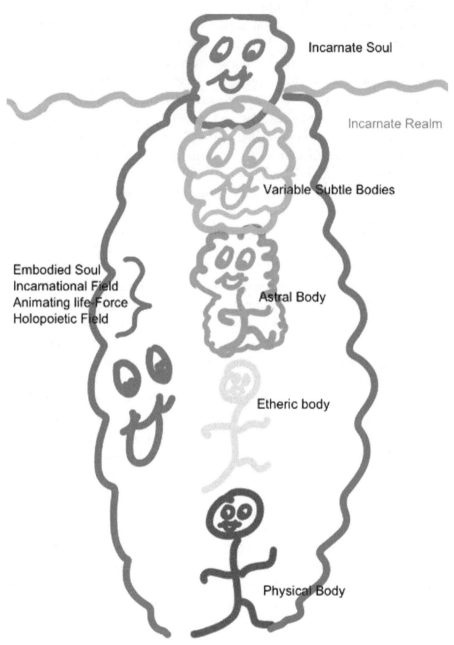

FIGURE 14

[Note: I'm not attempting a precise anatomical description of our subtle nature here. Think of this as suggestive of the wavelengths and patterns involved. These are levels I've experienced, but there may be more, and the arrangement between them is not truly vertical or linear as they blend with each other. Also, this picture only concerns itself with our relationship to the subtle environment of the earth and our "subtle" incarnation. There are other subtle layers to our consciousness that are part of the incarnate soul and of the soul itself.]

Let's start at the bottom of this picture.

The physical body is the "field of contact" with the physical realm. It is one of the bodies or "fields" through which the Soul engages the world and its incarnate realm.

The etheric body is the exact replica of the physical body within the subtle environment immediately around the physical earth. This body is in effect the energetic aspect of the physical body, holding the chi and prana and other subtle forces that directly interact with or emanate from (or are absorbed by) the physical body. It is also the energy body that feels the effects of other subtle energies in our environment, so it can also be thought of as an organ of subtle perception. I often refer to this simply as our "energy body."

The astral body is problematic for me. It is referred to all the time in popular esoteric literature, and people speak about "astral travel" and "astral glamour" and the like. From my perspective, it's not really a "body" like the other parts of the subtle field but rather represents a point of connection and interaction with what is usually called the "astral plane" but which I prefer to call the "imaginal realm." This is a part of the incarnate realm that is highly fluid and plastic, easily molded by thought, feeling and will. My inner colleagues sometimes refer to it as akin to an interstitial or synovial fluid, which is the semi-viscous fluid between bones and joints that keeps them from grinding on each other and allows freedom of movement. In effect, the astral plane has no true character or structure of its own other than to be a pliable, plastic medium that can be shaped by forces arising from the incarnate realm on one side or the subtle worlds on the other side. However, it is where thought-forms are generated and it can take on a whole imaginal character of its own shaped by human thought and feeling (among other things). If enough energy is poured into these thought forms or imaginal landscapes, they can persist indefinitely. We might think of the astral plane as the source of a "molding plastic" or "molding clay" that can be shaped by consciousness to create a mold around which manifestation can occur. For this reason, the astral substance has long been used in various forms of practical magic and manifestation. Our "astral body" is really an imaginal body we create that can allow us to engage with and manipulate this realm, but it's not really a structural body of incarnation in the same way that the other elements of our overall subtle field can be. Like any astral creation, an astral body, once formed, can persist throughout the lifetime, though it can take different shapes. I think it's more precise to say that what we possess is an imaginal capacity, an ability to engage with the astral realm, more than that we have an astral body. There are practical energetic reasons for this that go beyond the scope of this book. However, working with the astral can be a powerful and meaningful piece of work in our world given how prevalent and powerful astral influences can be within the collective human psyche (this is where most human "baggage" ends up). If anything can be called a "plane of illusion," this is it.

By Variable Subtle Bodies (VSB), I mean that when I look into this part of us—when I attune to it—I see a "cloud" of potential subtle bodies, or perhaps I should say, a subtle body that has a "cloud" of potential capacities, forms and manifestations. This may be purely a function of the limits of my observational capacities. It may seem cloudy because I can't see the definitions and forms well enough to discern exactly what's there. This is certainly a possibility to take into account. What I see, though, may be exactly what is there: a subtle field of consciousness that can "shapeshift" according to the need. Or there may be a cluster of subtle bodies that are in close systemic interaction, a kind of "one in many, many in one" phenomenon. (This is not an unusual perception for me in the subtle worlds where many things don't have clearly or rigidly defined forms but can shift from one aspect to another depending on the need or the circumstances.) This may simply represent a unifying field of different subtle connections and contacts, each of which has "body-like" aspects.

The etheric and physical bodies relate to the physical environment and its energy fields. The astral relates to an imaginal space which in some ways may be thought of as a tool of communication and manifestation. The "VSB," however, is that part of us that relates to the larger subtle environment and layers of the incarnate realm. Depending on which aspect of that environment or which layer or aspect it's relating to, it takes on a particular configuration. That's why I think of it as "variable." And if it's in contact with several different aspects of the planetary subtle field at once, it may be manifesting more than one such configuration. That's why I think of it as "bodies."

Simply—and simplistically—put, if it's not the physical body and it's not the etheric body or the astral connections but it's in touch with the subtle environment of the earth, it's a Variable Subtle Body.

Enfolding, holding and empowering all these bodies or fields I think of as the Embodied Soul: the will and life, love and presence of the soul within the incarnate realm. But I also think of this as the incarnational field and the holopoietic field that enables all these "soul fractals" or "self-fractals" to work together. This presence I also think of as the animating life force. When it is removed (as at death), all that holds these elements together with each other and in some cases within themselves vanishes. Thus at death, the physical body is no longer animated and comes apart in decay. The etheric body also disintegrates in the normal course of things. The astral body may become the body of incarnation within the lower levels of the post-mortem realm but it, too, will sooner or later disperse. The VSB may coalesce into a single subtle body in which the personality experiences itself as surviving death. Over time, this, too, will disappear as it integrates with the incarnate soul and then with the soul itself. But here I am anticipating Act III.

What is tricky here is that really everything I've described above, from the physical body to the variable subtle bodies is the Embodied Soul in action and expression. It's like one of those optical illusion photographs which seen one way is a vase but seen another way is two faces looking at each other. Looked at from one perspective, we possess a number of subtle bodies (or potential subtle bodies) but look at another way, there's only one subtle presence which is the Embodied Soul.

Finally, there is the Incarnate Soul. This is the embodiment or manifestation of the focus and intent of the soul to engage with the incarnate realms. The Incarnate Soul straddles the threshold of the incarnate realm and the subtle worlds beyond and is the energetic intermediary between the two.

This is the aspect of soul that holds the unique personal identity of a particular incarnation. This is where, in my case, David is found or David's soul—as contrasted with the Soul itself which is the soul of multiple incarnations, including David.

If I think of my personal identity and especially that David who survives physical death, this is where I will find that.

Before we continue, I should reiterate something I said (or at least implied) much earlier in the book: what I am offering here is a look at the self and at our identity from the standpoint of subtle energies. It can get confusing with all these "souls" and multiple bodies and identities running around—who the heck am I in the midst of all this?

But it can help if you remember that what I'm talking about here are really energy states of varying frequency and intensity. The Embodied Soul is a particular energy state (for that matter, so is the physical body) and the Incarnate Soul is a different energy state, and the Soul is different yet again. But these are differences along a continuum. X-rays are different from gamma rays and both are different from visible light, yet all of these are expression of electromagnetism.

This is one reason I usually talk about "fields" rather than "bodies" when discussing these things. Talking about subtle bodies is a familiar, comfortable way of speaking about these phenomena but it can suggest something far more distinct and solid than is the reality. Calling them fields suggest their energetic nature.

Each of us has just one "I" which exists in various states of energy manifestation and potentiality, configured to a variety of different environments which are themselves at different energy states. If the "I" could directly relate to the physical world, if the Planetary Soul or the Cosmic Spirit-Soul could directly relate to the physical world, it would. Why not? But the energy differential is too great—or at any rate, the difference in states of being is too great. Connection can't be made.

So the "I" manifests in a variety of energy states, each of which allows it to connect and engage appropriately with a particular environment. The challenge comes in integrating all these various manifestations—the different states and stages along the continuum of being, such as soul and body or soul and personality.

**ACT I, SCENE ONE: THE SOUL'S INTENT**

Earlier, I wrote about the initial impulse for an incarnation which begins with the soul's intent. I said at the time that this wasn't a plan in the way we usually think of a plan as a mental construct or an idea; it was more than that. It was a shaping of the living presence of the soul into a particular "shape" or configuration. To put it in our experience, it's the difference between thinking "I'm going to make a million dollars," and taking on the mental and emotional felt sense of having a million dollars, i.e. of being a millionaire. It's the difference between thinking of something and being that thing.

Please take a moment to refresh your memory of FIGURE 10.

This is a classic strategy in manifestation: embody or inhabit the felt sense of the reality of that which you wish to manifest—that is, take on its psychic and energetic "shape"—as this will begin to shape and configure the flow of probability, life and circumstances around you to bring that intent—that shape—into being.

There is another factor here as well. When we think of a plan, we usually think of something unfolding linearly through time. I think of where I'd like to be and what I'd like to accomplish "in the future." I am planning to reach a goal that lies ahead of me in time. But that's not how the soul experiences this. As best I understand it at this point, time for the soul is a "structural tool," a way of creating boundary and focus and giving something definition. I don't know if I would say the soul lives in an "eternal Now," as I'm not at all sure that's true, but it does inhabit and experience time as something a good deal more fluid and flexible and, well, different, than we do here, in part because the perception of time as we experience it unfolds as it does partly due to our brain and neurological structure, a particular limit with which the soul doesn't have to contend. So, when I have observed this, the best way I've found to describe it is as if the soul shapes what I think of as a "time-bubble" a kind of "phase space" for all possible permutations, manifestations, connections, consequences, and expected or potential emergent properties of a particular incarnation. (In physics and mathematics, a phase space is, according to Wikipedia, "a space in which all possible states of a system are represented, with each possible state of the system corresponding to one unique point in the phase space.") In this bubble or space the entire incarnation is present; the entire bubble and the qualities it generates is the soul's intent, and it is a present reality to the soul, not a future one. From womb to tomb and beyond, the entire incarnation is held in the body of the soul as a presence within itself.

And yet, this bubble isn't "realized" or "sprouted" (if I think of it as a seed). It exists within the soul, and yet it doesn't. It hasn't been "cooked" in the oven of incarnation. It's as if I bought all the ingredients for a great soup and laid them out on the table. I can see all together everything that will be in the soup, and yet, it isn't a soup. I could eat each of the ingredients separately or in different combinations, but I still wouldn't get the flavor or the experience as if I'd put them all in a pot and cooked them together. Or to use another analogy, I can hold the seed of an apple tree in my hand and that seed contains everything that tree can be, including the apples it will produce. But holding the seed will not give me the taste of a fresh apple, nor will "apple flesh" become part of my flesh. I can't eat the seed and get the same results as eating an apple. An incarnation is more than just its intent, more than the "time-bubble" or phase space that is its seed.

When I was working with John, he asked me to spend some time doing "readings" for people, which was an interesting form of training for me. A client would come and sit with me and I would contact John, and then we would have in essence a three-way conversation (though from the client's point of view, I was speaking for both John and myself).

During this experience, the number one question bar none that clients brought to me was "What is my purpose in life?" or "What is my soul's plan?" or some variation on this. And in most cases, this was difficult to answer because John would show me this "time-bubble" (this was my first introduction to this concept and experience) and there was no easy way to describe it. Most of the time, there wasn't a specific "mission" or "plan" in the way the client was thinking, no message saying "you were born to be a doctor," or "you were born to become President of the United States." Instead, the clearest translation of what John would show me or tell me was "your soul's intent is to be you." Needless to say, this wasn't satisfying to most of my clients who were looking for something more specific!

What I learned from this experience, though, was that in most cases (certainly not all), the soul's intent is much more holistic and systemic than a simple "plan" could describe. It placed great emphasis on the value, beauty, wonder and purpose of the whole life, not just some specific part of it such as the accomplishment of a particular goal. It made identity the purpose: you are here to be you.

The time-bubble that is the shaping and manifestation of the soul's intent holds all the time of the incarnation from beginning to end, from womb to tomb, as I like to say. But there is no sense of predestination about it; little is preordained in an absolute or limiting sense. However, there is at least one dominant pathway, and often secondary pathways as well branching off from possible decision points, that represents the most likely way the life will unfold. For example, my dominant pathway shows me becoming a spiritual teacher and seer, an explorer of the subtle worlds and a partner to subtle beings. But other pathways were potential, though not of high probability.

In this sense, the time bubble is a study in statistics and probability. It creates tendencies in certain directions and towards certain choices and experiences, and those tendencies can be strongly "grooved" or given an energy of high probability within the phase space. But it doesn't lock anything into an absolute pattern of unfoldment and direction. There is structure and likelihood, but there is also freedom and choice built into it, these being necessary to create the true fruit or flavor of the incarnation. Whatever else it is, this time-bubble or incarnational seed that represents the soul's intent, is an instrument of emergence as much as of destiny.

This is true because the realization of the potentials within this seed depend on its correlation, connection and collaboration with a number of other similar seeds held by souls whose interaction will be part of that phase space and with overall conditions on the earth and within humanity. The unfoldment of an incarnation is a collective endeavor; we are all in a sense co-incarnates of each other. For instance, for me to incarnate, I needed parents. Parents would have been included in my time-bubble. Were they the specific people who in fact were my parents? Probably not at this stage, but that would have become part of this seed later—but I'm getting ahead of myself.

The main point I wish to make is that this time-bubble or phase space or seed of incarnation doesn't stand alone but is a starting point for a process. It's like a blueprint the soul can then present to other souls or to whoever (or whatever) may help it with its incarnational process, soliciting advice, help, additions, changes, and so forth. So in my case, for instance, at some point in the process, seeing this intent within my soul, the souls who became my parents came forward and said, "Oh, we can fit into that. We can be your parents." At which point, one path within the phase space becomes more emphasized over another (the path in which these two particular souls with their particular incarnational time-bubbles become my parents as contrasted with some other path within my incarnational phase-space that would have been emphasized had two different souls with their different circumstances, energies, intents, time-bubbles, etc. been my parents).

FIGURE 15 shows a very simplistic picture illustrating this example.

In this picture, my soul has created a "time-bubble" or phase space in which all meaningful potential life-events are present as golden dots. The "birth-point" is indicated, or what is really the moment of conception when two people become my parents. If souls A and B are my parents, then my lifetrack—the dominant, high-probability path through the phase space, connecting various life events together in a sequence that will unfold through earthly time—goes in the blue direction, but if souls X and Y are my parents, it goes in the red direction.

The point of convergence is where these two potential lifetracks meet in a single event (for instance, if two divergent circumstances in my life led me to Findhorn, no matter who my parents were), at which point I could go along either the blue or red lifetrack from that time forward.

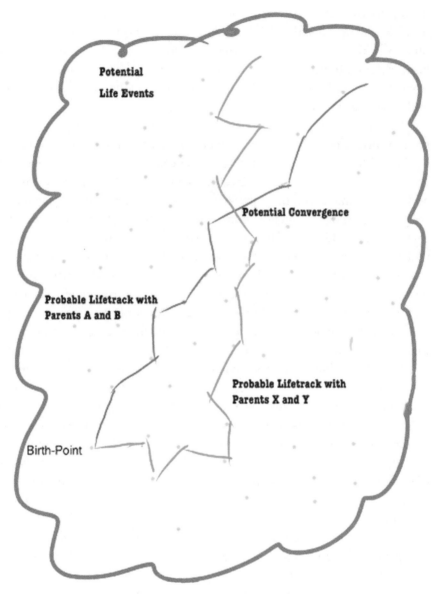

Incarnational "Phase Space"

FIGURE 15

When thinking about this "time-bubble," all the possible points (the golden dots in the picture) are present; they are all possible or potential as a result of the parameters set down that created this phase space in the first place, i.e. by the soul's intent. But not all will happen in the actual incarnation itself, Some will have a higher potential of occurrence than others. The lifetrack defines the path connecting these "highest-probability" points. It's possible a soul's intent may contain a very distinct lifetrack; it's possible it may have more than one of relatively equal probability depending on how circumstances unfold in the actual "cooking" or "living out" of the incarnation on earth; and it's possible there's no real life-track at all, that there's no one or two or three high-probability paths but that the whole incarnation is one of improvisation, spontaneity and emergence (this may happen if the soul if fairly new to the physical experience and simply wants to "try out" physical life and gain some experience but doesn't have any particular specific goals in mind other than that).

Why do I call this phase space a "time-bubble?" It's largely an attempt to interpret what I've been shown. It's just that the soul seems to use what appears to me as time or some aspect of time to form part of the boundary that creates this incarnational seed—this embodied intent. And there is paradox involved. For instance, using my earlier example of manifesting a million dollars, a person might hold and embody the felt sense of being a millionaire now and yet still know that this reality needs to "work out" or unfold in both linear and "synchronistic" time. He can have the felt sense of being a millionaire and still not have a bank account that tells his banker or creditors he's a millionaire. He holds simultaneously a state of "NOW!" and a state of "Becoming" and "Unfolding." There is work of some nature he has to do to translate the felt sense in himself into the tally in his bank account.

This "time-bubble" incorporates both the temporal wholeness of the incarnation—the sense of NOW—and the temporal energy to do the work of becoming—the sense of Now and Then, in which the "Then" is also important.

I'm not sure I can explain it more than that; attempting to do so just gets me into the metaphysics of time which I think diverts us from the real topic here. But I did wish to make the point that the soul doesn't simply live through time in the way we appear to do, moving from past to present to future, but uses time as a molding and creative force. And I wanted to stress that the soul's intent is not a goal, something that will happen "then," but is a condition of presence and intentionality that is complete in the "now."

### FROM INTENT TO INCARNATIONAL SOUL

When the soul forms its basic intent to engage with the incarnate realms and shapes its intent, Act I of the incarnation begins. The next step is that this embodied intent is itself transformed. It's first act as the seed of the incarnation is to generate a boundary of focus and intent that differentiates some part of the soul's overall consciousness and energy into a unique configuration. In my life, this would be equivalent to what happens when I decide to write a book. A part of my mental and emotional life (and physical life, too, as my fingers know only too well!) becomes dedicated to this book and become wholly focused upon its life and unfoldment. I have written of this before in the book.

Here's a picture:

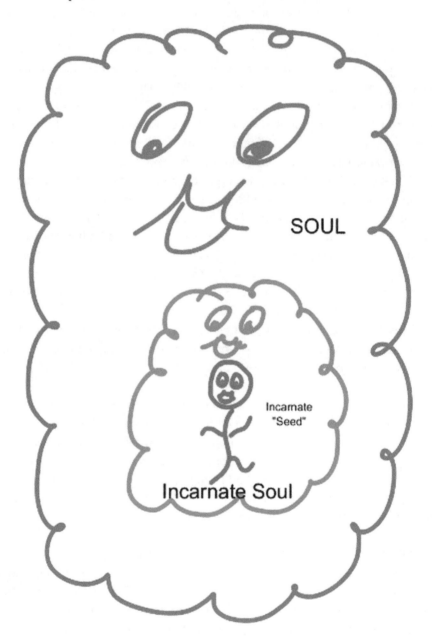

FIGURE 16

In this picture, the part of the soul that specifically starts to hold and shape and become responsible for the "time-bubble" or phase space of the incarnation—the incarnational seed—becomes what I'm calling the Incarnate Soul. At the same time, the growing influence and needs of the incarnational seed affect the soul as well, further establishing and defining boundaries around that part of the soul that is engaging with it. In this manner, a distinct part of the soul comes into being that is in some ways wholly unified with the soul as a whole and in other ways is a distinct and separate consciousness. Metaphorically, it's like the Great Red Spot on Jupiter, a giant swirling, hurricane-like storm that has achieved stability within the planet's atmosphere.

The Incarnate Soul begins the process of attuning to the incarnate realms and taking the steps necessary to create both the subtle and physical incarnations and to embed itself (a popular word these days) into the material world and into the collective consciousness of incarnate humanity. In so doing, the Incarnate Soul will itself become partly involved in the incarnate realm as I described earlier.

In effect, the Incarnate Soul becomes the theater manager or impresario who will oversee and produce the three acts of the incarnation.

As the Incarnate Soul—the increasingly embodied intent of the soul as a whole—comes into greater activity, it sharpens and brings greater differentiation and substance to the incarnational seed itself, heightening the probability of those lifetracks that will best represent and manifest the presence of the soul and its intent within the incarnate realm. The "time-bubble" begins to take on more definitive form and as it does it begins to attract those who can and will help it move into manifestation.

### ACT I, SCENE II: THE STAGE HANDS AND OTHER ACTORS

#### THE FOUR INCARNATIONS

As I said above, incarnation is a complex process. Souls need help and collaboration, guidance and advice from peers and from more developed souls and other beings. How much advice, guidance, help and collaboration depends on the development and skill of the soul and the nature of the incarnation.

Though we usually think of an incarnation as simply a matter of a soul taking on a body and living on the physical earth, it's more than just that. I've already referred to the "two incarnations," one into the subtle body of the planet, the subtle environment of the incarnate realm, and the other into physical matter. But to this I could add two others. The soul incarnates into the life-field of Gaia as it is currently manifest and it incarnates into the collective energy field of incarnate humanity. In effect, the soul takes on four "incarnations" in order to create its incarnate self. Here is a picture:

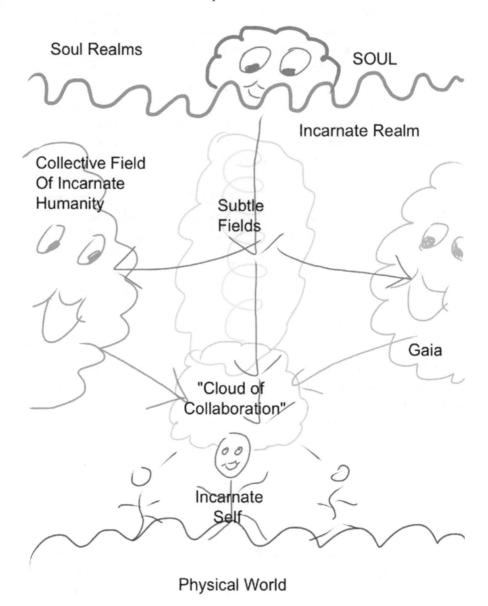

**Soul Realms**

**SOUL**

Incarnate Realm

Collective Field
Of Incarnate
Humanity

Subtle
Fields

Gaia

"Cloud of
Collaboration"

Incarnate
Self

Physical World

FIGURE 17

First, a broad picture may be helpful here. There is nothing static about the world into which a soul incarnates. It is a dynamically evolving system filled with diverse lives each pursuing their own destiny and evolution; Gaia itself is developing.

Thus the world a soul incarnates into in 2012 is not the same world that soul would have engaged with in 1912 or 1812 or 2012 BCE. Of course, on a physical planetary level, many changes are so slow by human standards that they may make no difference. But this is not true in the subtle worlds which can be much more dynamic and fluid.

But beyond these changes, from the point of view of the soul the world is not simply an environment in which to live but a living entity with whom to partner and engage. Gaia is incarnating, too, and when a soul enters into its life-field, it becomes part of that incarnation. We are each participants in the incarnation of Gaia.

This is also true for Humanity seen as a great collective entity. The Soul of Humanity spans both the subtle and physical worlds, and all of us participate in its ongoing incarnation and development. But on the physical level, the human collective field also is changing and much more quickly than that of Gaia.

Thus the humanity we incarnate into in 2012 is most definitely not the same humanity we would have incarnated into a hundred or a thousand or ten thousand years ago. We are the same physical species but we are not the same energetically or in the development of our subtle bodies. We face different challenges now than our ancestors did, and we have a different set of opportunities.

This is the meaning of the Time card in the *Soul's Oracle* card deck as shown here.

Note that even if we think of all our incarnations happening simultaneously in some eternal NOW, they are not all happening on the same earth. A life I may be leading in the fourteenth century is not within the same energetic structure and context of both Gaia and Humanity as the life I lead now. We know that a life in ancient Rome under the rule of the Emperor Augustus is not taking place in the same kind of culture and energy field as a life in New York City in the Twenty-First Century with Barack Obama as President. The same is true for the inner energetic structure of the human collective field and the "Gaian collective field," if I may call it that.

This is not to say there are not consistent elements and similarities. Some things change very slowly. But a Roman consciousness of the 1st century is dealing with a subtle energy environment and a set of evolutionary challenges quite different from those of a New Yorker or a Londoner or a resident of Tokyo in 2012.

The Greek philosopher Heraclitus said it best twenty-six hundred years ago, "No man ever steps in the same river twice."

So when the soul looks upon the incarnate world and contemplates its next journey there, it has to take into account the changes that have taken place. In a way, it's like considering how to jump on a moving train...two moving trains, actually: humanity and Gaia.

In crafting its incarnation, the soul has to consider the subtle fields and levels that it is going to be part of and create a subtle incarnation; this will become the initial matrix for the subsequent physical incarnation. In a way, this is the vertical axis of the incarnation.

It also has to consider how it is going to incarnate into Gaia and how it is going to incarnate into the collective field of incarnate Humanity. Just having a human body on the planet isn't enough in either case. It has to correlate and come into resonance with the current vibrational conditions of Gaia and Humanity.

In effect, it's all about making connections.

These issues are illustrated in the picture above by the arrows entering into the subtle fields and branching off along the "horizontal axis" of the incarnation into Gaia and Humanity.

There's a whole other set of connections, though, that need to be formed. In the picture I call these the "cloud of collaboration." These represent all the significant connections that we form with other souls who will be our parents, siblings, friends, even in some cases our enemies who will challenge us in ways that help us grow in important directions. These are all the other actors in our incarnational play, just as we are actors in theirs.

I mentioned above that the planning for an incarnation can take decades or even hundreds of years in earthly time. This is especially true if the soul is going to engage with the Souls of Humanity and Gaia in a way that will have a powerful impact, or the soul may even be taking on a particular "avatar" role, embodying some aspect of the Humanity Soul or the Gaian Soul in physical form.

This has its analogies in our everyday experience. A friend of mine who is an up and coming opera singer knows that next month she will be playing a role in one opera, then later in the year she'll be in a different role in a different city in a different opera, and then next year she'll be in yet another role. She plans her schedule out, as much as she can and depending on the roles she can get, as much as a year or more in advance. Each of these roles is like a new incarnation.

But these collaborations can be built "on the fly," so to speak. It's not always the case that a soul arranges while its future great-grandparents are alive who its grandparents and parents will be before those individuals have themselves taking birth. Remember that souls remain conscious and active in their own native realm. The fact that my soul is in incarnation as David Spangler in no way limits its ability to lead its live and engage in its own level of activity and relationships.

So it's quite possible that a soul seeking incarnation may collaborate with another soul who is already in incarnation, arranging for it to be one of its parents, say.

Here's an example. I have memory of having arranged with the souls who became my Mom and Dad that they would be my parents, and this was before either of them had yet been born as Hazel and Marshall. But about eight years ago or so, I was sitting in a friend's living room when a subtle being suddenly appeared before me. It was a sparkling, jolly, joyous presence, and it said to me, "Hi. I'm going to be one of your grandchildren." Then it disappeared. I have no idea which one of my kids will be its parent—none of my children are anywhere near having children—and I didn't recognize this being. It apparently had a soul relationship with one of my children and had just taken an opportunity to introduce itself to me. I have no idea, but perhaps it had just arranged with the soul of one of my children to enter into a parent-child relationship.

Those other souls—I think of them as our "co-incarnates"—who are part of our "cloud of collaboration" don't all necessarily take incarnation with us. Some of them may remain as partners and collaborators on the subtle realms (I call such close subtle partners our "Pit Crew") while others will enter into incarnation with us.

The fact is that most souls belong to clusters, not unlike soul families, in which a group of souls have incarnated together in a variety of roles and relationships over thousands of years. The intimacy and love between such cluster partners can be very powerful; when we meet someone who is part of our soul cluster we almost always know it, experiencing a sense of recognition and familiarity with this person as if we've known them for a long time. This is not always the case, as for particular reasons a strong veil may be drawn over the instinctive soul memory that each of us carries, but usually, members of a soul cluster will recognize or respond to each other in some manner.

Souls are not bound to incarnate only with members of their particular clusters, and these clusters are themselves part of larger clusters, like soul families that are part of clans and tribes. Souls are perfectly free to move outside their clusters and form partnerships and relationships for particular incarnational purposes with any other souls, but these clusters form powerful fields of resonance and capacity that can greatly augment what a soul can accomplish in a given incarnation. However, it's perfectly possible for a soul to "graduate" from a particular cluster and join with souls from other clusters to form a new cluster in order to develop together new capacities. In such a case, it always remains close to its "cluster of origin," just as most of us do to our birth families even after we marry and form families and circles of friends on our own.

As I understand it, the Incarnate Soul creates a presence, a life-field within the subtle realms of the incarnate realm, and this becomes the seed and contact point around which the subtle incarnation takes place. I suppose in a way the Incarnate Soul becomes a kind of womb within which the subtle matrix of the new incarnation takes form. I honestly do not know the details of this process, and I suspect that it can differ from one soul to another.

What I do know is that this matrix becomes a focal point for the development of what I think of as the "incarnational intelligence" or even a collaboration point for incarnational intelligences. By this I mean a particular kind of awareness and intelligence, one that is skilled at doing what needs to be done to organize and manage the incarnational process, just as we have a body intelligence that "runs" our body for us at unconscious levels so we don't have to think about it.

This incarnational intelligence is not a being or anything so specific or bounded; rather it's like the intelligence I might bring to repairing my car or writing a novel. I don't operate my life with that specific intelligence but it's there and it's handy when I need it.

Actually, "car maintenance intelligence" isn't a bad metaphor for what I want to convey here—and to be wholly transparent and truthful, for me it's only a metaphor, not an experience! What I know about car maintenance could be written on my little finger—more angels dance on the head of a pin than what I know about automobiles and how to fix them. I have practically zero mechanical intelligence! Ha! So we're partly treading in the realm of fantasy here, but it's still a good metaphor!

But assuming I did have a knowledge of cars and a feel for how they work and how to fix them, this would constitute a "car repair intelligence" within me. I could work on my car when it breaks down and fix it. However, this intelligence also includes knowing when to call in experts expert (actually, I'm VERY intelligent about this part! <g>) and include their intelligence in the process. In short, I can do some things myself and for other things, I go to a garage. As far as my car is concerned, though, the field of "car repair intelligence" that embraces it includes both me and the other experts.

When a soul seeks incarnation and is seeking guidance and help in creating both its "cloud of collaboration" and its subtle matrix (which, to introduce more jargon, we might start calling the "proto-personality"), there are plenty to offer that help and thus to augment the soul's own incarnational skills and intelligence. From the human side, these include members of its own soul cluster but even more, guides, advisers, and generally more advanced souls who may have a wider vision and perspective on personal and collective evolution than a given soul may have.

But there are non-human forces at work as well, angels and devas and a book of beings whom I think of as "human nature spirits" or "human elementals," beings whose task is to assist in the incarnational process.

The work of all these beings, human and non-human, is to assist in the creation of the incarnational seed matrix, the proto-personality, that will eventually provide the subtle structure guiding the cells in the formation of the body in a mother's womb, a process that itself is guided by intelligences within the mother's body and within the developing body of the fetus and embryo.

Part of their work is to form the appropriate energy connections to the current collective field of incarnate humanity and the current collective field of incarnating Gaia, as I discussed above. In so doing, a kind of intelligence forms to guide these connections and which will continue to do so throughout the incarnate life of the individual, for incarnation is a continuous process of connection and engagement, not something that happens once. This intelligence is like the "car repair intelligence" I mentioned above, a combination of skills within the self and skills brought by others.

As the proto-personality unfolds, there are four of these "fields of intelligence" that take shape. One regulates the connections with Gaia, one regulates the connections with the collective field of incarnate humanity, one regulates the connections with the body and the personal energy fields, and one regulates connections with the transpersonal, the Incarnate Soul itself and the Soul beyond.

These four intelligences or sentient processes—I'm honestly not entirely sure what to call them—form the basis of the incarnational system. In the Presence Exercise, I have at times referred to them as "selves," specifically our "World Self," our "Humanity Self," our "Personal Self," and our "Transpersonal Self."

## THE INCARNATIONAL SYSTEM

We're coming to the end of this chapter of the text, but I want to pause here in the narrative and say a bit more about the incarnational system as it plays such a central role in my understanding of the dynamics involved in incarnation.

The core idea here is that we don't incarnate into a body as much as we do into a dynamic system of interrelationships. This is true on the physical level as well. We think of our bodies as "My Body" in the singular, but in fact, a human body is a itself a system of interaction between cells, tissues, organs, and various metabolic pathways. Over a trillion beings live in us as our somatic cells and by rough estimate, about that number of microorganisms live on and in us as well, and most of these are absolutely vital to our health and well-being. Furthermore, as we will see, the actual incarnational system isn't limited to our subtle energies and subtle fields nor to our individual body but extends into our relationships as well. Part of our "body" of incarnation is a field co-created with others which I think of as our "relational body." It's obviously not as solid and highly defined as our physical body, but in many ways it's just as important and defining in providing a means for the soul to incarnate. There are aspects of our soul that incarnate—or perhaps I should say, become available and known to us energetically—through our group life that are not so We'll talk about this much more in the chapters to come.

The thing about a system is precisely that it is dynamic and in balance, and this balance can be thrown off. The system can be in a state of coherency or it can develop incoherencies. This is also one of the key thoughts that we'll be exploring much more in the chapters to come.

This systemic nature is obvious on the physical level but it's not always so obvious on subtle levels or in the realms of thought and emotion. If we are used to thinking of our bodies in singular ways—i.e. the body as a complete unit—then we are even more accustomed to thinking of that inner, subjective phenomenon of the psyche—the thing we call our "self"—as a singular entity. I am my self, we say, and at one level this is true. But from the standpoint of subtle energies and the fields that hold them, we are just as much a system at that level as on the physical plane.

The image of the four sides of this system—the Transpersonal Self, the Personal Self, the World Self, and the Humanity Self—is a very simple, and simplistic, representation of this incarnational system. It allows for the creation and practice of simple exercise of attunement to this system and to the Presence it embodies, i.e the Presence Exercise. It does represent elements of this system as I understand it and observe it, but it's not a comprehensive picture.

For example, the "World Self" in the exercise can be further divided into Nature (the biosphere), the Earth (the physical structure of the planet, the land, etc.), the Subtle Environment or etheric body of the planet, and Natural Laws (such as physics, chemistry, etc.), all of which combine to create the world as we know it—and we are connected to all of these, yet the connections are not identical.

So, for example, I am connected to the laws that regulate the composition and interaction of manner (my body exists as an expression of physics, chemistry, biology, etc.); I am connected to the biosphere (to the realm of animals, plants, microbes, and so on—and in fact, I am physically part of that biosphere as a member of an animal species); to the land (I connect energetically to the land and topography where I live, where I was born, where I am in the moment, and so son); and I am connected in subtle energetic ways to the subtle environment of the world around me.

All of these connections are subsumed in the exercise into the "World Self."

In a similar way, the "Humanity Self" could be further broken down into my connections with the people I meet and interact with on a daily basis; with the collective presence and activity of currently incarnate humanity; with the collective history or karma of humanity; and with the soul and collective subtle energy fields of humanity, both incarnate and discarnate.

My point is that the incarnational system is more than just what the Presence Exercise describes; these four elements are really categories of connection, all of which contribute to the ongoing and dynamic manifestation of a subtle energy system that creates a field to receive and hold the presence of our Incarnate Soul and provide a basis for an emergent self to appear.

Incarnation is a dynamic co-creative act between what the soul brings to the world, as focused through the lens and presence of the Incarnate Soul, and what the Earth provides (including what the collective field of Humanity provides).

It's as if you had to build a house in a wilderness. You bring with you some of the building materials, such as glass for windows, and your tools and even some furniture, but you also have to get many of your building materials from the land around you (such as lumber from trees you cut down). The kind of house you end up with is a product of what you brought with you, your own creativity and skill and what the land could provide. The house of a person building in the midst of a pine forest is going to be different from the house of a person building in the desert of the American Southwest or a person building up near the arctic circle. They might start out with similar furniture and tools, but one is going to end up with a log cabin, one with a house made of adobe and clay, and on with a house made of ice and grass from the tundra.

In the tradition of hermetic magic, in which the practitioner (magician, wizard, mage, whatever you'd like to call him or her) is invoking subtle energies and beings, a person working alone can draw in and hold a certain intensity of subtle forces. But it's well known that a group working together in relationship can invoke and hold a good deal more. One person trying to catch a 300-pound person jumping out of a fifth floor window of a burning building is likely to get squashed and injured, but a team of fire-persons holding a net can catch that falling body with no injury to anyone as the kinetic energy is distributed through the whole system. Something analogous occurs with subtle energies.

This is why magic and energy work is often done in groups. A system of interconnections and relationships can hold what a single individual cannot, assuming that system can maintain itself in integration and coherency (which sometimes is a big assumption!).

The same principle works with incarnation. I used the image of plasma being held in magnetic bottles to describe this. The incarnational system represents a network or system of relationships that creates a field powerful enough to both hold the presence and energy of the soul and connect that energy with the subtle and physical environments of the earth.

The "first incarnation," then, is the establishment within the subtle realms of this system and its holding field.

*(Note: I'll have more to say about the incarnational system later in the book when we discuss Act II.)*

### THE PAUSE THAT (I HOPE!) REFRESHES

At this point, I want to pause in the ongoing narrative (which is just about finished anyway) and pick up some loose threads and emphasize some important points. In the future, a person taking this book will have a book to work from in which all these ideas are presented in one fell swoop; you are having to read them piecemeal as I write them—and in a choppy way at that as I have to take breaks to rest my hands and arms. It's possible to lose the thread in this long, linear presentation of text. You can feel overwhelmed with ideas, images, pictures, new concepts, and so forth, though I hope no one is!

So let me take a moment to pause and refresh our minds about where we are, where we're going, and where we've been. (Ha! This is as much for me as for you, to make sure I don't lose the threads!)

Here are the important points I want you to know and remember from what we've covered so far:

The Incarnate Realm is made up of a subtle, non-physical dimension and a physical dimension. We incarnate into both.

The "subtle incarnation" consists of two things:

1. creating a field of energy and information that becomes a matrix for what will become the incarnate self or personality
2. creating a set of connections and relationships that generate a field to hold the plasma-like presence and energy of the soul.

These two fields become the foundation, as I understand it, for the emergence of the actual subtle bodies (etheric, variable subtle bodies, etc.) that we use during our incarnate life and which express both our personal life and our transpersonal connections. All of these subtle fields and bodies have an interactive and dynamic interrelationship that I call the "incarnational system."

Incarnation into the Incarnate Realm is a process of incarnating into systems. There are three major systems through which we embody and express ourselves:

1. the subtle "incarnational system"
2. the physical body
3. the body of relationships with others (and with things and places); this could be called the "co-incarnational body."

"Grail Space" (about which we'll be studying more later in the book) is a subset of this, a particular deliberately and mindfully created manifestation of an incarnational relational field.

Our overall incarnational field is the interaction of these three major systems creating a single whole. This whole is the field of emergence for the emergent self, which we experience for the most part as our everyday self.

Earlier, I said that the soul faced three challenges when incarnating. One is the challenge of how to fulfill its incarnational intent, a challenge unique in its form and substance to each soul and person. The other two were the challenge of differential and the challenge of integration. These two are intimately related and are generic in that everyone faces them, though in different degrees depending on soul development and skill.

The Challenge of Differential: This is the challenge of the difference in structure, complexity, and energy between the multi-dimensional soul in its native state and the conditions existing in the incarnate realm. This challenge is met through the creation of the incarnational system and the interrelationships suggested by the Presence Exercise.

The Challenge of Integration: This could also be thought of as a challenge of coherency and wholeness, and is a result of incarnating into systems. Systems are sets of interconnections and interrelationships that can go "out of sync" and become incoherent to some degree, something we'll be exploring in more detail later in the book. So the soul faces a holopoietic challenge of keeping all the elements of its incarnational systems (subtle, physical and relational) in harmony, integration, coherence, and wholeness.

The fundamental answer to these three challenges—the primary tool of holopoiesis—is love. Incarnation is all about learning the qualities, skills and capacities of love.

The soul's intent is manifest not as a "plan" in the ordinary human sense of that word but as a presence; it is a condition of being that is "planted" like a seed in the soil of the incarnate realm where it unfolds and develops, bringing for the fruit of new learning, new substance, and a deepening of the dimension of selfhood within the soul.

Here's a picture describing what I've been talking about:

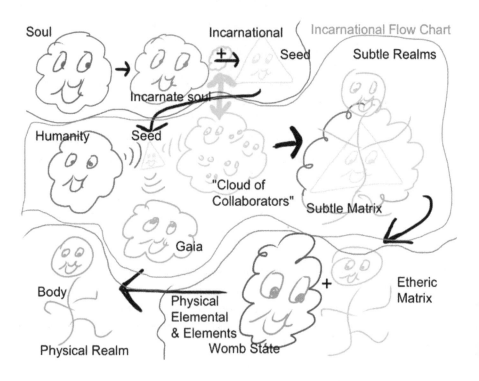

FIGURE 18

Here we have an "Incarnational Flow Chart." There is a great deal of presumption and assumption embodied in the very idea that something as complex, wondrous and profound as incarnation can be encapsulated in a linear flow chart, but hey, fools rush in where angels know better than to go! At any rate, I hope it clarifies the process I'm describing because the process itself lies at the heart of how I view the incarnate self.

So this flow chart covers essentially what I've been calling Act I.

We begin with the soul who has an intent. This intent becomes embodied and focused as what I'm calling the "Incarnate Soul" which manifests the soul's ability to carry this intent into collaboration with other souls and into contact and engagement with the different frequencies, conditions and vibrations of the incarnate realms.

The Incarnational Soul (or, if you wish, the incarnationally-oriented and focused consciousness of the Soul) engages with other souls (companions, advisors, teachers, members of the soul cluster, etc.) who are part of the "Cloud of Collaborators" for this incarnational project and out of this engagement comes an Incarnational Plan, the embodied intent for this incarnation.

This Seed is then taken within the Incarnational Soul into the Subtle Realms where it needs to connect to the current vibrational conditions of both humanity and Gaia. It needs to become part of the subtle fields and energies of the world. In this process, it continues to draw advice and help from its "Cloud of Collaborators," which now may have expanded to include non-human entities (devas, elementals, etc.) as well as other individuals who are closer to the earth plane and can thus help in the incarnational process.

Out of this process of connection, relationship, and engagement, a subtle matrix takes place which constitutes the incarnation of the soul into the subtle realms. This is a kind of "proto-personality" or "proto-personhood." It continues to act as a point of connection with the subtle worlds, taking on information and substance.

It's this subtle matrix that gives birth to the etheric matrix that, within the womb, guides the development of the physical body and its integration with its mental and emotional aspects, it's subtle bodies. This process is helped by an elemental entity working with physical elements to build and shape the body. This becomes the physical elemental for the newborn.

I call this the womb state because it is more than the womb in the mother's body. The new being is gestating and developing within a larger etheric or energetic womb co-created and shared by both the mother and father—and if there are any, perhaps by siblings as well. It's within this larger field that it draws in material from the surrounding mental and emotional—i.e. subtle—environments to incorporate (up to a point) into its own developing subtle bodies. Thus, although the mother carries the physical womb, both parents—when they are present—carry the womb state or the womb field within which the embryo develops.

Once the body is sufficiently developed, the body is born into the physical realm. The process of development, though, continues. That's the topic of Act II and the theme of the rest of the book.

As we end up our consideration of Act II, I want to focus on the process of transforming the intent of the soul, the incarnational seed, into the matrix that shapes and generates the subtle bodies—a process that continues on into and throughout our physical life.

In many ways, we are assembled beings. We are assembled from cells on the physical level. And in the subtle dimension we are "assembled" from subtle material and energy drawn in from the surrounding subtle environment—the thoughts, feelings, instincts, and other psychic materials drawn from humanity and nature both. In this sense, we're like the log cabin made by people living in a forest or an adobe house made by people living in a desert. As I said earlier, we bring a lot to the incarnational table from the soul and its connections (as well as from our own "I" and our sacredness), but we also draw on material available to us in the mental, emotional, and subtle environments.

In effect, when we incarnate into the incarnate realm, we enter into a sea of information, much of it manifesting as vectors (that word again!), bits and pieces of information of varying intent, intensity, and content.

On the whole, this sea of information is not random but is organized in various ways, often by frequencies and affinities.

One way I experience (and think about) this organization is in terms of the four categories I've already mentioned:

- information and subtle energies relating to and generated by activity and beings within the world (nature, the biosphere, the land, the weather, natural laws, etc.)
- information and subtle energies relating to and generated by activity and individuals within humanity.
- information and subtle energies relating to and generated by activity within transpersonal levels, particularly within a person's own soul, spirit, and sacredness.
- information and subtle energies relating to and generated by activity within an individual's personal incarnation, his or her body, thoughts, feelings, connections and relationships.

These make up the broad categories of the incarnational system as practiced and explored in the Presence Exercise (among other things).

The incarnational process, both prior to birth and certainly afterwards during our incarnate life, is one of fitting these different "puzzle pieces" together to create a coherent whole.

This brings us to the end of what I have to say about Act I.

Act II is the subject of the rest of the book.

Act III is what happens after death. This is really a whole book in itself, one that I have done occasionally under the title Death and Dying. I also discuss the Post-Mortem Realms in my book Subtle Realms.

While the topic of what happens to the self after the surrender of the physical body is certainly interesting and important, it's not the topic of this book. Given the amount of time we have and the material I do want to cover about the self as it manifests in physical life, trying to cover Act III would take us too far afield. The main reason I bring it up here is to say that the incarnate life—i.e. the life of the personal, incarnated self or personality—doesn't end with physical death. It simply shifts to a different environment. In Act I, the soul's life within the incarnate subtle realm is as an incarnational seed, a matrix taking form and gathering about itself what it needs to inform and shape its physical life. In Act III, however, the soul re-enters the subtle worlds generally speaking within a new expression of self that has developed over the years of earthly life. It's relationship to those subtle worlds is now different. It's not preparing a seed, it's harvesting its fruits.

I do not have a lot of experience with the Post-Mortem Realms. John took me on a couple of excursions there, which I recount in my book. And I've had occasion on a couple of occasions to act as a psychopomp, escorting a friend across the threshold of life into the afterlife. But such events are rare for me. My attention and work have been much more focused around what happens at the other end of life and on the relationship of the embodied physical consciousness with the subtle worlds while still active and alive in Act II of the incarnation. I simply don't have that much information or experience relating to Act III.

As I understand it, the post-mortem realms fall roughly into three layers (and this is very simplistic, I know). There is the borderland leading up to a threshold between the higher energetic layers of the physical and etheric realms and the actual territory of the subtle worlds, the true post-mortem territory. Then there is a "layer" dedicated essentially to resolving issues that the individual has with the incarnate realm and with the physical life just ended. Just what this resolution entails depends entirely on the person. It can mean anything from confronting and dealing with dysfunctional energies within the person or lessons left unlearned and incomplete to resting and recuperating to exploring new possibilities or developing talents that were potential in the physical life but never had a chance to unfold due to circumstances or individual choice. Finally the third layer is where the individual engages with pursuits attuned to the soul and does whatever is necessary to gain the skills and capacities necessary to fully enter the subtle worlds and reintegrate with the soul.

As I say, this is a very broad-stroke description.

Over the years I have had a few occasions to experience the threshold between the borderlands (which is where souls may linger if they are "earthbound") and the true beginnings of the Post-Mortem realms. Interestingly, this threshold has always appeared to me as a river. Whether this is because it genuinely is a river of energy of some nature or whether it's my projection or it's an image held strongly in the collective consciousness of humanity—based on such older images as the River Styx—I don't know. I just know that it always looks like a river to me.

I am told—I have not experienced this for myself—that some areas of the borderlands can be turbulent and difficult to navigate (though usually, I think, not for the departing soul itself unless it has rendered itself earthbound in some way). Some of this is due to the negative thought-forms and fears that humanity holds so strongly around death. But some of it is due to the death process itself. After all, there is a powerful process of dissolution of bonds and detachment from certain kinds of energetic connections going on. The various energies, intelligences and elemental forces that had been brought together during the life to make the incarnation possible are now dispersed and broken up, going in different directions. I guess it can be like an explosion, and one that is not always comfortable for the living to experience since it moves in a direction opposite to that which is maintaining our own life together.

Beyond this, I don't have much more to say in this book.

There is, however, one more thing I want to say to finish up this chapter's text about "Interiority and the Subtle Worlds."

### INTERIORITY AND THE SUBTLE WORLDS

One of the common synonyms for the non-physical worlds is inner worlds. I've certainly used this terminology, and in past years, it was the main way I referred to these dimensions. But the term is misleading on two counts. In the first instance, it can lead us to assume the subtle worlds exist wholly as a subjective, interior experience and thus are a product of our own consciousnesses. It adds to the supposition that the non-physical dimensions have no objective reality, they only exist within us. This is not true. What is true is that from the standpoint of physical awareness, the means of perceiving the subtle worlds are within us and are not objectively physical senses such as our eyes or ears. In other words, they are objective worlds that we perceive using inner senses rather than outer ones, generally speaking.

The other misconception, though, is more subtle. It is that the non-physical realms constitute the withinness or the interiority of the planet and of the cosmos beyond. This is one reason people in my experience sometimes conflate psychic experience and the perception of and communication with subtle realms and subtle beings as the same thing as a spiritual or mystical experience. This is not true. Experiencing a non-physical being or phenomenon is essentially no different than experiencing a physical person or phenomenon. Either one can trigger a spiritual experience, and both are ultimately rooted in sacredness, but otherwise, both are simply different vibrational realities and different modes of consciousness.

What I think of as the true withinness or interiority of our lives—and of the earth's life as well—is the domain of sacredness, the pure, unconditioned presence and flow of beingness and identity that is the Sacred. Sacredness as I define it is not a subtle energy. There is no differential between ourselves and that sacredness, none. The energy of a cosmic angel or stellar deva may be incredibly far beyond my own energy, and the complexity of its beingness immeasurably greater than my own, but this is not true for the Sacred. We are as close to the interiority of our being, our core of sacredness, as a cosmic archangel or a stellar deva is to its.

In other words, the least evolved being has access to the Sacred, the same access as the most highly evolved cosmic entity has. The experience of the Sacred may be different in each case; the lesser being will know and experience the Sacred in a manner appropriate to it, just as will the higher being, but the Sacred hugs the life within a pebble or the consciousness within an atom just as closely and with just as much caring and love as it hugs a cosmic, galactic high angel.

Our interiority is where our "I" resides, or perhaps I should say the Life and Presence from which our "I" itself emerges.

In all our discussion of incarnational systems, subtle levels, subtle bodies, souls, incarnate souls, and all the rest, we're really talking about the "engineering" and "architecture" of incarnation; its an exploration of the energy systems that make us what we are and shape our expression. But underneath all these things—within them, at the heart of them, at the heart of each of us—is an Interiority, a Presence that is our consistent Identity. In this place we may experience the most profound joy and the most profound sense of unity. We create multiple energy connections with our world, but in our Interiority lies the Connection of Connections, that Presence that makes connectedness possible in the first place. This is the home turf of Love.

As we explore all the different "selves" and manifestations of our incarnational process, it's important that we don't lose sight of the reality of this Interiority.

From my own experience, I would say that contact with subtle worlds is qualitatively different from contact with one's Interiority. Partnership with the subtle half of the world is important in its own right, just as partnering with our physical world is important, but neither is the same as knowing and attuning to our Interiority.

In the Presence exercise, the Presence that you attune to isn't necessarily the same as your Interiority, your sacredness, though I know that when people do this exercise they can slip into this deeper contact. In point of fact, there aren't hard boundaries within us. The holopoietic presence and identity that draws all the elements of the incarnational system together is certainly related to and draws its power from the deeper Presence of ones Interiority, and for all practical purposes, a person might experience them as identical. But they're not necessarily the same thing.

Dealing with the Interiority of life can be challenging. It seems to me that humanity has a history both of confusing higher realms of subtle energy and life with the Sacred Presence and of turning the experience of that Sacredness against the phenomena of incarnation and physical life. The Interiority is not in battle with the Exteriority, so to speak. The exterior worlds, whether non-physical or physical, are creative and loving expressions of the Life that is also the Interior of all things.

In this book, I don't usually wear my Mystic's hat (though in one sense it's always on my head, I suppose); instead, I'm wearing the hat of the subtle world explorer and the subtle energy engineer. But I want to give a shout out to the Interior, the Sacred, to that which is beyond energies and forms and manifestations.

I'll come back to this point from time to time just to make sure!

# Exercise for Chapter Three

## PACKING EXERCISE:

You live in a comfortable, beautiful home that houses all the things that make life wonderful for you. Out of the blue comes an offer to go on an expedition around the world. You will have the funds you need for this trip, and you will be visiting a wide variety of climates and countries on both sides of the equator. You will also be visiting with a wide range of people from poor, rural folks in villages far from cities, perhaps even in jungles to rich people in high society, perhaps even nobility or government ministers. You will need to fit in appropriately wherever you are and with whomever you're visiting. You're not sure how long you'll be gone, but it will be at least three months and quite possibly longer.

Your Task: There is one condition. You can only travel with one carry-on bag or backpack that can fit in the overhead rack of an airplane. You can't carry more with you, so whatever you take from your house will have to fit in this one bag. What do you do? How do you plan your trip? What do you take with you? How do you pack it? (Note: You don't have to pack a bag in reality for this exercise...unless you want to for the full experience! This is an imaginative exercise.)

Object of the Exercise: The focus of this exercise isn't really on what you take and how you organize yourself and pack. It's on what you feel when faced with this challenge. What is the felt sense of meeting this challenge, which is one of starting with something very large (your house and all your belongings) and ending up with something very small but able to meet your needs (your carry-on bag). That's what I'd like you to report on in the next Topic area.

**Variant:** If packing a bag to go on a trip isn't your thing or you'd like more excitement in the exercise, try this variant: A policeman shows up at your door and tells you that the dam upstream is about to break. When it does, a wall of water will sweep down the valley, carrying away your house and everything in it. You have at most one hour to pack up your car and evacuate. What do you do? What do you take with you? How do you decide?

Again, the purpose is to explore in yourself and experience the felt sense of going from what seems a spacious state to one that is more bounded and limited.

Have fun!

# CHAPTER FOUR, ACT II: THE SELF AND THE SEA

The title for this chapter's work comes from the idea that our incarnate self exists and unfolds within a sea of energy and information—a sea of "vectors," if you wish. We develop by absorb substance from this "sea," assimilating and integrating it, and by contributing to it as well. Some of this substance we call "ideas" and "feelings," but much of it is subtle energy of one kind of another. Hopefully, I'll be able to make this much more clear as we proceed.

Before we get into this, though, I want to explore some general thoughts and ideas with you.

First let me say that when I observe the self with subtle perception, it appears to me as a dynamic, somewhat polyhedral field of energy with a complex and shifting architecture. Various streams and currents of subtle energies and forces flow into it and out from it at different frequencies or wavelengths, as if part of us absorbed (and generated) radio waves and another part absorbed (and generated) gamma rays. It is beautiful beyond description, and because it is in constant motion, it is, as I say, very complex, at least as complex in its way—and perhaps more so—than our physical bodies.

Although I certainly have a mystical bent, the way I approach the self is neither as a mystic nor as a psychologist but as a kind of engineer or biologist, looking at dynamic interactions between energy structures and processes within this "self-field."

I imagine this perspective may be unfamiliar and I hope it's not too confusing or off-putting. I will do my best to keep everything as clear as I can make it, but please do make comments or ask questions as we go along.

As I suggested in the previous book texts, what we call an incarnation is really like several incarnations all happening at once. I've already suggested four of them: the incarnation into the subtle fields of the planet, the physical incarnation, the incarnation into the collective soul and energy field of incarnate humanity, and the incarnation into Gaia, which includes the biosphere, the land, and the natural laws of matter (physics, chemistry, etc.)

Another way to say this is that we participate in our personal incarnation, in the incarnation of our soul, in the incarnation of humanity, and the incarnation of the World Soul, Gaia. (What, you may well ask, is the difference between our personal incarnation and the incarnation of our soul? I'll answer that in a bit in more detail, but for now, just think of them as the difference between transpersonal and personal interests, objectives, and modes of being.) Each of these four will (hopefully!) benefit in some manner from our being here on the earth.

As I've said before, in the Presence Exercise I refer to each of these "incarnations" as a self ("World Self," "Humanity Self," etc.). Each can act with a certain degree of autonomy as if it were the locus of selfhood and of decision-making and choice, the focal point of agency.

Why these four? Because I can see them as points of intensification and activity within the dynamic structure of the field of self. They are not ideas or philosophical constructs; they are observations and perceptions.

Another way to describe them as perceptions is that they are like "receptor sites" within the overall energy field of the incarnating self: one such site is a place where Gaian and planetary energies are connected with, received, engaged with, and so on, while another engages with subtle energies emerging uniquely from the collective field of humanity, and so forth. In this sense, they are like the receptor sites on the cell wall of an single-celled organism (to which the energy field of the incarnate self bears more than a passing resemblance to me).

Of course, even though I am seeing certain phenomena, I am also interpreting what I see, so it may be that the manner in which I'm describing them (or even seeing them) isn't wholly accurate. I've said that before, and I just need to say it again. I'm sharing with you not simply what I see but my interpretation of it.

However, the energy field of the self can be observed from different perspectives. If I "slice" though it in one way, I get the four-fold image I've been sharing with you, the four "sub-incarnations" or "selves" of Humanity, World, Soul, and Personality. But this is not the only way the field can be sliced.

Another way is to see that part of us is oriented to the world system in which we exist as physical beings—I might think of this as a "horizontal incarnation or orientation or self." Another part of us is oriented to the ability to cross the thresholds into other systems, the ability to be "multi-systemic" or "meta-systemic." This might be thought of as a vertical orientation. And there's a third I'm aware of that is oriented to what I call the Interiority, which is neither "in the system" or "beyond the system" but something and someplace else altogether. This is an orientation that goes inward at "right angles" to both the horizontal and the vertical.

This three-fold description of a vertical self, a horizontal self, and an "inside" self (the "z-axis" or "depth axis") is simple and tempting to use. And in esoteric literature, it is used quite a bit. If I map the other four "selves" or "incarnational orientations" on this three-fold grid, I get the personal and transpersonal forming the vertical, meta-systemic axis and the Gaian or World and the collective Human forming the horizontal or systemic axis.

But this mapping can be misleading. What we have here really in this second way of describing who and what we are is a part of us that has the capacity to engage with all the elements of a particular system, a system with its own identity and coherency. In our case, this system is the incarnate realm. But as we've seen, the incarnate realm includes a non-physical as well as a physical dimension; it's the physical world around us but it's also the subtle environment around us, too.

If we think of "vertical" as meaning anything beyond or "higher than" the physical, then we miss this subtlety. We think of the subtle environment as outside the system of everyday life in the material world. Then we think of contact with nature spirits and elementals as being "vertical beings" when in fact they're not.

So the "system" here has both the physical and non-physical aspects, and that capacity (or "self") within us that can relate to the system because it, too, is part of it, isn't limited to just engaging the physical world. It can engage the subtle environment as well.

In effect, the incarnational process I described in the previous book texts, that is, what happens in Act I, is designed to create a kind of consciousness—a kind of self—that can live and interact within the world system on both its physical and non-physical levels.

But we also have the capacity within us to go beyond the system (which means going beyond the subtle environment and its psychic energies as well as going beyond the physical) and engage with what is outside the system, what is not bound to or bound by the conditions within the system. Which basically means everything that is not part of the incarnate realm. For us this would mean our soul. (The incarnate soul is basically the soul acting as part of the incarnate system.)

The ability to transcend a system, to go outside it and be a point of communication and circulation (as I described at the beginning of the book) between what's in the system and what's beyond it, is important. It's what prevents the system from becoming a closed system and risking stagnation. When we can reach beyond what is familiar and what we know, we open to new learning and insights, new energies and possibilities that allow the system itself to grow.

Reviewing what I wrote, I feel like I'm teetering on an edge here. On one side is a whole esoteric investigation, which I know from past experience can be a slippery slope, filled with strange concepts, jargon, and dense ideas, while on the other side is an overly simplistic portrayal of the ideas we're working with. I want things to be clear and accessible, and at the same time, we are wading into potentially deep waters that, for me at least, are challenging to describe in straightforward ways. So I apologize for any "brain-burn" anyone may be experiencing or the sense that somewhere in the past chapter you've tumbled down a rabbit hole.

I often have this experience in lectures when someone asks me what seems to be a simple question and it opens up a panorama of visions, images, and cascading ideas and connections that it would be easy to get lost in.

So let me back up a moment in the midst of these images of bits of incarnations, vertical, horizontal, systemic, meta-systemic, and so on and come at this from a different direction. (This is what comes of reading a textbook instead of a carefully planned book—you have to suffer through the raw stuff as it comes out: you are all my beta testers!)

A central idea, though, behind all I was writing earlier is this: how amazingly wondrous, beautiful, impressive, and jaw-droppingly, astonishingly splendid each of our selves is. What we call our "self" in a psychological, subjective sense is so often a far cry from the splendor of the system of energy and presence that actually holds our soul in engagement with this world. It's this beauty that I would like to convey.

So, backing up a bit, let me ask (and answer) a simple rhetorical question: what is the self?

For me, in its simplest form, the self is a divine instrument of learning. It is a way of generating experience, creativity and emergence (new learning) through differentiation and relationship. It is also a means of holding that learning and absorbing it. The self binds learning across time and space. I have a sense of myself because I have a sense of a continuous existence. Some of that felt senses may be illusory, but at its core, it's very real.

When I say "learning," I actually mean something more expansive and even qualitatively different from what we think of as learning, as when we say we go to school to learn. If anything, the soul learns through participation and assimilation; it learns by becoming, which is far more than just an act of mental storage or understanding. It's closer to what happens when we eat and turn "world-stuff" into our own flesh, into "self-stuff."

When the self or the "I" is young and undeveloped, it's learning is shaped and guided by others and by forces in its environment. But there comes a threshold on the other side of which it learns by positing and creating its own lessons, so to speak; it becomes an agency of its own learning, and that is when the fun really begins. Think of a young person learning chemistry in a laboratory under supervision and then when he or she has mastered the discipline being let loose in a lab to create their own compounds and set up their own experiments.

We long ago as the cosmic species Humanity (which, as I said earlier in the book, can take different forms on different worlds, it need not be hominid or anthropomorphic in shape) passed this threshold and gained a capacity to shape our learning. So for us Self means not only an instrument of learning but also an agency of learning, an agency of creativity.

Each self not only holds in its very texture and substance the "flesh" of its history—a living memory-being of divine exploration—but also a capacity for intentionality and will and the freedom to express it. We can be a source of new learning, not just recipients of it. We become generative.

So the self is a function that provides a) a core of divine being around which learning can occur and b) an agency, a generative source of will, love and creative power that can initiate such learning.

The I, the Spirit-Soul, the Planetary Soul, the Soul, the Incarnate Soul, the Embodied Soul and the Personality are all different ways of expressing this function of Self. Each of these different levels or layers or energy structures is temporary, though a particular level of selfhood might last for uncountable millennia of ordinary human time.

OK, here's a picture to begin bringing order into all these ideas and thoughts.

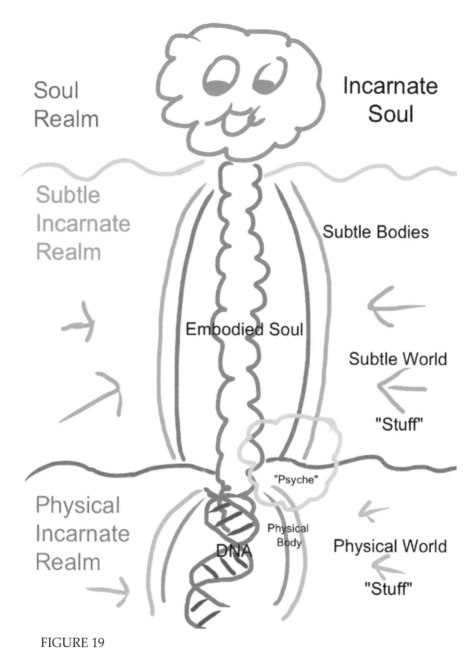

FIGURE 19

The challenge of incarnation for the soul is to extend its power of self (or "selfing") into the incarnate realms. The Incarnate Soul carries the pattern or matrix for the new life and is the instrument of engagement of the soul with the incarnate realm, as we have seen. Within it, the incarnational matrix or "proto-personality" comes into being; the soul becomes in the subtle worlds what it will ultimately manifest as its incarnate self. This is what I called the first or the subtle incarnation.

I described the process of this incarnation earlier using the metaphor of building a house in the wilderness: the settler brings some things to the process but it draws on is surrounding environment for the rest.

In FIGURE 19, we see the Incarnate Self extending its power of self, its life, its presence but not necessarily all its subtle energy, into the subtle world as the core around which the "house" or the incarnation will be "built." I call this extension the "Embodied Soul." It's part of our Interiority.

It's task is to provide the core stimulus around which subtle bodies will form. Remember, these subtle bodies are basically energy constructs, but they will become infused with the function and power — the presence — of self. They are the means through which the soul — the self — connects with the subtle dimensions of the incarnate realm.

These subtle bodies, from the etheric on up to what I called the "variable subtle bodies," are shaped in part by the incarnational matrix the soul brings with it and which it extends and projects as a kind of musical note or vibration out into the "sea" of information, subtle energies, "vectors," and so forth that make up the subtle dimension of the incarnate realm.

An metaphor that I find useful here is the accumulation of crystals from a supersaturated solution around a string. As a kid, I could buy this simple toy which was really a small chemistry experiment. I would dissolve a packet of colored crystals in water, creating a supersaturated solution, one in which the particles are dissolved but there are more of them than the volume of liquid can really hold. The excess will begin to precipitate out as crystals again given the slightest provocation or stimulus. This provocation came in the form of a string that I would lower into this solution, leaving it overnight. In the morning, I would discover the string had been covered by a crusty coating of colorful crystals (which as this chapter's exercise you need to say three times very fast!).

Something akin to this happens in this subtle incarnation. The "string" is the embodied soul and its "covering" of the incarnational matrix, which supplies some crystals of its own into the surrounding "solution" of the subtle realms. Now subtle material is attracted and begins to align and connect, becoming or at least adding to the "flesh" of a subtle body.

So we end up with subtle bodies that are partly made of "soul stuff" and partly made of "incarnate subtle world stuff." I'm being very generic and simplistic here, and trying to portray this using physical images is inherently distorting. But the process is important to understand as it's one that goes on in our lives all the time and constitutes one of the reasons, as we'll see later in the

book, why the incarnational system breaks down and develops incoherencies—
i.e. why good selves go bad.

A similar process occurs in the incarnate physical world. Here the core
identity is not the field of the

Embodied Soul but our DNA (which itself, I believe, is shaped and selected
to varying degrees by the soul itself prior to and during conception). Our DNA
is our somatic identity; it creates and guides the processes that take "world stuff"
and shape it into our own personal body, our "physical self stuff."

Here, too, the body and its immediate etheric counterpart are shaped in part
by what the soul as the settler brings to the mix and in part by what is drawn from
the environment. Our body is embodied soul but it's also embodied world.

The image of the string in the supersaturated solution around which crystals
precipitate out and form is suggestive but as a process it's far too passive. The
means by which the soul is shaping itself in collaboration with its environment
is much more dynamic, active and deliberate. It is intelligence at work, both
the intelligence within the soul (and within any helpers it may have in this
process) AND the intelligence within the environment—or perhaps I should
say, intelligences.

To fully understand this, we need to appreciate that everything is alive and
sentient. There is nothing in the cosmos that is not alive and sentient. When
I talk about subtle energies, I'm also talking about living, sentient forces, not
something apparently dead and blind like electricity.

Sentiency doesn't mean the same as consciousness. Not everything possesses
consciousness or self-awareness. Sentiency is a capacity to be aware of the
environment and a capacity to respond. It's the power of appropriate response.
If I project love towards my coffee cup or the lamp beside my desk, I will get an
energetic response back. At some level, the energetic substance that forms the
matter that forms the coffee cup recognizes it's being loved and responds as best
it can. This may not be a conscious response as I would understand that term
in a human context—the coffee cup doesn't have self-awareness, personality,
and so forth—but it's still a response. Love comes back to me, not merely as a
reflection like light bouncing off a mirror but as something generated within
the depths of the matter that forms the cup. There is a sentient, though not
necessarily a conscious, response.

We live at all levels of the incarnate realm in a "sea" of sentient, living
energies and the sentient forms such energies can take, some of which can be
complex and coherent. More on that later.

If you wish, you could see this living sentiency as part of Gaia, and you
would be right—and on a deeper level it's part of the life and presence and
awareness possessed by the Sacred. That perception would be right, too, though

I might instead say that the Sacred makes the existence of sentiency and life possible and all things in creation share that possibility.

There are many ramifications that come with this point of view, which historically might be seen as the shamanic viewpoint. My earliest memories are of encountering our physical world as filled with these living, sentient fields. As a child, I knew the sofa and the chair in the living room were alive and each possessed its own particular "field of sentiency." This is more than what psychologists like to call "magical thinking" or "projection," projecting a sense of life similar to ours onto inanimate objects. It's a genuine psychic or subtle perception, and for me it continues to this day. As I child, I imbued the sofa with personality characteristics that in fact it did not possess, and that truly was projection or magical thinking, but the underlying perception that there was life and sentiency residing in the matter that made up the sofa was not.

A body is a means of connection, engagement and communication with a particular environment. It isn't the only such means available to a soul, but it's the primary one assuming the soul wishes to have a wide range of options for activity and engagement in that environment.

I can illustrate this with the example of my subtle colleagues. They can be present in a room but only those who are sensitive in some way to their subtle energies and non-physical presence will be aware of them. A subtle being like John can stand in a room and talk to people forever and only a few, if any, will be aware of him. On the other hand, if John takes on a physical body and walks into that room, then all the people can see and be aware of him and if he talks, people will hear what he has to say.

This probably seems painfully obvious, and it is, but it's also the reason why the incarnational process involves a collaboration or partnership with the life and sentiency of the environment and a taking on of the substance of that life and sentiency. A physical body can communicate with other physical bodies because it's made of the same stuff.

The soul doesn't incarnate because it needs a body; it already has a body on its own realm. It generates a new body because it wishes to incarnate. The body is itself an instrument of communication and communion with the new realm, and it is such because it is made in part of the living substance of that realm.

It's like going into a strange, foreign land where you don't speak the language and attracting people from that culture who will be your representatives and translators.

I'm probably beating this point over the head. The key point is this: the systems we inhabit when we incarnate are formed partly from material emanating from the soul and partly from material drawn from the environment. And all such materials are sentient and alive.

Anticipating what we'll be exploring later in the book, it's this joint "parentage" of soul plus planet that creates a sense of division within us that historically has led to the idea of a "lower self" and a "higher self," a "good self" and a "bad self," a "false self" and a "true self." As St. Paul said in his letter to the Romans, "For the good that I would I do not: but the evil which I would not, that I do."

This kind of dichotomy plagues all of us at one time or another; we say it's part of the human condition. Seen energetically, though, it's a manifestation of incoherency within the incarnational system brought about in most cases by engaging with a "sea" of sentient energies that carry with them their own "vectors" or intents and not being able to fully assimilate, digest and alchemize what we take in or take on, making it our own.

It's as if we had rabbit for lunch and chicken for dinner and our body failed to fully transform the "rabbit vector" or the "chicken vector" into who we are, with the result that occasionally we start hopping or begin pecking at the ground.

As I say, we'll explore this more fully later in the book. Right now I'm just establishing a foundation for that exploration.

Here is our basic principle: the incarnating and embodying soul holds a matrix of intent and identity that gathers to itself subtle energies from both the soul and the world, from which the structure or "chalice" of the personal self emerges.

It's as if the "picture" of the self emerges as the various jigsaw pieces are assembled.

The thing is, unlike a jigsaw puzzle, this process doesn't happen once but is happening all the time as we add our energies to the sea of information, identity and intentionality in which we live energetically and in turn take in "bits" of energy containing information, identity, and intentionality (the "vector") which we incorporate into ourselves.

These "bits" come from a variety of sources. Some major categories are cosmic sources (solar and stellar, i.e. subtle energies entering the world system from the sun and from stars much as sunlight and starlight bathe the earth); subtle energies from the subtle worlds; Gaian energies coming from the biosphere and nature and from the World Soul itself; subtle energies of thought, feeling and spirit coming from the collective field of incarnate humanity; Lunar energies; and subtle energies from the land and the physical planet itself.

Here's a picture:

FIGURE 20

The way in which these energies are received and absorbed is more dynamic and complex with more intentionality involved than in my previous metaphor of the string lowered into a supersaturated solution. If anything, it resembles the activity of receptor sites in a cell membrane, which are the way a cell perceives and receives information from its environment (which shows my bias as a former biologist!).

Here's a picture:

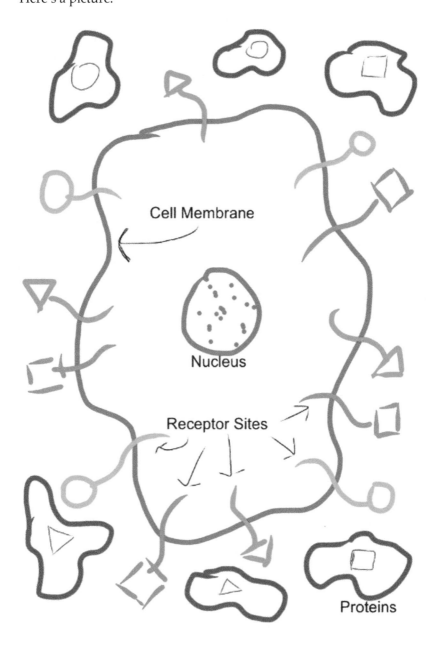

FIGURE 21

A receptor site is really a protein molecule extending through the cell membrane into the surrounding environment. Each such molecule has a unique shape, represented here by the triangles, circles and squares. When such a molecule encounters a protein or other substance in the environment that has a complementary shape, it attaches itself like a key fitting into a lock. This causes the receptor molecule to change its shape, which sets up a cascade of other molecular changes within the cell itself, conveying information to the organism.

A human being is more complex than a cell, of course, but in a way we have receptor sites as well. In our case, it's more like having radio-or television-like capacities to tune into certain frequencies and receive information and energy from them.

This is not necessarily a conscious activity; indeed, in most cases it isn't. There are a great many vital processes and activities that our bodies perform minute by minute that are necessary for our continued physical life but of which we are wholly unaware. It is possible to gain that awareness, especially through advanced yogic techniques, but most of us never need it and get along just fine without it.

It's the same with the subtle energy transactions that go on at the boundary of our subtle field.

Here's a picture:

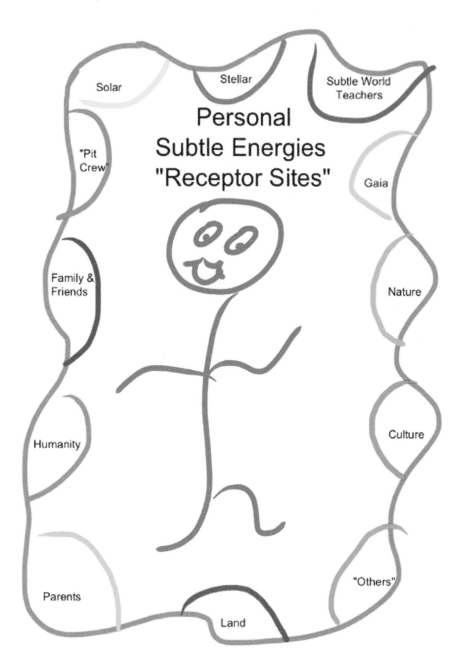

FIGURE 22

This, of course, is not meant to be a detailed list of all the frequencies and wavelengths of subtle energy, presence and information to which we can be attuned, but these are many of the main sources of the "energy bits" that we draw to ourselves to shape and build our personal incarnate energy field.

Pit Crew, by the way, is a term I use for those inner beings who are specifically attuned to and supportive of our incarnation (like the pit crew of a NASCAR racer who help keep him in the race). "Other" simply means that there are many other sources that we can draw upon.

Note that this picture—and this discussion—says nothing about the quality of the energies to which a person attunes and from which that person draws material for his or her energy body. One person might draw noble, inspiring, and loving energies from humanity, another might draw energies of pain, suffering, violence, and even evil.

Here's another perspective on the same thing but arranged to illustrate the relationship of these receptive capacities to the Presence Exercise:

Here we see the individual. Within him or her is the core energy that I think of as the Embodied Soul, our animating life force and interiority. In one sense, it and the Incarnational Soul from which it flows are part of the Transpersonal side of the Presence Exercise, but attuning to our Interiority is more like the "Within" at the center of the circle. Otherwise, I think of the Transpersonal side of the Presence Exercise as relating to the subtle worlds, pit crew, cosmic energies, transcendent forces, etc., all the things that take us beyond our personal boundaries.

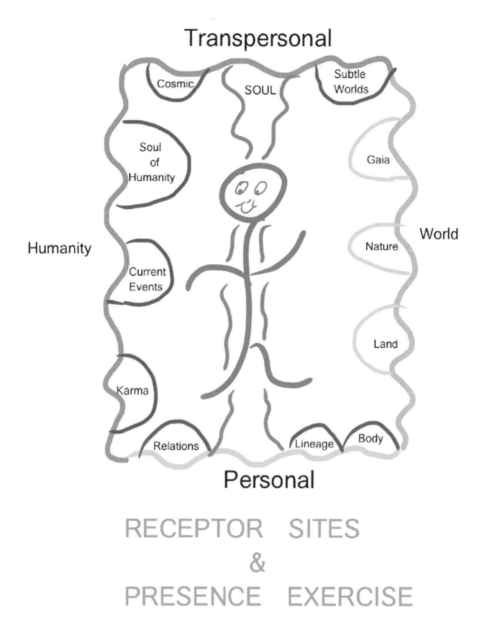

FIGURE 23

On the other hand, at the bottom are elements that make up the personal side of the incarnational equation, including attunement to the body, to our lineage (past history, family history, karma, etc.), and to our relationships with people close to us or who have an effect on our personal lives. This is the domain of what I think of as our "Everyday Self"

The World and Humanity are the other two aspects of the Presence Exercise, and you can see some of the possible receptor sites related to these larger categories. I discussed this earlier in 9:42 where I listed some other sub-categories.

Let me come back to the idea that what these "receptor sites," representing the capacity to attune to a particular frequency and type of subtle energy, are dealing with are sentient, living energies. More often than not, these energies are the emanations of other living beings, both physical and non-physical.

Because of this, our interaction with these subtle forces and energies isn't as passive as simply receiving a particular frequency or wavelength of information, like a radio tuning into and receiving a particular broadcasting station. It's more like a conversation, a process of analysis, filtering, engaging, agreeing, disagreeing, and so forth. It's an intelligent process, part of the overall incarnational intelligence operating within us.

For this reason, I think of each of these receptor capabilities as intelligences with me: an intelligence that knows how to receive, process and integrate cosmic energies, an intelligence that knows how to receive, process and integrate energies from nature, an intelligence that knows how to receive, process and integrate energies from human society, and so forth.

Here's an illustration of this:

# The Intelligences Within

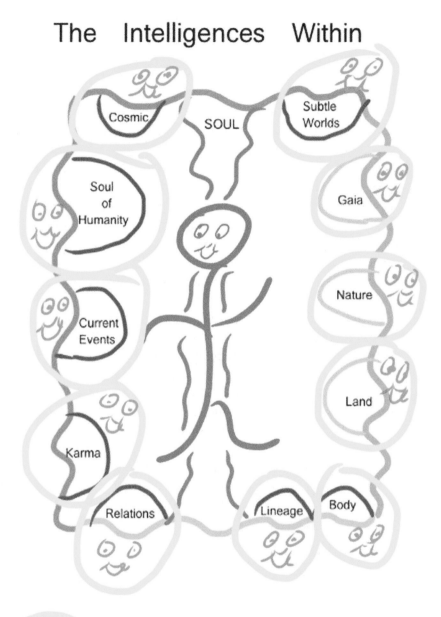

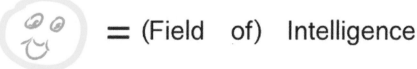 = (Field of) Intelligence

FIGURE 24

If at this point you're thinking, "Omigosh! First we've got all these souls and now we've got all these intelligences?! I'm feeling a little crowded inside! Who and where am I in all this?" I don't blame you. We haven't even gotten to the everyday self yet—to the part of us that says, "Hey, I'm David" or "I'm Jeremy" or "Mary" or "Suzie" or "Ian."

But bear with me a bit longer. There's still a bit more to come of these esoteric bits and pieces and then we'll look at the everyday self. I promise all this will tie together into a wholeness....someday! <G>

But the picture in FIGURE 24 is really no different than saying that there's an intelligence in my liver or in my heart or my spleen that guides their unique processes within the overall context of my body. And there are some advantages to this perspective when it comes to working with exercises designed to enhance our expression of self, all of which will be coming up in a chapter or so.

The thing is we can communicate with these "intelligences" within us. They aren't passive organs; they are dynamic expressions of our own sentient, living energy in dialogue with the sentient, living energies in our environment, and this is one dialogue we can participate in with the right attitude and a little bit of patience and attention.

There's another reason for putting things this way. Incarnational Spirituality rests on a partnership cosmology, which in turn rests on a sense that we are in a living cosmos with which we really can communicate—and this communication and relationship is an integral part of incarnation. When I was told years ago by an inner being that humanity's problems stemmed from not being incarnated enough, this entity didn't mean we had to get more physical; he meant we weren't in sufficient communication and connection with the world around us. We're like that awful guest at a cocktail party who doesn't socialize with anyone, and certainly not the hostess, but who drinks all the drinks and eats all the food as if he's the only one there.

If I begin to think of all the intelligence and sentiency and life and consciousness that surrounds me on every level, and I realize that my own body, my own energy field, my own incarnate being is also bursting with its own complementary intelligence and sentiency—wow! Then I find myself in a living world that is rich beyond compare. There's nothing I can't be in some kind of communication with whether it's within me or outside me. That awareness is the beginning of everything, I feel. It's the foundation on which subtle perception is based...and the foundation for healing and transforming our world.

That's why I point out that those capacities or elements or receptive areas in our energy structure that put us in touch with a wide band of life and information from the cosmic to the atomic, the spiritual to the material, are in their way intelligences.

And this perspective will be important as we consider why and when things go awry and dysfunction, suffering and yes, evil, enter the picture.

Incarnation is not entirely a top-down process. It is a collaboration, a partnership, between the soul and the earth. The body that we inhabit is shaped in part by the information and energy provided by the soul, but the body is also the product of millions of years of evolution, as well as being the product of a particular family genetic lineage. Here's a picture:

The history of humanity's involvement with this world, as I wrote about during the first chapter, goes back for millennia. I don't know at what point the connection was made—what I see with subtle perception doesn't translate well for me into linear chronology—but I do know that either in anticipation of Humanity's arrival and engagement or as a result of this, Gaia began to shape and develop a body suitable for the kind of intelligence and spirit that Humanity brings.

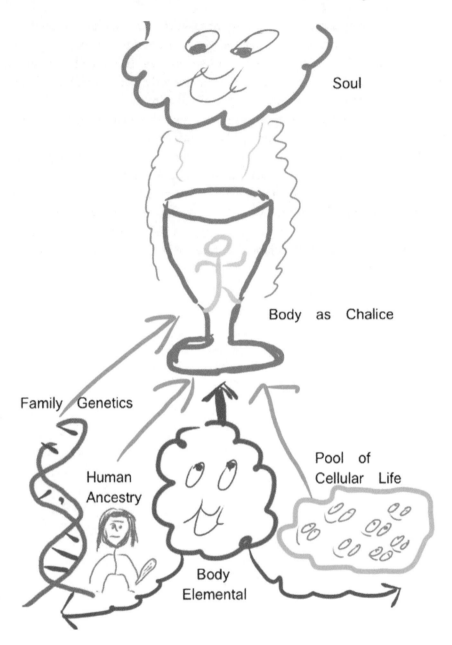

Soul

Body as Chalice

Family Genetics

Human
Ancestry

Pool of
Cellular Life

Body
Elemental

FIGURE 25

While the body as a "chalice" to hold the energies of the incarnating soul is partly shaped by the incarnating soul, it is in its way an evolving intelligence in its own right with a long history of relationship with Gaia and the subtle realms. Folklore and legends speak of the mating of the gods with the sons and daughters of ancient humanity, giving birth to the human race as we know it, and there is a deep esoteric truth to this.

When we incarnate, we come into partnership with an entity I call the "Body Elemental." I think of this being as a species of nature spirit but one specialized in its association with the human species. It is with us our entire life and is in a way the overall intelligence regulating and assisting the body as a whole. It's rather like a top sergeant in the army!

When a body comes into being, there are a number of forces that influence its eventual nature. One of these, of course, is the whole lineage of human ancestry and evolution—and of course, pre-human evolution before it. These stages are replicated by the embryo in the womb as we know. There may be "karma" or habits that arise from this lineage, which is further specialized by the particular race and ethnicity to which the body belongs. The physical karma or "habits of evolution" of a Chinese body are not exactly the same as those of an African body or a European body.

Then there is the effect of family genetics. There may also be influences from the family spirit and from family karma, but here I'm just thinking of the particular genetic heritage this specific family line has to offer the incoming soul. If this family line has no genes in its history for red hair, chances are very small (though not impossible) that the soul will be able to fashion a body with red hair, for instance.

Then there is what I call the "pool of cellular life," which is where our cells come from. This is not an actual physical reservoir, of course, but rather an inner pool of life and intelligence belonging to the microbial world. Cells evolve, too, and are life forms with consciousness and spirit; they exist in the subtle world in their own realm as much as we do in ours.

We don't pay much attention esoterically to the microbial world but we should. It does, after all, make up the largest amount of biomass on the planet; this planet is really "owned" by microbes; we just rent space from them. The intelligence within the microbial world is powerful and elemental, and all physical life forms partake in it or are affected by it.

Our physical bodies are made up of microbial life, both somatic (belonging to our particular body, like a liver cell) and not (like the microbes that live in our stomachs and help us digest food but which possess their own unique DNA). There is spirit here and consciousness. It's a far cry from our own consciousness to be sure, but we would not have physical life without it. It's another form of intelligence with which we share our incarnation.

The body elemental is the entity that receives the imprint of the soul—the incarnational matrix emerging from the soul's intent for the incarnation—and works out on a practical, physical level how to implement it in the form of a body. This body is not an empty vessel that the soul enters but an entity in its own right with which the soul partners, even though elements of this body-entity with its body-mind and its own body-feelings are shaped by the soul's intent.

In short the soul enters a physical system that has its own structure, its own tendencies, its own link to the past, and its own link to the microbial world and to Gaia. And this is in addition to entering the subtle system made up of subtle bodies shaped in part by existing energies within the planetary subtle field, as I have described. Systems within systems, all of which the soul needs to inhabit and draw into its own unique pattern of integration and coherency, all within a world that is alive with flowing, sentient energy.

A being once said to me that incarnation was like building a house of matches while standing in a flowing river!

The body elemental is one of our most intimate and closest allies in helping us do this.

Incarnation is not a simple process. It's a very dynamic one and behind it is the magnificent and awesome intelligence of the soul supported and partnered by other magnificent and awesome intelligences in the subtle and physical worlds.

What I'd like you to do at this point is to take a moment and honor and appreciate this intelligence within you. You, in yourself, in your soul, possess and express an incarnational intelligence so spectacular in what it accomplishes that next to it the smartest human mind is like the village idiot. What we call our intelligence, wondrous as it is, is only a part of the intelligence of our soul that makes incarnation possible.

And this incarnational intelligence is you. It's your intelligence, operating behind the scenes but capable of being drawn upon in your everyday affairs.

So I just want you to appreciate yourself. In your everyday human self, you may at times feel limited and that you don't amount to much (though I'm sure no one in this book feels such a thing for very long!) but just remember what you are doing to enable you to be in contact and engagement with this plane of existence. It's fantastic, and I want you to appreciate yourself and honor this deep intelligence within you.

### THE PERSONALITY

Now we're getting into the realm of lingo. I define personality in a specific way. To me the personality isn't the "mask" we present to the world; I call that the "incarnate self" or the "personal self" or our "everyday self." Personality to me is a function that makes that individual, incarnate self possible. It's a function of particularization. The personality takes all the energetic and psychological impulses coming in from the material and subtle worlds and makes them particular to the person, individualizing them. In a sense, it is the counterbalance to the pull towards the universal and the transcendent. It's not that the personality gives us the ability to say "I" — that comes from our Identity manifesting through the soul; rather, the personality establishes boundaries for this "I" and gives it specificity and particularity within the material world.

The personality as I see it is rooted in the body and the body-mind. To a considerable degree, it is shaped by the body. In this psychological age, we think of our personalities as shaped by our experiences, memories, relationships, self-reflections, and so on, but for me, this describes our whole incarnate self. What I mean by personality is shaped more by the structure and dynamics of our bodies and by the incarnational matrix created by the Incarnate Soul. I see the personality more as an automatic way of expressing ourselves, an organic default position when we're not exercising attention and intention, i.e. when we not making choices from a self-aware and self-directive place within us. The personality is the subjective expression of the body and the body-mind.

The personality, to me, is supposed to be self-orienting and self-oriented. You could say it is the naturally selfish part of us, and it's supposed to be that way in order to preserve our boundaries and our autonomy within the incarnational process. But it's only one part of the whole incarnational system and isn't intended to be the driver for our lives. Its default positions can always be overridden, changed, expanded, and redirected by conscious choice and self-direction

I know that in our culture we use the term personality in a broader and looser way. I couldn't think of another term to use to describe this function, and since it the way the word "personality" is used seemed to me often to refer to this function, I decided to use it in this way. I apologize for any confusion.

I don't use the word ego much. In psychology, I know it means the self-function and having a healthy ego or sense of self is important. In this context, this is basically what I mean by the incarnate self. But I don't have a psychological background. I come out of a religious, spiritual, esoteric, New Age background, and in that context, ego usually means something negative, a selfish part of us, or even the separating, individuating function. Many times I remember hearing people say that we had to rise above our egos or get rid of our egos. There is a truth here, but I resisted turning the ego into a distinct piece of us, a kind of inner self with which we had to do battle. Remember that my training has been to avoid the kind of internal conflict in which we regard one part of ourselves as "lower" or "false" or "bad" and which we therefore have to defeat or rise above. This internal conflict works against wholeness. So to the extent that ego came to mean for many people on the spiritual path a "bad" part of us, I have avoided the term. We'll talk about this much more later in the book. Here, I'm just seeking to clarify my language.

For me, if a person is acting in a separative or selfish way, rather than say he's coming from "ego" or that his "personality is in the way," I prefer to say simply that that person is acting in a separative or selfish way. In other words, rather than label the action as coming from a particular part of the self, I prefer to describe the action and see it as coming from the self as a whole which in that moment has decided to act in that particular way.

Anyway, for me personality is a natural and important function, an ally to the soul. But as we shall see, any part of us can act out of coherence with the other parts and in so doing, create problems. The personality isn't the problem in our spiritual journey, but it can at times be a problem. But then, so can the soul! And I'm anticipating myself, so enough said for now.

I think at this point I should tell a story about this. But first I want to say that the way I use the word "personality" is not cast in concrete for me. This is an area where I simply haven't found good terms that I'm comfortable using. I realize, as I said, that the word is used more broadly than I do, and I certainly don't insist that anyone change this to use "personality" as I do.

So here's my story. Back when I first began working with my mentor, John, he often said that our work was to explore how the personality and the soul could be integrated as partners. I noted that in all the years we worked together, John never used the term personality in a derogative manner...nor for that matter, did he ever use a term like "false self" or "illusory self" to describe any part of us. Indeed, he once said that there were no illusions, that everything was real because everything could make an impact on us. It might not look like what it seemed to be, but that was another matter entirely. So if I saw something coiled in a dark corner and thought it was a snake, I might be mistaken in that it could be a rope, but if I reacted to it as if it were a snake, then in that moment, it was a snake as far as its impact upon me went.

Actually, the context in which John said this wasn't a discussion on illusion vs reality but rather a discussion about honoring and loving the physical world. The matter had come up because I had been asked about teachings that said the world was simply a dream, an illusion from which we needed to awaken. John's reply was that while our view of the world was often incomplete and we didn't see everything that's there, this didn't make the world illusory. But his main point was that if we viewed the world as a dream, it could interfere with our ability—and willingness—to love and bless and honor the world. Why honor something I feel doesn't exist and which I feel is obscuring me from the true world behind it somewhere. This lack of appreciation and honoring in turn diminished connections which diminished incarnation.

Likewise, if we viewed part of ourselves as false or illusory, we might fail in honoring and loving ourselves sufficiently. Why this is important is a topic for later in the book.

So John was scrupulous in honoring all parts of us, even parts that were functioning in limited or limiting ways. He did talk about the "lower self" but never in a pejorative or dismissive way and never in a hierarchical way. He meant it in energetic terms as that part of us that occupies a lower level in a spectrum of energy differential, such as I've already discussed in this book. "Higher" and "lower" for John were not synonyms for "better" and "not so good."

At the time I began working with John, I'd been associating with metaphysical and esoteric groups for five years, and if these groups had one thing in common, it was a disdain for and at times even a fear of "the personality." Getting rid of or going beyond one's personality was *de rigeur* for spiritual progress to be made. So when John didn't follow this "party line," I was curious. Why did he have a different view of the personality?

John never denied that people could act in selfish, hurtful, negative, thoughtless, stupid, careless, violent, and even evil ways. He simply did not see that kind of behavior as originating from a single part of us. He said once, "You can engage in evil actions but if so, it's because you choose to do so, not because you have an evil part of you making you do it against your will." Or, as he said later, it might be because a person had fallen into "incoherency" and thus into vulnerability to "outside forces." Indeed, there could be many reasons why a person would act in negative and hurtful ways, but he did not list the personality as one of those reasons.

John's perspective on this obviously came from his perception of who and what we were as incarnate persons. His desire for me to honor the personality in the teaching work I was developing and seek for ways in which soul and incarnate self could be partners was the beginning back in the sixties of what forty years later developed into Incarnational Spirituality. When I began some twelve years ago or so to actively research the process of incarnation, seeking to understand what John had seen and known about us was one of my priorities. In following through on this, I observed this part of our energetic field that took energy from the surrounding environment and transformed it into "self-stuff," into our particular, specific incarnational field. It was not interested in becoming "universal," it appreciated being separate because that was what it was designed to be, and it's allegiance was to its own incarnational process, not to anyone else's. It was selfish, but in a necessary way. In many ways it held the boundaries that differentiated each of us from everyone and everything else. It did not reflect the universal inclusiveness of the soul, but it wasn't supposed to. Other parts of the incarnational system took care of that. It wasn't against such inclusiveness; it just wasn't its particular function. It seemed to me at the time that it embodied some of the traits that, back in the day, had been seen as negative qualities of the personality, only now I was seeing them as positive elements within a particular and specific context. So I decided to call this sentient function the "personality."

### BIRTH

If incarnation is like a theater production, we've now come to the moment when the curtain rises and the soul takes the stage in the physical world. So let's see where we are, remembering that for any play when the curtain does rise, a whole new element enters the equation: the audience. Here's where we are at the time of conception:

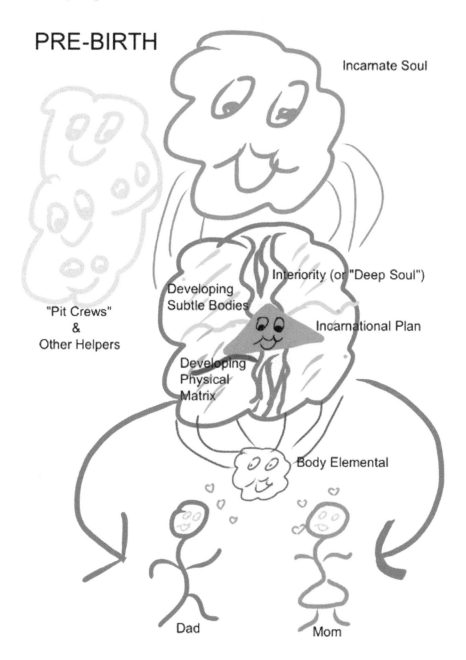

FIGURE 26

Here we see all the elements we've talked about over the past chapter poised to take the incarnational drama the next step into the physical realm. We have an overall incarnation matrix that is a kind of proto-personality or proto-self, the seed for the incarnate self. It has developing subtle bodies. It also has a developing (most likely etheric) physical matrix, the latter being nourished and empowered by the body elemental which has been called forward by the Incarnate Soul and is in partnership with it.

This proto-self has within it its connection to its own soul and sacredness. I call this our Interiority or "Deep Soul." And there is a "manual" of sorts that is guiding this development, an incarnational "plan" that in effect determines the initial resonances that control what kind of sentient energies are attracted from the subtle worlds to incorporate into the developing subtle bodies. This "plan" includes past memories the soul may have from previous incarnations, memories that might act as habits shaping the formation of this new life. These include what are popularly known as karmic patterns.

In effect, this incarnational "plan" is like the blueprint for the development of the incarnational seed as a whole. And it's this seed that will link with the embryo in the womb and help influence its development as well. It is, in fact, the seed of the soon-to-be emerging self. It can play a role in bringing together the man and woman who will be its parents, particularly if all three have agreed to this relationship from a soul level.

This process is also overlighted by other helpers in the subtle worlds, including what I call the "Pit Crews" of all those involved.

### THE FOUR WOMBS
Birth is a story of four wombs, only one of which is physical. The "soul-seed" or "incarnational seed" is held and developed in each. These four are:
- The Womb of the Soul
- The Womb of the Mother
- The Womb of the Parents
- The Womb of the World

The Womb of the Soul is really what we've been discussing for the past chapter. It's the enfolding embrace of the Incarnate Soul within which the elements that will form the new life are woven together in an energy matrix, creating a template for the formation of the subtle bodies as well as for the physical body. Here is where the originating intent of the soul is embodied and shaped and given form within the subtle realms of Gaia. The end result is a "proto-self," a "soul-seed" or "incarnational seed" that connects to a body elemental and then to specific physical cells at the time of conception. This soul-seed is then passed from the field of the Incarnate Soul into the body and field of the mother. At this point, physical incarnation commences and the soul encounters the full energy impact of the world.

The Womb of the Mother is where the physical body is nourished and developed, but it's also where the subtle field of the child begins to develop in resonance with the physical world. The mother's energy field also takes on womb-like characteristics to further this inner development and also to protect the child's energy field if necessary.

The Womb of the Parents, when available, is a larger subtle field that holds the developing child and nourishes its developing subtle bodies. The child can pull directly on material within the energy fields of the mother and father—i.e. within their thoughts and feelings—to incorporate into its own personal field. This parental womb can be as important in the health and development of the child overall as the maternal womb is to the health and development of the physical body. Unfortunately, in today's world, more and more women go through pregnancy without the help and support of a father or a surrogate male who can also provide inner support and love. Of course, the mother can draw upon supportive energies from a variety of sources—family, friends, relatives—to augment and support her own energy field. The parental womb is not a necessity, obviously, but when it can be present, it is a hugely influential resource in the development of the child.

The Womb of the World is my way of talking about the influence of the world itself with all its subtle energies arising from nature, the land, weather, the collective field of humanity, etc. The effect of the world can be mitigated and modulated by the parental and maternal wombs and by the soul itself, but it's still there. Depending on circumstances it can have a powerful effect or a lesser effect, but it will be felt. From the get-go, the incarnating soul begins to draw on this wider environment to build and shape its inner resources and subtle fields.

In an ideal world, all four of these work together seamlessly to support, nourish and foster the developing embryo so that when the child is born it has a fully integrated, fully harmonious, fully functioning incarnational system. He or she is born as a whole person.

But as we know all too well, we don't live in an ideal world, so these wombs don't always work together smoothly. However....

The incarnating soul is not helpless. Even in the womb it is exerting a certain amount of control and influence over the process. The developing body and body-mind begin exerting their intentionality and the "soul-seed," now becoming the incarnational self, does so likewise, drawing on the incarnational "plan." Even if the wombs turn out to be less than satisfactory in ways the soul had not anticipated, it still has power to influence its development in ways it wishes, though how much it can do so depends on variables such as the strength and skill and experience of the soul itself.

# Exercises for Chapter Four

Here is an exercise that is not just for this chapter but which you can work on throughout the rest of the book. I call it making a "Personry."

### OVERVIEW

One of the traditions of contemplative practice is that of using prayer beads or, in the Catholic tradition, a Rosary. While a Rosary is in essence a mnemonic device for keeping track of the number of times one has said a particular prayer within a particular devotion or "mystery," more generically the beads can also be used to symbolize particular events or qualities in themselves. This is particularly true if each bead is different in size and shape, thereby facilitating attunement to a specific quality or event.

In this book, we are exploring—and celebrating—your energy and spirit as a unique individual. The Path of the Self is one of attuning to those specific spiritual and energetic resources that you have by virtue of being an incarnate person, resources that arise and develop through the process of incarnation itself. It might be understood as a contemplative or mystical practice of the self, leading to deeper oneness and attunement to your own unique beingness. In particular, it's a practice of attunement to and expression of a quality I call "Self-Light," about which I'll be writing much more in a chapter or so.

To begin this practice, you can make a variation of a Rosary which, because its intent is to help you attune to your own unique energy as a person, I'm going to call a "Personry."

The Personry can represent a number of things depending on how you identify the beads and how you construct it. In this particular case, it's a mobile version of the Presence Exercise.

### WHAT YOU WILL NEED

You will need beads, probably of various shapes or colors. (You don't have to use beads, by the way, just something that you can attach to a string—could be buttons or shells or anything you wish, but beads are probably simplest—for that matter, it could even be knots on a string, as long as you can make them different sizes). You can use as many as you'd like.

I would like you to have six special beads (or buttons or whatever) that are larger than the others so that they stand out and can be used to divide the prayer beads up into sections, just as with a Rosary. These will stand for the four elements of the Presence Exercise plus one for the Interiority and one for You as the Emerging Self, the Agency, the source of intentionality and choice within your everyday life.

You will need string or something equivalent on which to attach your beads or buttons or whatever.

## HOW TO DO IT

Basically, you tie a knot in one end of the string and then put the beads on one after another in the order you wish.

If you'd like a good book on the making and use of prayer beads, here's one I've found useful: *A String and A Prayer*, by Eleanor Wiley and Maggie Oman Shannon, published 2002 by Red Wheel/Weiser books.

The number of beads will determine how long the Personry is and their size will determine how large. There should be, as I said, six beads that stand out and act as separators, dividing the Personry as a whole into six different sections. These six special beads can be different colors, but they don't need to be as long as you can tell one section from another and know what each section represents for you.

Here are the six sections:

1. Deep Soul — Your Interiority
2. Transpersonal — Incarnate Soul, Subtle Worlds, Pit Crew
3. Humanity — Soul of Humanity, Culture, Collective Human Energy Field
4. World — Nature, Biosphere, Land, Gaia
5. Personal — Body, Relationships, Autobiography, Individuality
6. YOU — Emergent Self — Yourself as Agent, the "Decider," the Source of Intentionality and Choice, The "Amalgam" of the other five elements

Your Personry can look however you wish it to. It can be a linear string, a circle like a bracelet, a combination of the two, and so on. It can have as many beads as you feel comfortable putting on it, but from experience, shorter is better!

Here's one example of what it might look like. Note that I've used the order listed above, but you could arrange the sections any way that makes sense to you.

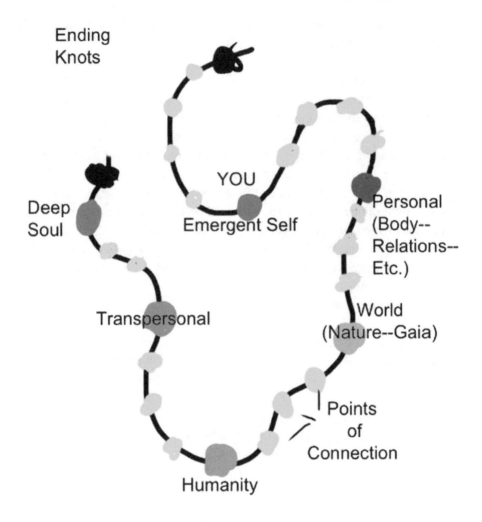

# THE PERSONRY

FIGURE 27

The gold points represent the beads (or knots or buttons or whatever) between the Section Separators. There can be as many as you wish, but again the longer the Personry, the more unwieldy it can become.

The exercise focuses on these points of connection. Each represents an experience or an insight or some point of connection for you with the energy and presence represented by the Section. For example, a bead in the Deep

Soul Section might represent an experience you have of the sacredness within you, while a bead in the World section would represent some connection or experience you have with nature. If you wish, you could correlate the beads with the "Receptor Sites" and the "Intelligences Within" that I suggested in FIGURES 23 and 24. The important thing is that whatever you choose to put on the Personry is personally meaningful for you in the context of the particular Section and can connect you with the spirit of that Section just as if you were doing the Presence Exercise.

### HERE'S THE PROCEDURE:

Pick a bead (or button, knot or whatever) to represent a point of connection. Choose a particular experience, insight, or felt sense of attunement which this bead can represent. Meditate on why you picked this particular connection point and how it represents the Section to you. Enter into a felt sense of that connection and feel the energy of your attunement flowing into the bead as you put it on the string. Most importantly, take time to love this part of you, to love this connection and feel love flowing back to you in return. Overall, this exercise is about honoring and appreciating yourself, the parts that make you up and you as a wholeness.

Take time between each bead in order to "clear your palate," so to speak. You want each bead to have a clear, unique meaning to you as a point of connection to your Deep Soul, to the Transpersonal side of your life, to Humanity, to the World, to your Body and individuality, and to your felt sense of yourself as a whole person, the YOU on this string.

We haven't talked about this Emergent Self—the You in your life—yet, so if this is unclear, just leave this part of the Personry unfinished for now. Basically the difference is that the "Personal" section refers to those elements in your life, such as your body, that "personalize" you and make you the unique individual that you are. They could include the specific important relationships in your life, your autobiography, your dreams and goals, and so forth.

The YOU, though, is you as the one who implements this individuality on a daily basis through your choices and decisions, actions and reactions. The YOU is where your sovereignty resides (another concept we'll discuss more later). It is the "amalgam" of the other five sections or the holopoietic point that draws them into a coherent, integrated wholeness.

As I say, we'll discuss this more in future book text. Hopefully, though, this gives you enough information to get started.

What do you do when you've made your Personry? Well, how you use it is up to you. It can be a tool for meditation, for reflection, for reminding you of who you are as a whole person, as a personal energy talisman born of honoring and loving the various parts of you as well as you as a wholeness.

And by the way, what do you think the string represents in this Personry?

Have fun!

## CHAPTER FIVE, ACT II: THE INCARNATE SELF

When I teach or write about Incarnational Spirituality, I step mentally and energetically into a large field of presence; it's a bit like walking into a very large university research library. Since the material isn't "stored" like books on shelves but is literally—at least as I experience it—a living presence (though not a specific being, if that makes sense—like the presence one might feel in a beautiful library), I in a relationship. At times it can feel a little overwhelming as I want to share everything I'm experiencing: the flow can be immense. The challenge isn't so much one of finding what to say but what not to say, how to channel that flow and create boundaries so that it can manifest in a world made up of time, space, words, ideas, concepts, and images, all of which are very particular and conceptual in ways the original presence isn't. My task is to bring this to earth while retaining for you (and me) the link with the presence itself so that hopefully you can feel it in your lives in ways that transcend the limits and boundaries of the words themselves.

This is why each class I teach (and this resultant textbook) is an emergent experience. A class for me is really a dynamic and evolving relationship between the participants, this living presence of Incarnational Spirituality and its field of energy and knowledge, and myself. I never quite know in advance just how this will unfold.

Well, enough of that. Suffice it to say that I began to see some new pathways into the material that I hadn't seen before—thank you very much—and I've been trying to clarify them for myself so that I could present the material clearly to you. Let me do that by looking quickly at where we've been and where we're trying to go. It's my way of getting back into flow and making sure the flow I'm getting back into is connected to the flow we've already had!

My objective here is to give you some tools to enhance and empower your incarnational experience. These tools surround concepts like Self-Light, Sovereignty, and Generativity. I would like you to experience yourself as a "star," a radiant source not simply as a soul but as embodied soul, as a personal, individual, unique incarnate self. And I would like you to experience this not simply as a cognitive concept, an idea, but as a very real felt sense, a presence of being that in the midst of the challenges of life you can fall back upon and rely upon, a kind of "spine" to hold you upright in your generativity and creativity.

Just like a wrench is designed to fit bolts and not really to hammer nails, these tools are designed to fit an incarnational understanding of self. They work best if I can see how I am composed of systems and connections, relationships and partnerings, much as my physical body is composed of cells, for the tools are designed to create wholeness, integration and coherency within such systems. They are holopoietic tools. The tools do not work well if my understanding and image of who I am is binary. Here are some examples of binary self-images:

- I am a soul in a body.
- I have a "higher self" and a "lower self."
- I have a "true self" and a "false self."
- I have a physical self and a spiritual self.
- I have a "good self" and a "bad or evil self."

Binary self-images tend to collapse into conflicts and opposition. We tend to privilege one side over the other or try to eliminate one side in order to be the other side purely and exclusively. Such conflicts prevent the whole incarnational system from experiencing and acting with coherency.

The tools also do not work as well if I think of myself solely in physical or psychological terms. They work best if I can experience myself as a flowing, interactive being of spirit, subtle energies, psyche (the psychological bits), and body, understanding that while there are boundaries or thresholds that define these four different areas, they are—as long as we are incarnate—inseparable partners in a larger system. The edges or boundaries between them are not hard walls but regions of soft, flowing, intermeshing communication and communion. Spirit becomes energy becomes thought or feeling (psyche) becomes cellular material and interaction (i.e. the "chemicals of emotion," the "neurochemistry of thought," and so forth). And it works the other way: body states become psyche which generates subtle energy forms which blends with spirit.

If I have a sense of myself living within and as—and emerging from—this interactive, blended incarnational system, then the tools work very well and can be life-changing.

In the preceding chapters, we've looked at the incarnational process from an energetic point of view. We've considered the cosmic and planetary circulation of which incarnation plays a part, we've looked at the nature of the soul, and we've explored the means by which the soul inserts its energetic presence into the incarnate realms, weaving for itself sheaths of subtle matter (the "first incarnation") and then, through conception, gestation and birth, a physical body (the "second incarnation"). At the same time, we've seen how the soul weaves as well new patterns of connection and relationship with Gaia and the forces of Nature and the Earth on the one hand and with Humanity—and in particular incarnate Humanity—on the other, which might be likened to "third" and "fourth incarnations" (though no special sheaths or bodies are produced as a result, the effects of these connections being woven into the subtle energies and physical body of the soul's incarnate life). These four sets of connections and relationships—with the subtle environment, with the forces of personalization and particularization, with Humanity, and with Nature and Gaia—make up what I think of as the incarnational system. It's with this system that our holopoietic tools work.

The soul doesn't make this journey alone. Incarnation is not a solitary undertaking but a collaborative one. Each of us is really a co-incarnate. And in a strange way, it might be said that the soul fashions its incarnational vehicles from the outside in. It operates from outside the incarnational system. But there comes a time when this takes a dramatic shift, and the soul fully enters into the bodies of its incarnation, including the physical. At which point, it begins operating from within that system, looking, as it were, from inside out and experiencing a whole new world from before.

It's as if a person visited a neighborhood while supervising the construction of a house in which he or she planned to live. This person moves in and out of the neighborhood and is not yet rooted in it, so to speak. He or she looks upon that neighborhood from a particular perspective, being both in it and detached from it. But when the house is done and this person moves in, now he or she sees the neighborhood through the windows of the house and as a neighbor and inhabitant. Nothing has changed, and yet everything changes.

This is the threshold of birth, and this is where we start this chapter's book text.

### BIRTH AND THE "MANGER MOMENT"

When we left the incarnating soul, it was in the process of being born, assisted or at least influenced by its "four wombs."

I do not know the details of all that goes on in this process, any more than I know the details of the chemistry of digestion or the biophysics of signal transfer at the nerve synapses. I have no doubt that it's a very individualized, tailored process. But there are some general remarks I can make.

When does the soul actually enter the physical realm (i.e. the physical body)? Some people say at conception, some at birth, some that it doesn't really make connection until sometime within the first seven years of life. (I could argue that I've met adults whose souls have yet to enter or make contact, but that's just being snarky, and it's not true anyway...still, it can sure seem that way at times!) As I understand it, the soul "enters" in stages, or perhaps more appropriately put, expands it presence and influence over the body, body-mind and the etheric in stages. In one way, this happens all through our lives; as the emergent self (our "everyday self") develops in its capacity to hold the energy and presence of its overlighting Incarnate Soul, more of that energy and presence enters the incarnate life and becomes part of the daily life. But there is a tipping point at which the consciousness within the Incarnate Soul fully commits to and "snaps into" the incarnate personality.

Let's look at this a little more closely. As we've seen, the Incarnate Soul has gone through a process of shaping and surrounding itself with sheaths or fields constructed from appropriate subtle energies and substance. The life force, the intelligence, the presence of the Incarnate Soul extends itself into and becomes one with this material, becoming in effect now the Embodied Soul. Remember that this material by our physical standards is very fluid and wispy, very refined. In a sense, these are the subtle sheaths of our High Self, the subtle bodies of our "Higher Mind" and "Higher Feelings," if I may borrow terms from esoteric literature. Yet they are definitely part of the incarnate realm and resonating to the subtle fields of Humanity and Gaia, as I've described.

As conception approaches, there is a gathering of etheric and subtle energies arising from the physical plane, generated by the thoughts, feelings and physical forces generated by sexual attraction and intercourse. These energies, guided and shaped by the physical elemental, become a chalice, a power sheath that pulls the Embodied Soul into deeper contact and engagement with the physical plane. At conception, the living energies are quickened by the intent and life force of the soul and a child is conceived. The processes are set into motion for the development of a physical body.

This is the normal pattern. Deviations from this pattern can occur, or so I'm told, but I don't have the impression they are that common and often involve pulling a soul that is energetically close to the physical plane for some reason into incarnation before it is ready. The vortex created by sexual energies and intercourse can be very powerful!

The subtle energies surrounding conception play a role in what kind of energies the incarnating soul can initially connect with its physical body as well as affecting the initial quality of the material from which it builds its mental and emotional fields. A child conceived in violence, pain, fear and suffering as through rape will have those energies to contend with in its initial contact with the physical realm. It is not a given that such negative influences will "infect" or "corrupt" the subtle field of the embryo; other factors play a role such as karma, the quality of the mother's field, the strength and skill of the incarnating soul itself, the support and love of others in the environment. But still, the presence of such forces means the soul has to deal with them in one way or another, which could be strengthening or could be weakening. By contrast, when the sexual union is between two people who love and honor each other and delight in each other's presence and in the possibility of attracting a child, this creates a smooth and welcoming passage for the soul's life force and energy to enter the physical realm.

This is the rationale behind the kind of magical conceptions that were attempted in some ancient temples and cultures. In such events, the man and woman would go through a ritual process designed to purify and heighten their subtle energies in order to create the best possible field of attraction and portal of entry for a soul, the idea being to give birth to highly evolved individuals—or at least individuals who could bring more of their soul force through into the initial stages of their incarnations. However, as I understand it, a couple doesn't have to go to such lengths to attract "high quality" souls. Any union of love and joy and mutual giving where a child is wanted will create a perfectly acceptable and broad field of connection under most circumstances. Obviously, the more mindful the union, the more coherent and purposeful the energies will be. If two people are mainly thinking of themselves and their own pleasure during sexual intercourse, this narrows the field because they are not opening to the full extent of the energies possible if they could reach beyond themselves and into the other.

A final thought here. Earlier I talked about how I define the personality. The personality as an energy function that personalizes, individualizes, and particularizes emerges as part of the developing body and body-mind. This is what shapes the initial chalice that receives the soul and provides a kind of default mode of expression as the soul is gaining control over its physical vehicle. It is in no way a "lower self" or an obstacle to the soul but an ally. It has the job of building and expressing structure, whether that structure is physical, emotional, or mental. It uses habit as a structural tool. What it cannot do on its own is act in freedom outside of its function and structure. Freedom is a gift and power of the soul.

I have a compelling memory from my infancy. It is, in fact, my first and earliest memory. It has two parts. The first part is a memory of dying at sea, drowning in cold water as a great ocean liner is sinking nearby. It is dark, nighttime, and the ship is lit up as she sinks into the ocean. There are lifeboats about, but I'm not in one. The interesting thing is that I don't remember the actual instant of death. What I remember is wanting desperately to find help and realizing, somehow, there is another ship nearby, just over the horizon. I am flying through the air—obviously, in retrospect, out of my body, death having already occurred though I didn't know it at the time—towards that distant ship, calling for help. Suddenly, the sky to one side of me brightens with the most beautiful and colorful light, just as if the sun is rising. I immediately turn towards it and fly into it. Looking back at that memory now, I realize I am leaving the earth plane and moving through a passage of Light into the realms beyond. That's the first part of the memory.

In the second part, I'm still seeking to get help for the passengers of the ship, many of whom are now drowning in the water. But now, inexplicably, I am surrounded by bars, as if caged. I grip the bars and call out, "Help! Help! Someone come help us!" But what comes out of my mouth are just wails and inarticulate sounds. Then, a being appears, a giant woman who reaches down and picks me up. What is this? What is happening? Then, as I look at her and at myself, I have this moment of crystal-clear realization: "Oh my god! I'm not an adult anymore. I'm a baby!" And at that moment, my consciousness shifts, all awareness of my adult self disappears, and I am wholly a baby in my mother's arms, picked up from my crib where I'd been crying.

This memory, looked at years later, suggests a number of things when viewed from my perspective. It suggests that as I took up embodiment in this life, I was presented with lingering memory traces either from my own previous life and the moment of my death or that for some reason I drew on a memory of someone close to me in the subtle worlds; coming back into embodiment put me in the "vicinity" of this memory, so to speak, just as if I traveled back to the home of my boyhood, I would be presented with memories of childhood otherwise long forgotten. In some way, this memory was a tie back into the earth plane.

But more importantly, I view this as the moment that my soul fully engaged with the physical world and surrendered itself to the "consciousness of matter." This was my "plunge" into my body, because from then on, I did not have that kind of soul perspective on my life—i.e. viewing my life as if I were someone other than David Spangler—until I again awoke to my soul level of consciousness when I was seven. To use the metaphor I used previously, this is when I stopped "camping out on the front lawn" of my new house and actually moved in, becoming an inhabitant of the neighborhood.

At conception, the soul commits its life energy and the resonance of its unique Identity to physical embodiment, though it may still have the capability of pulling away, which would cause the embryo to die in the womb. The soul has the power to self-abort a life at any time, more or less, and while accidents and unexpected terminations can happen, for most of us, when we eventually die, it's because the soul has willed it. We've reached the end of the pattern we've set for ourselves prior to incarnation and there's no compelling reason to extend it.

This commitment of the soul, however, at conception is not the same thing as the soul fully engaging with its developing body, body-mind and personality. There is very little the soul can do from within the field of the embryo. It can do far more "camping on the lawn," that is, having its focus in its developing subtle bodies, sort of "hovering" over and around the embryo and, after birth, the baby The internal processes of gestation and development are quite well handled by the intelligence of the emerging body itself and the body elemental. A body-based consciousness is developing, what I've been calling the body-mind, all of which is participating in what I've called the "personality function." The intelligence within the body and the body-mind is very capable; it draws on millions of years of evolution. More specifically, it draws as well on ancestral forces, the subtle energy lineage (and karma) of the family as a whole with its two genetic lifelines extending back through maternal and paternal lines of ancestors; and it draws, as I said in the earlier book text, on the subtle energies in the immediate subtle environment, invoked and held by its parents or at least by the mother. The soul can participate in this, but as I understand it, it basically overlights the process with greater or lesser skill depending on its own development and awaits the moment when it can leave the lawn and fully inhabit the house. What the soul really provides is the "spiritual DNA," the force of the "strange attractor" (to use an image from chaos theory), the organizing power of the four principles of incarnation: Identity, Boundary, Relationship, and Emergence. The living intelligence of the body and the body elemental are gathering what is needed from the mother's body, from the subtle environment, and so forth, but it's the soul that's providing the unique stamp of identity, the "note" or resonance that alters "world stuff" into "self stuff."

There comes a time when it steps across the threshold and through the door. This may or may not be at birth or close to it. There certainly is a progressive process as the soul deepens its embodiment in stages during the first months and years, but by age seven the soul should be fully ensconced in its new abode. However, there is that unique moment when the fundamental shift takes place, and the soul "out there" becomes the soul "in here." The locus of embodiment tips from the subtle into the physical world. I call this the "Manger Moment."

Actually, what I call the Manger Moment can't really be located as an event in time. It really describes a relationship that progressively evolves and emerges, but it's still one that has a beginning. And we can attune to it at different stages of its unfoldment...or perhaps I should say, different stages of its intersection with time.

Here's what I wrote about it a few years ago:

There is a condition where we emerge from the soul as a specific seed of intent around which all the elements of our incarnation develop . This is the moment when the soul's will impacts and penetrates the membrane of the incarnate world, setting into motion the incarnational process. In Christian symbolism, I might think of this as the "Manger" state, for the manger is a powerful image of the moment of incarnation of the sacred into the physical world represented by the manger itself and attended by the forces of nature (shepherds and sheep and other animals), of humanity (the kings), the inner worlds and the overlighting Soul (the angels and the Star), and the personalization and particularization into a unique and individual human being, (Joseph and Mary as specific human parents and, of course, Jesus). Here these elements are blended together into the Light of the Christ, the personhood of sacredness, love and intent at the heart of each and every incarnation.

The idea of the "Manger Moment," like the Presence exercise, is a way of focusing attention on the active presence of coherency and integration—the holopoietic presence, if you wish—at the center of our incarnation. Even more, it is a metaphor for our own "Big Bang," the creative moment and condition in which our presence, our living power of self, soul and sacredness, appears and begins to act from within the incarnate realm and in particular from within the physical plane.

Continuing with the metaphor of the Christ and the Nativity, in Christian tradition Christ (as a facet of the Divine) exists prior to the birth of Jesus (for that matter, prior to the creation of the world itself). It was an overlighting sacredness whose presence was known to the mystics and priests and sages of old and whose coming into incarnation was foreseen and foretold. The Three Wise Men in tradition had advanced knowledge and warning of the forthcoming birth, and this set them forth on their journey to find the new born Christ. For that matter, Joseph and Mary had known in advance Who was being born as their child. So we have an image of the Christ acting outside the physical realm preparing the way for its birth. The Christ didn't come into being when Jesus was born; it was already present and active in the world.

But there's a significant difference in Christian tradition between the Christ as Spirit and the Christ as Jesus, an incarnated person. The whole drama and meaning of Christendom revolves around "the Word made flesh," the actual presence of sacredness in incarnate form in the physical world, the Christ not as spirit alone but as matter as well. The Nativity—the "Manger Moment" of the Christian tradition—represents this important threshold and difference. Before, there is Christ as spirit enfolding the world, "in the neighborhood," so to speak, an overlighting force; after, there is Christ enfolded by and in the world, "in the house," a participating, connecting, engaging presence, part of matter, part of humanity.

The Christ drama can be—and certainly has been—interpreted and understood in countless ways, used as metaphor, illustration, inspiration, myth, and parable as well as being seen as actual history.

And that's what I'm doing here, for in this drama of the Christ and the Incarnation we can see symbolically the same processes at work that surround each person's incarnation. I guess that's why I like using the Nativity story as a symbol of our own Manger Moment, our own Big Bang, when we come into being as a spiritual force in the world and of the world and not simply as soul acting in the subtle worlds.

In many Nativity pictures, the baby Jesus is depicted as glowing like a small sun.

This is appropriate, too, as a symbol in IS, for this "Manger Moment" when the soul steps across the threshold and shifts into full embodiment generates energy, just as the Big Bang did; there is a radiance that results, and I call this energy our "Self-Light." I'll have much more to say on this next chapter in the book.

I want to emphasize that even though I'm calling it a "moment," as if it were a specific event in time, the "Manger Moment" — the appearance of our own soul's presence in the manger of the world, the manger of our body, the manger of physicality — is more a condition than it is an event, a condition that may unfold over a period of time, depending entirely on the individual.

Before leaving this image, I want also to emphasize another reason why I like using this particular symbol from the Christian tradition (which, after all, is at heart an incarnational tradition). It is said in the New Testament that Jesus was born and the Christ came to earth because "God so loved the world." But that is fundamentally why each of us comes here. Love in general and love for Gaia and the world and humanity's role in the world specifically is the prime motivating force behind our incarnations.

Oh, there are certainly many other motivations, too, which can be specific and individual — and collective. But underlying them all is love.

So in Incarnational Spirituality, we say that the soul in each of us so loved the world that it gives a portion of itself to embrace and bless and serve the earth.

With that in mind, let's talk about embodiment and the emergence of the personal, everyday self.

### THE EMBODIED SOUL

When a naturalist lays out a plant to study on a laboratory table, he can dissect it into distinct, separate parts: leaf, branch, stem, flower, petal, bark, root, and so on. Further, if our scientist turns away for the moment and looks elsewhere, he can be confident that when he turns back, a leaf will still be a leaf, a flower a flower, and a root a root. The leaf won't have suddenly morphed into a branch or vice versa while his back was turned.

I as a subtle naturalist cannot always be so sure. The phenomena I observe and study are fluid.

Boundaries are not hard and fast or operate in ways I don't always understand or may not perceive. I can't always be sure that the "leaf" won't become a "root" the next time I see it—and then be a "leaf" again after that. What something "is" may be related to the processes or relationships in which it is participating in the moment, and these can change in dynamic ways. There is nothing static about what I observe.

Of course, this may be due to the limits of my skills of subtle perception as well. Subtle observation is an interpretive art as much as anything, and my interpretations may not always be as accurate as I would like. In fact, I'm sure some of the problem is due to my own perceptional limitations and the failure of my descriptive abilities. This is one reason it's important that more people than just me engage in this kind of investigation—and why your experiences, intuitions and perceptions are important in this book, as you may see something or experience something that I do not. There are no "experts" in this process, only fellow seekers and learners faced with the wonder and awe of the non-physical side of creation.

But the fact is that subtle reality, unlike physical reality, truly is more plastic and flowing. In the wholeness of a tree, metaphorically speaking, because of their connections and interactivity, it can be difficult to pinpoint just when a leaf stops being a leaf and becomes a branch or a branch a root, and so on.

I bring this up because this is the challenge I run into when trying to describe the Embodied Soul.

You may have noticed that I fall back on several different names for this phenomenon: Everyday Self, Incarnate Self, Embodied Soul, Personality (sometimes), Psyche, Emergent Self.

That's because what I see with subtle perception aren't clearly demarcated and nicely defined layers, but a dynamic, swirling, meshing mélange of patterns, processes, functions, and "selves." Again, this may be simply a function of my own limitations as an observer—and I'm sure this is part of the problem for me—but I believe it's also the nature of the beast.

The paradox is that it is easier for me to "see" the forms and patterns on the higher energy levels than close to the physical. They are in one sense more "pure," more clearly what they are. But the incarnate state is such a mix of elements, it's not always so clear what's happening. And it's also true that as an incarnate person, I'm in the midst of it, too. It's like being in a crowd of people dancing on the street and seeing a helicopter hovering overhead. It's easier to see the helicopter because it's in a different environment than it is to see everything that's going on in the crowd around you.

Frank Capra, the great movie director, once said that we "are a divine mingle-mangle of guts and stardust." How true that is! And the Embodied Soul is at the heart of that mingle-mangle.

OK, having stated my caveats, let me get on with describing what I can. I've drawn a series of pictures, and here's the first:

This is one of the most crucial ideas I wish to communicate this chapter. When the Soul, acting in focus and intent as the "Incarnate Soul" engages with the physical world, something new comes into being that has never existed before. That new phenomenon, that new self, is you...and me...and each human being who incarnates into this world. It is a blend of soul stuff and earth stuff.

The familiar old metaphor is that the body is a car and the soul enters it as a driver, but in fact, it's as if the soul melts itself into steel and plastic, rubber and fabric and glass and becomes the car. Only that's not quite it, either. It's as if steel and plastic, rubber and fabric and glass are melted together into soul and poured into the shape of a car.

A dozen years ago or so when I was starting my inquiry into the nature of incarnation, I asked how incarnation came about. I was shown an interesting image. A man walked into a large patch of muddy ground and lay down. When he got up, there was a perfect impression of him in the mud. This impression then got up as well, a mud-man.

This is what incarnation is: the soul impresses itself into the substance and vibration of matter. But the reverse happens as well: matter impresses itself into the soul. What results is an amalgam. Matter becomes "soul-ified" and soul becomes "matter-ified."

The Embodied Soul that results is qualitatively different or maybe I should say vibrationally different than the Incarnate Soul or the greater Soul beyond. It is now of the earth, inside matter, part of matter as well as being part of soul.

When Jesus is referred to as the "Son of Man" as well as the "Son of God," this is what it means to me. He is not all "Heaven" nor all "Earth" but a being manifesting both.

And this is true for each of us.

This is one reason for the energy differential between the Soul and the incarnate self, the Embodied Soul, which I wrote about earlier. And in thinking about this, it is very important that we don't think of the human incarnate self as "fallen" or "lower." It is simply different, a whole new kind of soul that begins to emerge and function as a part of the incarnate world.

This creates more than just an energy differential, though. It creates a consciousness differential, a perspective differential, a beingness differential.

And yet Soul is Soul is Soul.

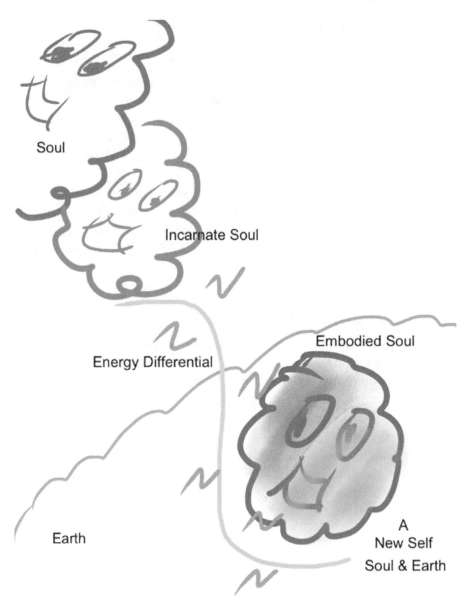

Soul

Incarnate Soul

Energy Differential

Embodied Soul

Earth

A
New Self
Soul & Earth

FIGURE 28

Here's the next picture:

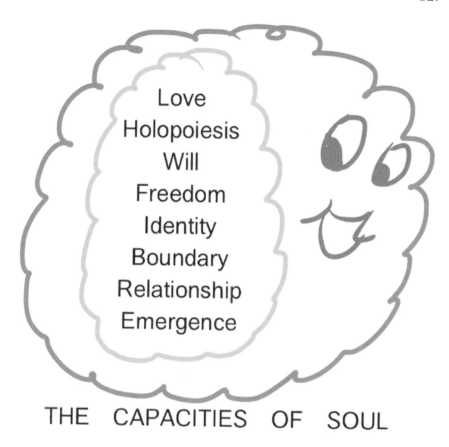

Love
Holopoiesis
Will
Freedom
Identity
Boundary
Relationship
Emergence

THE  CAPACITIES  OF  SOUL

FIGURE 29

A crucial idea here is what makes soul "soul." What is soul? Is it simply the non-physical part of us, the part that lives on a higher plane of existence? Yes, but Soul is also a function, or perhaps capacity is a better term. It is the coherent, integrated capacity to consciously hold and express Love and Holopoiesis the four principles of incarnation (Identity, Boundary, Relationship, and Emergence) as well as the qualities of Will and Freedom, among other things.

It holds and manifests these qualities, forces and principles whether it's operating on a cosmic level as Spirit Soul or a Gaian level as Planetary Soul or within the incarnate realm as Incarnate Soul or in embodiment as Embodied Soul. These different levels or "types" of Soul differ in structure and energy but not in capacity. The structure and energy may determine how Soul expresses itself, but not what it can express. The essential capacities and functions are constant across the continuum of "soul-dom."

# SOUL   IS   SOUL

Cosmic  (Spirit)  Soul

Planetary  Soul

Incarnate   Soul

Embodied   Soul

FIGURE 30

Our incarnate, human capacities to create wholeness, to express love, to manifest will, to hold an identity, to create boundaries, to form connections and relationships, to learn and grow and emerge new capacities and qualities, and to act in freedom all come from being Soul. They all come from the impression of soul into the "mud" of our earth-stuff. This is what Soul brings to the amalgam that is the human being.

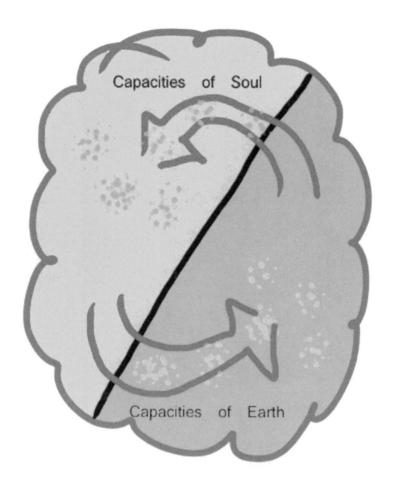

# BLENDING  CAPACITIES
# 1

FIGURE 31

In incarnation, the soul is enabled to take on capacities and qualities held by matter or if you wish, by the earth or by Gaia. Incarnate matter, in reciprocation, takes on capacities and qualities held in the soul. The earth becomes more soul-like; the soul becomes more, well, Gaia-like. A unique "amalgam" is created.

# BLENDING   CAPACITIES
# 2

FIGURE 32

You and I, as Embodied Souls, are each unique manifestations of this amalgam.

Here is a picture shown earlier in FIGURE 2. It's of the circulation between earth (Gaia) and its cosmic environment. As I said at the time, incarnation is a manifestation of that circulation.

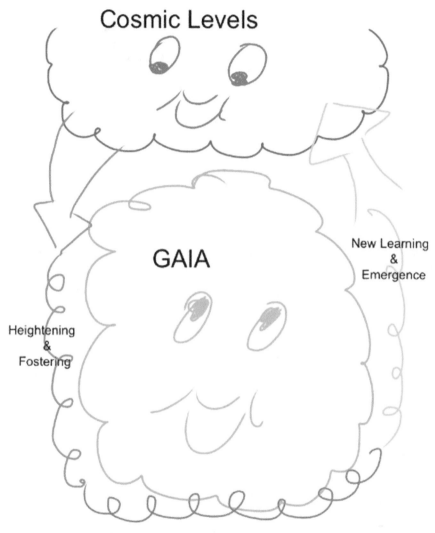

CIRCULATION & METABOLISM OF COSMIC ENERGIES

FIGURE 33

Here is a similar picture. As you can see, this is one aspect of this larger cosmic and planetary circulation.

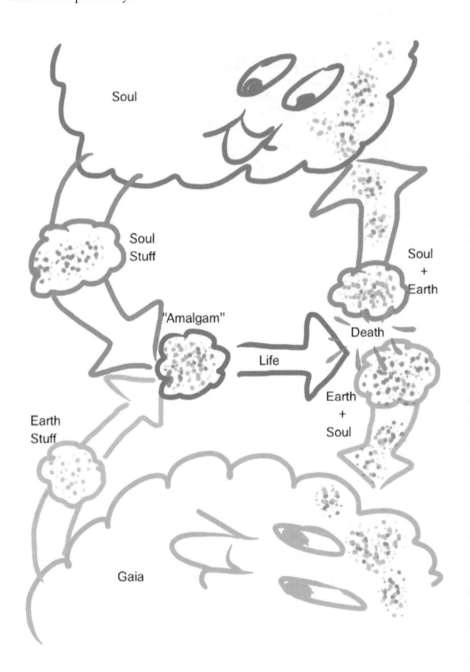

FIGURE 34

Here there are two circulations, one from Soul back to Soul and one from Gaia back to Gaia or earth back to earth.

In the first instance, "soul stuff," including the capacities presented earlier, moves into contact with the earth and its subtle and physical levels through the presence of the Incarnate Soul. It draws to itself planetary subtle and physical substance, which with the help of the body elemental among others, rises to meet the incoming soul forces; this "earth stuff" carries with it evolving and functional capacities of Gaia manifesting as matter. These meet in the Embodied Soul, which now becomes an amalgam, a wholly new form of Soul that lives an incarnate life as a human self. At death, this amalgam dissolves, so to speak; the earth substance returns to the earth but now imbued with soul resonances and capacities, however faint. The Embodied Soul itself, now freed from its physical shell, moves back into the soul realms carrying with it a new kind of soul vibration, one resonant with the gifts of the earth.

There has been learning and emergence on both sides.

This, as I understand it, is the large picture—and the main reason it's not accurate to speak of the soul as something totally separate from the earth and from physical matter, simply "riding" about in the body as if it were a car.

Here's a picture we've seen before in FIGURE 26:

# PRE-BIRTH

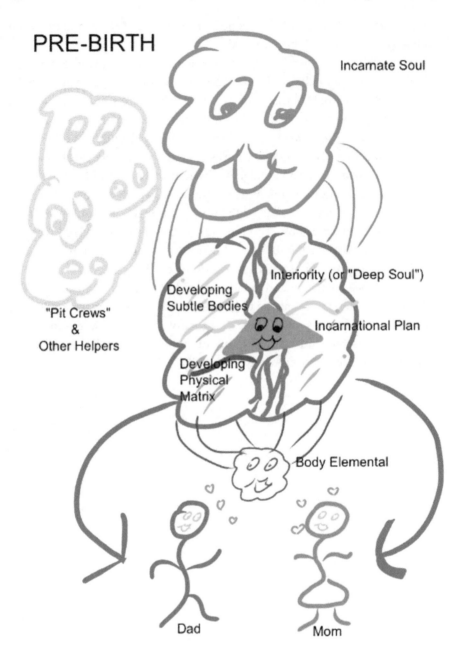

Incarnate Soul

Interiority (or "Deep Soul")

Developing
Subtle Bodies

"Pit Crews"
&
Other Helpers

Incarnational Plan

Developing
Physical
Matrix

Body Elemental

Dad                    Mom

FIGURE 35

In this picture, the soul is beginning to embody—the "Manger Moment" has begun—but it has not yet quite entered into the physical plane. The amalgam is forming, but it hasn't been "sealed," so to speak, by the actual transformation of part if the Incarnate Soul's consciousness. To use an earlier metaphor, it hasn't stepped over the threshold into the house yet.

But when the physical body is conceived and the embryo begins to grow, this changes. As I understand it, the soul dips in and out, forming more and more linkages with the body and its consciousness, impressing the "mud" more and more deeply and taking into itself more and more of the impression of the world and of matter.

And then, at some point—it doesn't really matter just when it is—the soul surrenders completely to matter and vice versa and gives its presence to becoming the amalgam. It enters the house; it is born in the manger. It is in and of the world. This, to me, is the true Manger Moment, the one that finally gives birth to our personal self and to the Embodied Soul as its interiority.

This is when, as shown in a previous picture from FIGURE 26 that the consciousness that represents the amalgam—what I call the "psyche" comes into being, the beginnings of our everyday mind and its various psychological depths and functions.

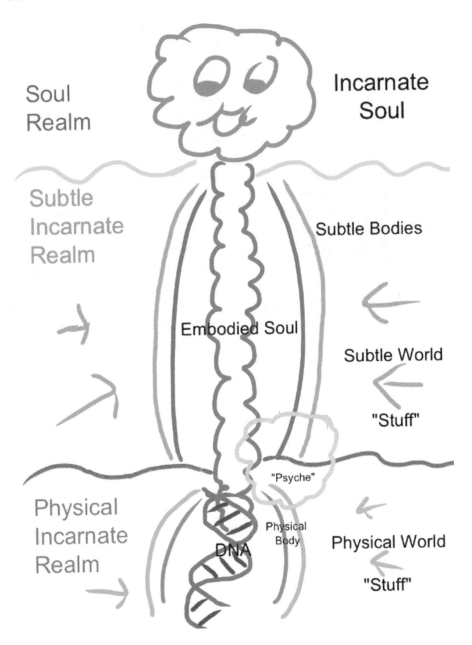

FIGURE 36

With this context, let's look more closely at this Embodied Soul, at psyche,
and at the everyday self. Here's a new picture:

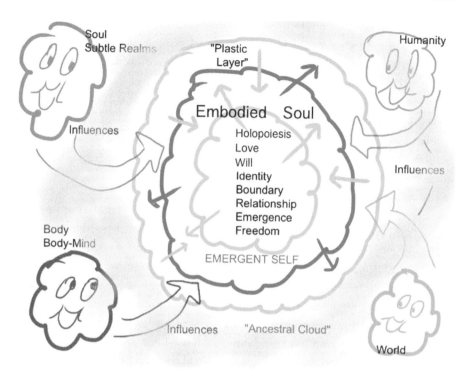

FIGURE 37

This picture is not complete, but it is suggestive—and it gets us started.

This picture is a map of subtle energetic relationships and influences. The Embodied Soul is now the incarnate self, the "amalgam" as one of my inner colleagues once called it. At the core of this embodiment and permeating it with potential and capacities is the quality of "Soul" itself, the presence of the "I" and of our sacredness. I think of this as our Interiority. It's important to remember that this core presence of Soul is essentially at one with and thus connected to all other manifestations of Soul (i.e. Incarnate Soul, Planetary Soul, etc.). Remember that soul is soul is soul.

Initially, the Embodied Soul is the essential structure of intent formulated in the Incarnate Soul; it is what I was calling the "proto-personality" earlier or the matrix of the incarnate self. But as it is now exposed to experience in the world, it begins to grow, change, and develop. It may do so along planned lines, but it may also do so in unexpected and novel ways as new experiences bring new learning and new insights. In this way an incarnate self begins to emerge. The core Embodied Soul attempts to influence the direction of this emergence as much as it can, but it is also influenced by a host of other forces. I show this in the picture by the four elements in the corner, familiar to us already from the Presence exercise among other things. Thus there is an influence from collective humanity, from the world of nature, from the subtle worlds and from the Incarnate Soul, and also from the body, the body-mind, and the Personality as an individualizing and particularizing function.

There are also influences from what I'm calling here the "ancestral cloud." By this I mean those forces connected to the incarnating person from its history and lineages. These could include influences from the planning done by the soul, i.e. the soul's intent, karmic patterns, past life habits rising up as the soul re-encounters the physical plane, and so forth; influences from the literal ancestors of the soul's new body (parents, grandparents, aunts, uncles, etc.), the genetic lineage, etc.; influences from the past history of humanity, lingering thought-forms from past human actions and beliefs which may be present in the subtle environment, etc.; influences from the evolutionary past of nature.

Some of these forces are quite specific to the individual and others are more general and diffuse; altogether, they represent the individual's encounter with the "Past," with what has gone before and the influences this Past generates.

Around the Emergent Self is a zone I call the "Plastic Layer." Of course, I'm not referring to any kind of petrochemical product here! I want to suggest that the boundary where the new amalgam, the Embodied Soul and Emergent Self, is meeting and engaging its subtle and physical world is very dynamic. It is fluid and constantly changing shape as subtle energies in the form of thoughts, feelings, impulses, and the like are taken up, held for a moment and then either discarded or taken in.

We experience this every day. Thousands of thoughts, feelings and images flicker across our awareness, most of them fleeting; but some of them grab our attention and hang on for awhile, and some of these are taken in and adopted as our feelings, our thoughts, our beliefs, and so on. They become part of us, and if they become part of us deeply enough and enduringly enough, they become part of our Emergent Self. They become part of who we are, shaping us and influencing the path of our becoming.

As we live our lives, experiencing the world, forming our own thoughts and beliefs, forming habits, and so forth, the "plastic layer" can become more complex, just as our emergent self becomes more developed and complex. Here's the first of two pictures:

As I've said in various ways at various times in our book, we live in a sea of information and subtle energies. Just as the earth's atmosphere and magnetic field are bombarded by charged particles from the sun, so our personal energy field is constantly being impacted by subtle radiations from the people and world around us. This can have a number of different effects which this picture seeks to describe.

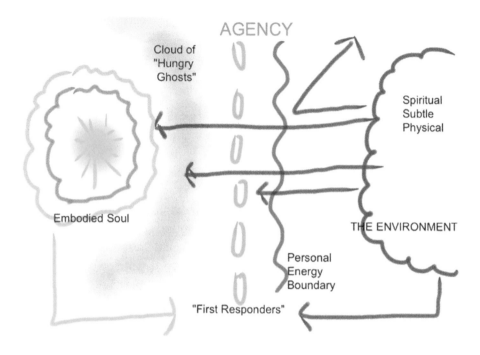

FIGURE 38

The energetic influences can reach us from several levels of the incarnate realm and beyond. They can come from spiritual and soul levels, from the subtle environment of the incarnate realm, and from people and places in the physical world around us.

Each of us is surrounded by our own personal subtle energy field with its boundaries; importantly, this can function as a "ring-pass-not," a protective boundary against many of the subtle forces to which we are exposed. Keeping this energy field healthy and vital is part of what I call energy hygiene.

Many, perhaps most, of the subtle energies and vectors that we encounter just "bounce off" us. Nothing in us resonates with them, draws them in, or attaches to them; we might feel them—the subtle field around us is also an organ of perception, much like our physical skin—but that's all.

Some of these impulses (ideas, feelings, and other subtle energies of different kinds and qualities) may catch our attention in some way; at some level (either consciously or unconsciously) they have a resonance with us, or their vector (intensity and direction of energy) is strong enough that we can't help but register them and pay attention in some way. Thus for some reason they penetrate the boundary of our personal energy field.

At this point, depending on just what the energy is and how we relate to it, different things can happen. Here are the broad strokes.

We all have elements that I think of as our "first responders." These may be physical, psychological, or energetic in nature and they represent our first response to a particular stimulus. They are almost always automatic, often unconscious and may take the form of habits. They may well be based on experience or arise from information I take in from the environment. They may also arise as conscious decisions and choices made by the Embodied Soul and the Emerging Self.

There's nothing mysterious about this. Here are some examples, some trivial, some not so.

Having had food poisoning as a child from creamed corn, my first response to the sight of corn kernels (not corn meal or ground corn) is to say no and to refuse any food containing them. This is an automatic response now, which I can override by conscious choice. I can, for instance, eat and enjoy corn on the cob, but I have to make an effort to accept it in the first place.

A man is raised in a family with strong homophobic feelings. He has gay friends, but it was an effort for him to overcome the first response of rejection when confronted with a gay person.

A woman picks up a vibe of danger while walking down a street at night. She hesitates; part of her tries to convince herself not to "be silly" or "afraid," that "nothing can happen." But she listens to her first response of fear to something she has picked up on and turns back and takes an alternate route. As it turns out, a mugger was lying in wait for prey down the street that she turned away from.

A person hears the President talking about increasing health care; his first response, based on things he's heard or read, is to say, "Oh, that's socialism. He's trying to take away my freedom." He becomes angry and turns the radio off. Or he might say, in spite of his initial feelings, "Oh, let me think this through. Is this really socialism. Exactly what is the President proposing?" In this latter case, he may come to new insights.

A woman in one of my classes years ago told me she loved what I was teaching but was bothered by me. I made her uneasy and she found it hard to listen to me. We were both puzzled by this as there was nothing I said or did that would have led to such a response. Sometime later, though, she came to me and said, "I know where these feelings are coming from. You look like my ex-husband from whom I had a bitter divorce." An image in her unconscious memory provided a "first response" to me; her interest in what I was teaching enabled her to override this, but it still bothered her until she figured it out.

A woman described to me once how she met a man who matched an image she had of an ideal mate. She opened up to him and ended up giving him a large sum of money, after which he skipped town leaving her high and dry. She didn't blame him as much as she blamed her own images that had led her to say yes to him as a first response.

I'm sure you can come up with many examples of your own. It's a common phenomenon. Such "first responders" can say yes or no to incoming stimuli and to subtle energies that are felt or sensed, depending on the circumstances, but in either case, the response is more likely than not to be an automatic one without much conscious thought or deliberation. These "first responders" represent mental, emotional, and energetic reflexes. If we take time to think through and evaluate what we're experiencing, we may come to a different conclusion and set of behaviors than the first responders would have prompted.

Normally, we think about these "first responders" as psychological and physical habits and complexes, and they are. But they are also subtle energy patterns and structures in our personal energy field and can be perceived or detected clairvoyantly. Psychology is often energy and vice versa.

"First Responders" can stop a subtle energy vector or pass it through. If it goes through, then it can become part of what I call the "Cloud of Hungry Ghosts," borrowing an image from Tibetan Buddhism. It basically represents a field of unintegrated subtle energies (which could be thoughts, feelings, qualities, etc.), material which we haven't fully made part of who we are but yet we haven't rejected them either. They are unintegrated parts of us, disassociated parts, which can become centers of focus and will for our outer behavior.

Before I explain this "cloud," I need to say something more about how I understand the nature of the subtle energies that surround us in the world.

There are many different kinds of subtle energies, and they emanate from a wide variety of sources. All of them, as I've said before, are sentient, living energies, and many of them—particularly those generated by the thinking and feeling of human beings—possess qualities of will and direction as well as intensity, what I call "vectors." In a way, they are mini-thought forms. Most don't last long—they don't have the energy to do so—and they don't propagate very far. But like physical micro-organisms, they can exist for a time in an environment where we can pick up on them.

FIGURE 39

In effect they are like small bits of information, bits of thought and emotion containing some impetus of will. If we pick up on them, that information—that thought and emotion and will—can be transferred to us, and we may experience them as if they were our own.

This picture is just a cartoon illustrating two extremes, the energies emanating from an angry person and the energies emanating from a happy person. The fact that I've drawn them as clouds of particles is merely an artistic device (or lack thereof!); they are not particles as such or even waves as such. I'm not sure how to describe them. Many are blocked by our personal energy fields, many by our "first responders," but some we take in, and they can become part of our "cloud of hungry ghosts," at least for a time.

There are often three parts to these subtle bits of information: a motivation or force, the sense of desire, of wanting or willing something; a quality that defines or colors that desire, which might be fear or anger or love or joy; and possibly a target or an object, such as a thought form that says "I fear Moslems" or "I Love Everybody."

The subtle bit of information may not be that precisely well-formed and articulated (though it can be) but it can have enough quality and direction to it to generate more specific thoughts and feelings when taken in to our own energy field, particularly if we already fear Moslems, say, or have a generous feeling of love for people in general.

In electricity, an ion is a free and unattached particle that carries a charge. In the subtle environment, the kind of subtle bits I'm describing might be thought of as subtle ions, looking for something to connect or attach to. They are looking for an "ecosystem" to be part of that can help them fulfill the "charge" that they carry. It's in this sense that I think of them as "hungry ghosts." They are seeking to fulfill their intent by attaching to a source of will and substance that can give them form and expression.

Imagine a bit of anger that has no way of being angry at something or discharging its anger; it is sentient energy frozen in a particular configuration by human thought and feeling, and it seeks to unfreeze, to fulfill its charge. It is hungry for expression, and when it is negative in its nature, it fulfills the definition of a demon (and if it's positive, it's akin to an angel).

When we take on such a bit, we might take on the specificity that gave it birth. We might find ourselves suddenly for no reason feeling an antipathy towards Moslems or a fear of gays or whatever it might be—or we might have a sudden rush of warm and loving feeling or of joy, perhaps also towards a particular person or group. Or that specificity may not survive its journey into our own field but it triggers a vague kind of unease and anger or goodwill and joy. We may then assign that anger or joy to a target of our choice, giving it specificity once again.

A good friend of mine, Catherine MacCoun describes demons as "fragments of human psychology that have become detached from their original human hosts."

Catherine is the author of a most excellent book, *On Becoming an Alchemist* (a book, by the way, I highly recommend). On this topic, she says,

"In my book, I described how thoughts, feelings and impulses get projected into the collective thought environment, aka the astral plane. Sometimes we do this on purpose, as in the case of art, advertising, propaganda and even, sometimes, prayer. Other times we do it by forcefully rejecting some part of our own content, declaring it "not me" and doing our best to get rid of it. In dying we may also shed obsolete personal baggage, which can persist in the astral as physic debris.

Many of our cast-offs simply "biodegrade," causing little or no ecological harm. But some cast-offs resist dissolution. The force with which we reject a thought, feeling or impulse may add to its power, launching it into the astral like a projectile. Some fragments of human psychology acquire so much momentum from the casting-off that they have a volitional quality, a will of their own. That's what a demon is: a thought, feeling or impulse that has acquired independent volition, so that it persists as a seemingly autonomous being."

Here Catherine is describing exactly the kind of subtle energy bits that I'm talking about. Some can be quite powerful and long-lasting, others dissipate quickly and easily. Some carry strong volitional charges, others weaker ones. But when we absorb them, their volition, their will, becomes active in us and can lead to behavior that later we wonder, "Now where did that come from?"

What I call our "Cloud of Hungry Ghosts" is the place where such material accumulates, whether generated by us and then disowned or rejected or taken in from our environment, however unwittingly.

The main characteristic of the material that exists in this "cloud" within us is that it is essentially unintegrated. It is part of our field of personal energy — part of our self — but it isn't connected or integrated with the Embodied Soul. Yet it can draw upon our energy and our power of will to sustain itself and even to express itself. Much of this material is what psychologists think of as the unconscious, and it is unconscious for the most part. But it isn't purely psychological, though it can have psychological manifestations. It is a subtle energy phenomenon.

Finally, we may take subtle energy in a variety of forms in from the environment that truly reaches the Embodied Soul, shaping the "plastic layer" in some way and even becoming an integrated part of our emerging self, perhaps for the rest of our lives. Note that this doesn't necessarily mean that it's "spiritual" information or energy that does this; it can be anything that touches us deeply enough and which we take on and integrate into our life and way of being — which is not a "hungry ghost" anymore because we are actively accepting and fulfilling it, feeding it by making it a living part of us.

If I suffer or witness suffering in ways that give me a deeply felt anger or hatred, one that I acknowledge and accept and form my life around, it is part of my emerging self. It shapes the way my Embodied Soul manifests. It takes the capacities of soul and builds a hateful identity with boundaries against what is hated and which forms connections accordingly; what may emerge is a purpose-driven life focused on destroying that which is hated. The core of the Embodied Soul, that which holds love and the holopoietic capacity may despair that this is happening, but it may be powerless to stop it without some kind of helpful intervention.

Let me give you a more benign example of a "hungry ghost." For all the years that I knew him, my father wanted to write books. He had two or three topics that he particularly wanted to explore, and over the years, he would start working on them. But he never got very far. Dad could write very well, but he wasn't a writer. It wasn't in him to do the kind of work necessary to see a book through to completion—and he had many other kinds of work going on in his life as well that took his time and energy.

His image of his books, however, were like hungry ghosts within him. They were always there as a kind of unfulfilled desire, something he felt he should do even though he didn't really have the will to do so. As he entered his eighties (he was 89 when he died), he would say to me, "I can't die until I finish my books."

Dad lived in Ohio and I lived in Washington State. A mutual friend called to tell me he had died. Dad and I had just been speaking the night before on the phone and he'd sounded strong and vital, but apparently he had a heart attack early the next morning. When I didn't feel him around on the inner, I became concerned that he might have become "earthbound." His hungry ghost of needing to write and finish a book had become so strong in him that I thought it might have bound him to the earth. It was a relief when Julie and I went back to Ohio to settle his affairs and I discovered no evidence in his home that he was earthbound, no sense of him at all.

Months later Dad showed up in a vivid dream. We were sitting in our kitchen here in our home and he was telling Julie and me that when he died, he knew he had to go immediately into a tunnel of Light that had appeared or else his sense of unfinished business would have kept him close to the physical plane. So he left, and this dream was the first time he'd been able to come back into the incarnate realm without the pressure of his desire to write his books potentially trapping him. He had shed his hungry ghosts in the post-mortem realms.

One thing that I am often asked by people is why they can't perceive or contact the subtle realms, or for that matter, their own souls. The reason is personal for each individual, but this picture, drawing on the idea of the amalgam and the transformation that the soul undergoes as it becomes part of the physical world, suggests some of the underlying dynamic of this issue.

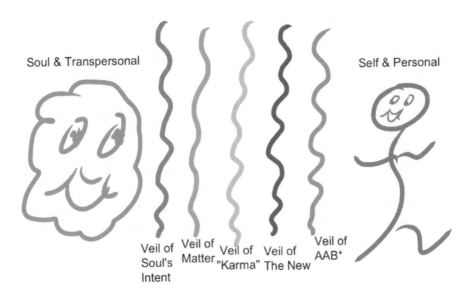

Soul & Transpersonal

Self & Personal

Veil of Soul's Intent    Veil of Matter    Veil of "Karma"    Veil of The New    Veil of AAB*

*Attention, Attitude, Belief

FIGURE 40

What stands between us as incarnate selves and our own souls, or the transpersonal and subtle worlds in general? This question goes beyond just exploring how to make contact with subtle beings; contact with Soul is a vital technique in dealing with the "cloud of hungry ghosts" and other subtle energy issues that complicate our Incarnational System and prevent us from achieving the level of coherency and wholeness that we wish. So what gets in the way?

These five veils represent possible obstacles. Not all five are always present, and there may be other "veils" not represented here.

**Veil of AAB:** AAB stands for Attention, Attitude and Belief or more generally for our psychological state. We may fail to make contact with our Interiority or our Soul or with the subtle worlds in general simply because we don't believe they exist, or we don't think we're worthy or able to make such a contact, or we fail to pay attention to the clues and sensations that indicate contact is present. The most difficult veil of all for the subtle worlds to overcome in their attempts to connect with us is our indifference and disbelief. And if we believe we can't do it anyway, well, that can be a game stopper right there. Attitude, Attention and Belief are very important.

**Veil of the New:** This represents the challenge created by the differences between the subtle worlds (and the soul) and ourselves as incarnate beings. It's the veil created when the "amalgam" comes into being and we become something new, no longer just soul but soul plus earth.

**Veil of "Karma":** There may be specific reasons in a person's life why he or she cannot make contact with subtle dimensions (though a person can always make contact with his or her own Interiority in some manner—karma cannot cut a person off from his or her sacredness or from the Sacred). Perhaps the individual needs to focus on his or her earthly life and not be distracted with subtle world contact. I met a man once who was totally insensitive to any kind of subtle perception or contact; as it turned out, he had been a psychic in a previous life who had used his talents and inner contact to deceive people and exert control over them. In this life, that contact was being denied him because he had misused it before.

**Veil of Matter:** The physical world and the subtle worlds are simply very different. Sometimes it is hard for communication to bridge the gap of this difference. It takes energy and work to do so, which may not be possible under some circumstances. And misunderstandings can arise when physical world assumptions and ways of thinking and doing things are projected upon the subtle worlds and applied inappropriately; the reverse can happen, too. I have had inner contact with beings who cannot understand why I can't do certain things which they can do with ease. The reason, of course, is that I am a being of matter and earth as well as of spirit, something they cannot fully understand.

**Veil of Soul's Intent:** This is similar to the Veil of Karma. For some particular reason, the soul doesn't wish its incarnate self to contact it, at least not as an outside source; discovering the qualities of soul within one's earthly life is another thing altogether. In any event, the soul may have reasons that we're not aware of that keep us from making contact with transpersonal or subtle realities. It may simply be a matter of timing, that something that will be OK at one stage in a person's life could be problematic or a diversion at another stage.

As I said, there may be other reasons as well, but these are the main ones. Most of them can be changed or overcome, but sometimes we just do the best we can and are patient until the time is right for contact to be made. However, in my experience, the soul truly wishes a deeper, clearer contact, and the subtle worlds themselves are actively seeking greater contact at this time. This suggests to me that while some of these veils may present challenges of understanding, interpretation and comprehension, the main obstacle is our lack of attention, attitude and belief. We simply don't think it's possible or real.

The irony is that even though we may have difficulty achieving conscious contact with the subtle worlds, we are in unconscious contact most if not all of the time. We live in a subtle energy environment as fully as we do in a physical one, and we have subtle perceptions at some level of our consciousness (or subconsciousness) just as we have physical perceptions. The trick is learning to pay attention to them and to be aware of them. They are, after all, subtle!

So, where are we now in exploring the incarnate self?

Here's a picture that sums up where we have reached in our exploration:

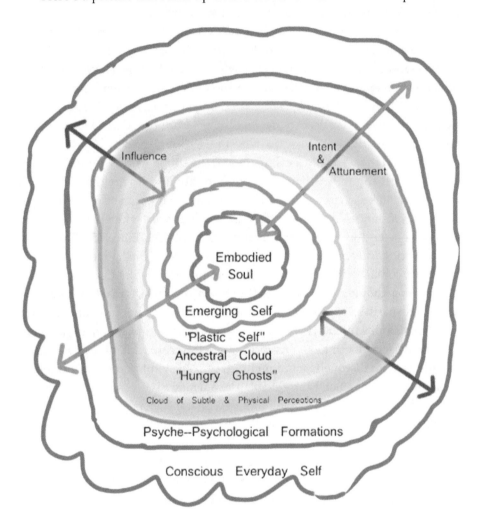

## SELF & PSYCHE

FIGURE 41

We could say that each of us is a blend of four dynamic elements: Soul (or, if you prefer, Spirit), Subtle Energy, Psyche (and psychological processes and structures), and an everyday consciousness which has the capacity for agency, i.e. decision-making.

In this picture we see these elements. There is the Embodied Soul, the Emerging Self (our deep structure of identity, belief, memory, experience, character, and so forth), and the "Plastic" self or our growing and "shape-shifting" edge. Then, as we've been discussing, there are the energetic elements of the ancestral cloud, the cloud of hungry ghosts, and the cloud of subtle and physical perceptions that are going on all the time: the continual impact upon our senses and our energy field of stimuli from the physical and subtle environments. There is a part of us that is aware of all this, even though only a tiny fraction actually rises to the level of conscious awareness. One way it does arise is often through the phenomenon we call intuition.

Atop all this, so to speak, is our psyche, the layer of psychological structure and its body-mind correspondences. Here is where we tend to find the "first responders" I wrote of earlier. Here we find habits of mind and emotion (habits of energy are located deeper in the self).

And the thinnest layer of all is that of our everyday consciousness. So much is going on within us all the time that we are not aware of. But it's at the conscious level that we can exercise mindfulness, awareness, decision-making, choice, evaluation, all the things that give direction to our lives. And it is on the conscious level that we can activate the holopoietic principles to foster integration and wholeness within our incarnate self. It may be a thin layer, the tip of the incarnate iceberg, but it's where the work of incarnation is done.

To complete describing the picture, there are two sets of lines, one red and one blue. The red line represents our conscious ability through intent and some form of attunement to link the conscious, everyday awareness to the deep presence of Soul and to other deeper or more subtle levels and layers of our being as well. This, as we shall see, is a most important capacity.

The other line suggests that our conscious mind is also influenced and shaped, sometimes in ways we don't always realize or expect, by forces arising from the Embodied Soul, from ancestral influences, from our own "hungry ghosts," from unconscious physical or subtle perceptions, and, of course, from our various psychological processes, which themselves can be shaped by subtler energy structures and processes.

It is not always clear just who is in charge in our lives, and that is the challenge of incarnation.

Before going on, I want to say that I realize how presumptuous all this seems and...how shall I say it?...how clinical or how mechanical it may seem compared to the actual wonder and beauty that is our incarnate life. I look back at my pictures and I laugh, for our consciousness is hardly limited to this layer or that layer but swoops like an eagle up and down through the whole of our being from the peaks of our daily awareness to the depths of our Interiority.

The point is that we are an energetic ecosystem in which many elements participate, not always harmoniously, not always in touch with each other. The soul within us is like the sunlight, shining on all of it, warming it all with its life. But that part of us that dares to call itself I, the part from which we look out on our world and think ourselves a unique person, draws on all those elements, on all parts of the ecosystem, and seeks to make it a whole. And it can do so, not by itself alone but by the power of its sovereignty and direction, its capacity to choose, to decide, to be mindful.

I hope beyond my words and my pictures you can glimpse the wonder of all you are. The miracle of each of us is that so many elements of creation come together and work together to bring something new into being. And that something new is who we are and what we are becoming.

### THE BODY—OUR PARTNERING INTELLIGENCE

Incarnation is a partnership endeavor. On the one hand, there is the soul in its various manifestations engaging with the Gaian field of planetary energy and substance. And on the other hand, there is the physical body, Gaia's gift to the incarnational process. The self that we experience as "I" is a product of the partnership of these two fields of intelligence; it is an amalgam (or perhaps more precisely, an alloy) of the qualities of these two forces.

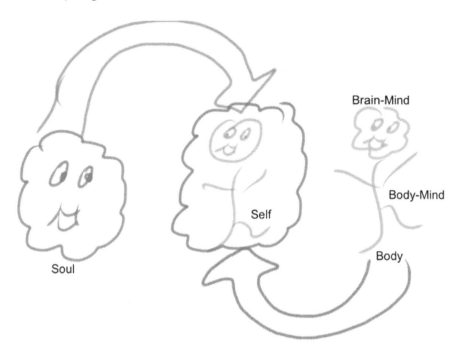

FIGURE 42

Older metaphors of incarnation portray the body as simply a vehicle that houses the soul, but in fact it's a good deal more than that. It is an ancient and powerful intelligence in its own right—one might even say a hive mind, since it's an integrated system of over a trillion somatic cells operating more or less in harmony (not to mention the trillion or so non-somatic cells or microbes that also inhabit out bodies inside and out and which are vital to the smooth running of our physiological processes and therefore of our physical life). Indeed it has been estimated that our bodies contain more cells than the number of stars we can see in the nighttime sky! Each of these is an evolving intelligence, an evolving spirit or "I" in its own right, much further down the evolutionary scale of consciousness than our own intelligence but very powerful and aware on its own level of functioning.

Here are some of the elements that are part of or engaged with the body as a physical field of substance and energy.

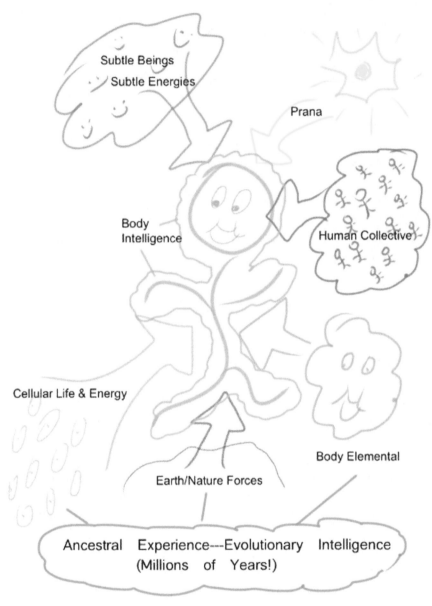

Subtle Beings
Subtle Energies

Prana

Body
Intelligence

Human Collective

Cellular Life & Energy

Body Elemental

Earth/Nature Forces

Ancestral   Experience---Evolutionary   Intelligence
(Millions   of   Years!)

FIGURE 43

At the bottom in this picture we see that our bodies are the product of millions of years of evolution; they are packed with what I might call "ancestral experience" and evolutionary intelligence.

Then there is the cellular life, energy and intelligence arising from all the cells that make up our bodies and who, as a result of these millions of years of experience, know just how to be what they are and how to "do" a body—how to work together to create our body. When people talk about the healing intelligence in the body, this is often what they're referring to. There is great wisdom embodied here.

Then there are earth and nature forces to which the body is attuned and upon which it draws. One of these in particular is what I think of as the body elemental, which might also be thought of as the "group mind" or "group soul" of all the cellular life that makes up the body.

The body is attuned to vital energies in the environment, such as prana, an etheric force which in esoteric tradition is generated by the influence of solar, life-stimulating forces. The body is also attuned to planetary magnetic forces, rhythms of tides, the moon, and so on. In short, it is a "cosmic citizen."

The body also is sensitive and attuned to the energy field of the human collective—in other words, it's attuned to other bodies, and aspects of this attunement are not limited by distance.

Likewise the body has its own attunement to subtle energies and to the subtle environment, including at times subtle beings.

All of these influences feed into the field of the body and manifest as a body intelligence and what I think of as a "body-mind." (Part of this body-mind is specifically the "brain-mind" which arises from the activity of neurochemistry and neurobiology.)

So the body has its own intelligence which is ancient, powerful, and integrated.

The energy field of the body just as a physical instrument, leaving aside for the moment its subtle counterparts, turns it into a powerful antenna which is attuned to a wide variety of subtle forces and energies arising from the planet, from humanity, from nature, from the sun and moon and stars, and from the subtle environment. It is constantly receiving and processing information from all these sources, and most of this happens without our conscious intervention or knowledge.

## BODY AS ANTENNA

FIGURE 44

However, one effect of this is that we can find ourselves thinking thoughts or feeling feelings that do not originate with us but which we are picking up from others. This may be more subtle than a telepathic reception, closer to empathy, but it isn't exactly that either. If we identify with them, we can make them our own, but this isn't always a wise thing to do. Who wants to take on another person's anger, for instance? And yet this kind of transference happens much more than people realize as our physical bodies (not to mention our subtle bodies) function as highly attuned antennae.

The point is that the body is designed and built to participate in the vast subtle fields of consciousness that surround and permeate the earth. It is so much more than just a "physical vehicle."

I've written before about the Personality and how I define it. The Personality, for me, is a sense of self arising from two interacting structures. One is the structure of the body which determines how it perceives, how it receives information from the environment, how it physiologically processes and holds that information and so forth. The other I might call the structure of the soul's intent, all that is held by the Incarnate Soul, the karma of the life, the "incarnational plan," and so forth. This is a subtle structure which establishes boundaries and vectors for the incarnation every bit as much as the physical body does in its unique way.

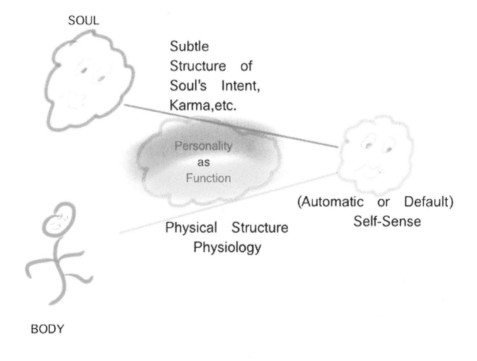

SOUL

Subtle Structure of Soul's Intent, Karma,etc.

Personality as Function

(Automatic or Default) Self-Sense

Physical Structure Physiology

BODY

FIGURE 45

As I've written before, I think of the Personality as a function that takes the more complex and fluid nature of the soul and particularizes it. It individualizes us in particular and specific ways, and it does so by establishing boundaries. Where the soul is inclusive, it is exclusive. It's a kind of subtle or psychic immune system, determining what is "I" and what is "Not-I."

The effect of the personality and the structures (and their function) upon which it is based is to generate in us a "default" and automatic sense of self, which in more general parlance we call our "personality." This sense of self is limited but it's designed to be such.

However, it's not intended to be limiting or to determine just who we are. It gives us a place to start, but then we can mindfully, consciously transcend these boundaries and limits, these "default" and automatic reactions and expressions to build an emerging, mindful self that has this personality foundation to fall back upon when needed but which is not limited by it. More on this in a bit.

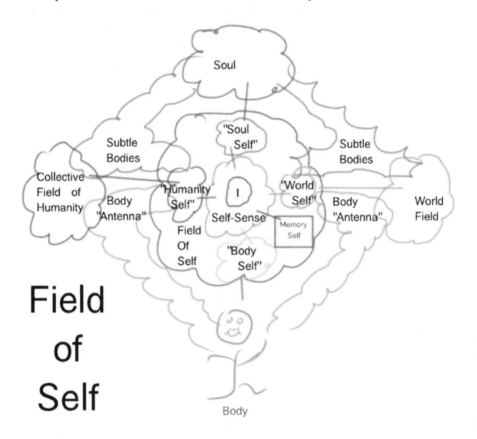

FIGURE 46

Let's summarize a bit, using the Presence Exercise as a template.

We each have a sense of who we are as a person; we have a "self-sense"

We all know this can change from one day to the next, even at times from one minute to the next. At one time we may feel confident and have a good sense of ourselves, and at another we may feel vulnerable, even weak, and have a poor sense of ourselves.

But on the whole, there is a continuity to our self-image and self-sense, the awareness that for all the changes we go through, there's something there in us that is, if not exactly permanent, at least long-lasting and very slow to change. In the picture, this is at the center and I label it "I". This is the source of our Agency, about which I'll have more to say in a bit.

Around this "I" is the field of our "self-sense." Many things feed into this, creating for us a sense of who we are and what we can do—our self-image, if you wish. In a way, in the total "field of self," there are different "selves" that contribute to this self-sense.

The two primary sources, as I've been discussing, are the soul—in this instance, the Embodied Soul—and the body and the personality they create between them. These are two great intelligences now working in partnership— and really, more than partnership as there is a blending of energy and essence to create the incarnate self as an alloy or amalgam of soul and earth, soul and body, soul and matter.

Each of these generates its own field of intelligence and identity within us, one as a "soul self" and the other as a "body self."

As the individual lives his or her life, memory and experience accumulate; a new sense of self begins to emerge. So what I call here the "memory self"—which could be body memory as well as psychological memory or spiritual memory (i.e. soul memory)—is another major source of information for our sense of who we are.

Our subtle bodies, which constitute, you will remember, the "first incarnation" of the soul into the subtle environments of the incarnate realm, put us in touch with the collective subtle field of humanity—what Teillard de Chardin called the Noosphere—and with the collective subtle energy field of Gaia and the world. But as I've discussed above, the body also acts as a powerful and sensitive antenna to these fields as well, albeit to a different frequency, one closer to the earth if you will. Between the sensitivity of the physical body and the sensitivity of our subtle bodies, we take in information and impulses arising from Humanity and from Nature or Gaia.

These act as forces within us, too. They constitute a diffuse field of influence that in the Presence Exercise I call our "Humanity Self" and our "World Self." Often their influence is felt in what I've called our "Cloud of Hungry Ghosts," the disassociated yet volitional bits of subtle energy or of thought and feeling, that we pick up from the human and natural environments around us.

All of these feed into and influence to some degree our sense of who we are and what we are. We take in concepts and ideas from our culture, from others around us, and we take in feelings and emotions, too. If I'm around someone who is depressed and angry, I may start to feel anxious myself. If I'm walking a piece of land where the subtle flows and energies have been disrupted, perhaps by human interference, I can feel that disruption as dissonance in my own energy field, which, if I don't know better, I might take on and identify with as a personal dissonance, anger, or upset. And I can take on positive and uplifting vibes as well.

In other words, our individual Field of Self is a dynamic, interactive field of energy in constant, multiple conversations with the world around us, taking in information that may, and often does, shape how we think and feel about who we are.

WHO AM I?

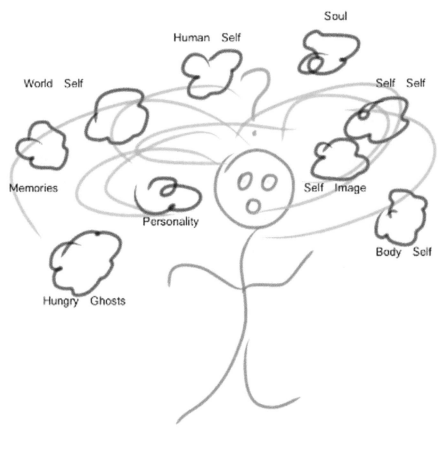

Soul

Human Self

World Self

Self Self

Memories

Self Image

Personality

Body Self

Hungry Ghosts

But.....Who Am I?

FIGURE 47

In the midst of all the "selves" and fields and intelligences and influences that swirl around us and within us, it's fair to ask "Who am I?"

I have three answers for this question:

1. We are who we choose to be
2. We are the center of a community of selves
3. We are the Self that is part of Soul—we are the emergent self of the Embodied Soul

Let's look at each of these in turn.

1. We Are Who We Choose To Be
   (or We Are Who We Are in the Moment)

We've all had the experience, embarrassing and painful at times, of behaving in the moment as if we were "someone else." We say, "I'm just not myself today." But then, whose self are we? It's obvious from such feelings and statements that we each have a sense—a self image, perhaps—of who we are or at least of who we'd like to be in our dealings with the world. And it's obvious that we don't always express ourselves accordingly. We say that we "don't live up" to our "true identity."

This is an internal, subjective assessment; it's something we experience within ourselves. But imagine that you are meeting someone for the first time and that someone is in a grumpy mood and not expressing their "best self." How would you know? The self that you experience from them may be, as far as you know, the way they always are. You may leave the encounter thinking, "What a grumpy person!" What they may experience as a temporary grumpiness becomes for you the definition of who they are, the nature of their self.

When I was in training with my mentor John, he made a point of discouraging me from thinking that somewhere inside me was a good and proper self and that when I didn't live up to it, I was not "being myself." "You are always yourself," he would say. "Do not deny who you are in the moment, even if it's not who you would like to be." Or he would say, "Who you are right now is exactly who you are. This is the self you choose to be, even if the choice is one of not choosing and simply reacting automatically."

John's approach to this was not psychological but energetic. "Your self in the moment is defined by the energy and quality of the relationship you are forming with the world. Your presence in the world makes this relationship possible. You do not have a false self because you do not have a false presence in the world." This was John's "Self as Relationship" approach.

But the more important reason for him lay in maintaining energetic integrity and wholeness and not becoming divided into warring "selves" or complexes of energy. "If you say this is your 'true self' and this other aspect of you and your behavior is not, then you set yourself up for civil war within your being. You may not like who you are being—the relationship you are forming—in the world right now, but take responsibility for it. Inhabit it as who you are in the moment. If it is unpleasant, then you have the power to change it, but not if you disassociate from it and push it away as another 'self' within you. Then your only option becomes conflict."

In short, I am always just one self, just as your Personry has one string running through it, though there are many beads or buttons or knots attached to that string. Not blaming some other part of me for bad or limited behavior helps me see past the bead to the string, to the presence that underlies my incarnational personhood. That presence, that "string self," is where the "buck stops."

For John, our self would have been the whole Personry, not just the string, not just the beads, but the whole system they create together. If there is a cracked or faulty bead—one of our "hungry ghosts," perhaps—it's still part of the Personry, or put more precisely, the whole is still a Personry.

We can certainly have "false" or limiting, negative, less-than-holopoietic relationships with the world. We definitely can have cracked or ill-fitting beads on our string. But it I say, "Oh, that bead's not really on the string at all; it's not part of me—it's an illusion, a false bead," then I lose my ability to deal with it and to change it. With responsibility and accountability comes the power to change. When I say, "Yep, that damaged bead is me, too, it's right there part of my Personry," then I can take actions if I wish to change the bead.

I understand that there are psychological issues here and complications, and that "changing a bead" is not always an easy thing to do. My point here—and John's point—is that I can look at a Personry and see just the beads or I can see the Personry as a whole. If the former, I may energetically get caught in "bead wars," as I pit one bead against another in my quest for a "perfect Personry." If the latter, though, I may still have damaged beads I want to fix or replace but I'm approaching this issue with the holopoietic energy of the whole self, the whole Personry, string, beads and all. Energetically, it makes a difference.

This difference begins simply with my acknowledging that the self I'm expressing—the energetic relationship I'm forming—in the moment is who I am. It may not be all of who I am, but I won't get to that "allness," that wholeness, by denying the part. If I accept the self of the moment, then it is energetically easier for my whole self to be present, or perhaps I should say, for my Presence to be present, if that's not too tautological! If I accept the bead, it's easier for the spirit of the whole Personry to be present and not just that bead or the string it's on.

## 2. We Are the Center of a Community of Selves

The Personry is made up of beads (or buttons or knots or whatever), and we are made up of "selves" or what in Psychosynthesis, for instance, are called "subpersonalities." I'm sure there are various terms in different psychological systems for these semi-autonomous parts of us. Yet at the same time, there is an Identity or Presence—a Big Self, if you wish—that links all these lesser selves together into a whole, incarnational system. There is a string self on which the beads are attached to make the Personry.

In this context, I can think of one of these lesser selves—the "beads"—as an energy structure, which may be simple or quite complex, which can focus my subtle energy and life energy into a specific connection, engagement, and relationship with the world around me. The nature of that connection and relationship depends on the structure of that energy. It can be very wholesome and benign, it can be distorted and violent; it can be meaningful, it can be automatic and carry little meaning. In short, it can be a beautiful bead or it can be an ugly, broken bead, but in the moment, if that's the bead I'm touching and the one that has my attention, it's focusing the presence of the Personry.

This is a converse to the first item above. In #1, I was asking you to acknowledge and honor the specific, individual bead, even if it's ugly or broken. In #2, I'm asking you to be aware of the string on which the beads are strung—the string self, if you wish. This is what links all the energy complexes—all the "selves"—together in one field of subtle presence.

In #1, the practice is to say, "Right now, I am this bead," whichever bead is being "touched" by the world. In #2, the practice is to say, "I am the self that holds all the beads together; I am the Self at the center of it all. I am the string."

The beads on the Personry at one point existed as simply a pile of beads, disconnected from each other. Your act of putting them on the string created a relationship between them, a relationship we're calling the Personry. It's the string that makes this relationship possible. It is the connective tissue, so to speak.

Who we are includes all these subpersonalities or "lesser selves," but it also includes the Self as connective tissue, as the presence that holds all the other selves in relationship. Even the "hungry ghosts,"—whether they are complexes that we have created and which have become disassociated within us, perhaps through trauma, or whether they are bits and pieces of subtle psychic energies we have taken on from our subtle environment—are less "hungry" as part of our field; they are sustained by being energetically "on the string." They are energetically shaped in part by being included in the Field of Self.

This is an important point. Two people may experience the same trauma and suffer the same kind of disassociation—what a shaman might call "soul loss"—but the energy of that disassociated complex, that "hungry ghost," will be shaped by the overall subtle energy of its host, the person that it is part of. I may have a "hungry ghost," but wherever it came from and however it came to be part of my field, it's my "hungry ghost" in a very specific way and not just a generic pattern of psychic and energetic hunger. It may be a disassociated element within me, but it's still a part of and expressing the energy of my Self. It has been "colored" and "flavored" by the overall quality of my personal field. (There are exceptions to this, as it is possible to "trap" in our auric fields certain kinds of subtle energies or even subtle beings that resist being there and resist being shaped by our own energies, but that's a different kind of pathology and one I'm not that familiar with; I don't regard such "trapped" elements as "hungry ghosts" in the way I'm using this term here in this discussion. Considering such elements takes us into areas of energy hygiene and exorcism that go beyond the boundaries of this book.)

In #1 above, the practice centers around taking responsibility for who one is and what one is doing and expressing in the moment, not trying to fob accountability off on some other "self." The focus is on not splitting oneself up into warring factions. It's on recognizing that the individual "bead" is not an isolated phenomenon but is still "us," still part of the Personry.

In this instance, #2, the practice centers on love. The emphasis is not simply on the fact that we may have multiples complexes of "self," i.e. multiple "beads," but that they are part of a community. This is the corollary to #1, that we embrace all the parts of ourselves in a loving and holopoietic manner, drawing them into wholeness, even those parts that we would rather not be part of us and which we would like to get rid of, the ugly and broken beads. It's not a matter of permanently accepting such beads; it's a matter of emphasizing the string on which they are attached and from the level of that presence doing whatever is necessary to heal, transform, and change the undesirable condition.

In this practice we are affirming that indeed there is a part of us that has the power to create loving connection and wholeness; we have the power of the string, so to speak. I can think of this as my core self, my emerging self, my mindful self. It possesses the power to be different and to make a difference, to make choices that supersede automatic reactions and express mindful action that transcends the reflex response of the "bead" level of consciousness.

3. We Are the Self that is Part of Soul—We Are the Emergent Self of the Embodied Soul

Continuing to use the metaphor of the Personry, it has three parts: the beads, the string, and the whole concept and presence of the Personry itself. So we have selves that are like the beads, we have a self that is like the string, and we have a Self that is the Personry itself. I think of this as the Emergent Self which hopefully continues to develop, grow and unfold throughout our life, just as I can add new beads to the string, lengthen the string, and so forth.

There is nothing static about the Personry.

But this Emergent Self is also the part of us that is the presence of the Embodied Soul, the Presence that is at the heart of the Presence Exercise.

I think of it this way. Beads cannot create a Personry, though they are part of and necessary to its creation. A piece of string by itself cannot create a Personry, though it, too, is part of and necessary to its creation. It takes a Personry—the idea and vision and spirit of the Personry and what it represents—to create a Personry. It takes a wholeness to attract, assemble and organize the parts into a manifestation of that wholeness.

In our lives, our Embodied Soul is that wholeness, that holopoietic presence and force.

Look back at figures 28 and 29. Here I present some of the qualities and capacities that define "Soul." ( Here again is one of the pictures)

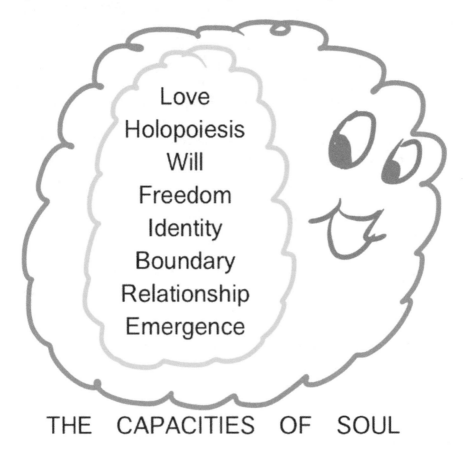

Love
Holopoiesis
Will
Freedom
Identity
Boundary
Relationship
Emergence

THE   CAPACITIES   OF   SOUL

FIGURE 48

The Soul is what holds the capacity to express love, freedom, will, holopoiesis, and the four Principles of incarnation, Identity, Boundary, Connection (or Relationship) and Emergence. These capacities do not originate from the beads or the string, though they can take advantage of them and express them. But when they do express one of more of these capacities or qualities, they are being soul by doing soul. They are functioning as fractals of soul, but in the final analysis, it's the presence of soul within the incarnational system that gives them that ability.

Soul is like the oxygen that fills the system that enables everything else within the system to breath and live. Take away soul, as happens at death, and the system falls apart. It loses what gave it life as a whole system.

So, when I look for an answer to the question "Who am I," I acknowledge that I have "bead selves" and a "string self," but I am the Embodied Soul emerging and shaping itself in relationship with the world, holding and bringing the capacities of soul into the world for its blessing.

Never Mind the Being—Who Does the Doing?

In one way, the question of who I am is less a question of being—what is my being or who am I as a being—and more a question of doing. Who is the actor? Who is the Agency? Who is doing the doing? And this can come down to who or what makes the choices in my life, responds to the world, and forms my connections and relationships.

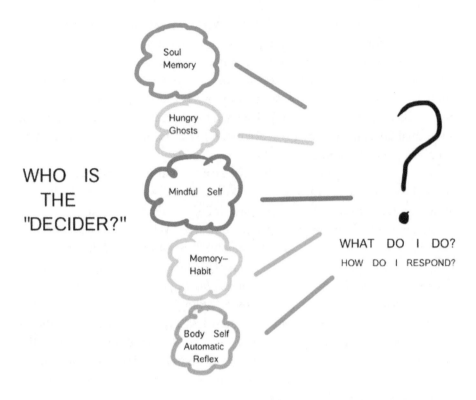

FIGURE 49

In this picture I offer some examples of possible "doers" or "deciders" within a specific situation.

- Our actions and responses might be stimulated and guided by "soul memory," i.e. karma or cues that exist within the Embodied Soul to trigger certain actions and relationships. For example, I know that Julie and I chose before either of us was born to be partners in this life. Neither of us "remembered" this at first, but the cues were there in our unconsciousness (or, if you prefer, in our soul consciousness). So when we met at Findhorn in 1971 (wow! forty one years ago!) these cues were triggered. We each had experiences (dreams, intuitions, and the like) that impelled us towards each other, leading eventually to love, marriage and the baby carriage (didn't someone write a song about that once?) Although technically we were each free to ignore or reject these cues (and there are times when the incarnate self may not recognize or may reject such cues for one reason or another), in fact they were so strong within us that such "freedom" was not a factor. Our "doing" and our response to each other was shaped by the soul's memory of our love and our agreement to be together as partners in this life.

- Our actions can be shaped by one or more "hungry ghosts" within our field, by habits, traumas, unintegrated, dissasociative material, volitional complexes, and the like. I've already told the story of an early student of mine who wanted to be in my classes but felt a conflict with me. It turned out that she had a "hungry ghost" in the form of an unresolved and unintegrated memory of a bad relationship and divorce from her ex-husband, a man whom I superficially resembled. She was projecting her conflicted feelings around her ex upon me, and that influenced how she at times related and responded to me. This is an area that psychology deals with in numerous excellent ways. Note that a hungry ghost doesn't have to be a psychological complex, however. It can be something as simple as a "meme" or "mind virus" implanted by advertising so that when I see a particular product in a store, I'm attracted to it or feel compelled to buy it. Hence the "Big Mac Attack" hungry ghost (which is likely to strike when we also have a hungry body!).

- Likewise, there may be experiences and memories from this life and habits I've built up and developed that kick in and make my decisions for me, as it were. Some of these may arise from trauma, some may arise from training. The memory and habit of how to drive is very useful as I go down the freeway at seventy miles an hour, particularly if I have to act on reflex to avoid an accident. Less useful is that I can fall into habits of relating to particular people so that when I'm with them, I go on "automatic." This may be useful in some circumstances, but in others it drains the relationship of life and awareness.

- Our body also has certain structural and physiological ways of acting and responding to stimuli, usually in automatic and reflexive ways. We can also train such reflexes. Much of the training that goes into preparing a soldier for combat (or a martial artist) is one of developing reflexive, instinctive muscle memory so that the person will act without having to think about it.

What all of these four potential "deciders" have in common is that they are what I call "structures." They are simple or complex feedback loops that act without mindfulness or creative thought in the moment; they are, in the language of some spiritual traditions, modes of sleepwalking through our lives.

The important thing about such structures is that they don't possess the freedom or capacity to change themselves from the inside out. A habit doesn't decide on its own to become a different habit or to dissolve itself and become no habit at all. Habitual patterns can be changed, of course, and learning can take place, but this happens through some form of intervention from another level of consciousness. Any of these four deciders and others like them can shape our doing and our responding and in this sense act as selves (sometimes very capably and appropriately so and sometimes not). But they do not possess or embody the capacities of soul. They are products of those capacities in most likelihood, not the holders of the capacities themselves.

For this reason, the fifth "Decider" in the picture above is the one I think of as the actual incarnate self, the expression of the Embodied Soul, and I call it here the "Mindful Self."

### THE MINDFUL SELF

The wonderful and important quality of self is that it can be mindful and aware  Out of that mindfulness come options and potential choices, the ability to move and act in unexpected and unprecedented ways that can go beyond the habits of physical and psychological structures. Mindfulness and freedom go together, for it takes freedom to be mindful and mindfulness enhances freedom.

Mindfulness certainly incorporates the ability to just observe and not react, which is a kind of mindfulness that is taught in some schools of philosophy and spiritual practice as "mindfulness training." It involves quiet, non-judging, non-duality. For me, though, mindfulness—or perhaps I should say, the mindful self—consists of three elements, each important as part of a "trinity of mindfulness."

When I began working with John, he gave me four practices to guide my daily work. I've written about these in the last chapter of An Introduction to Incarnational Spirituality. They are:

1. Attunement to Self and the Personal
2. Attunement to Sacred
3. Attunement to the Subtle Worlds, Soul and the Transpersonal
4. Blessing

Leaving aside the attunement to the subtle worlds for a moment as this was an explicit practice of attuning to and communicating with John twice a day, the other three form the three parts of the Trinity of Mindfulness. They are Self-Knowledge, Deep Witnessing, and Blessing. These could also be phrased as Mindfulness of Self, Mindfulness of the Other, and Mindful Action.

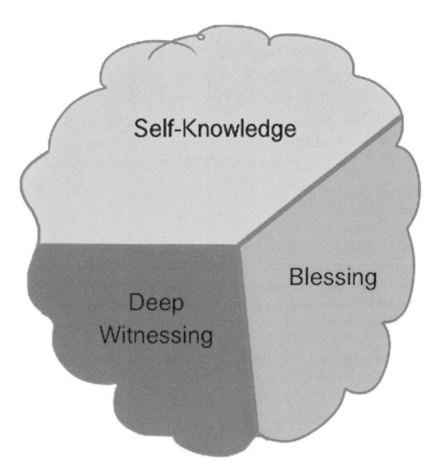

# THE MINDFUL TRINITY

FIGURE 50

Let's say a few words about each of these:

**Deep Witnessing** — This is mindfulness as non-reactive, unconditional and non-judgmental observation. It is an attentive awareness of what is happening in present time and of the reality or nature of what is observed. I think of it as "deep" witnessing because one progressively deepens one's awareness of what is being observed, moving from surface appearances to deeper layers of connection, interaction, and being, right down to the sacredness of what is being observed, or, put another way, to seeing how that which is being observed emerges from and participates in the Sacred as primal oneness and generative mystery. A characteristic of this deep witnessing is that it is quiet or silent and serene. It does not react to what is being observed. It holds that which is being observed in loving acknowledgement in a manner that allows it to unfold its nature.

**Self-Knowledge** — This is mindfulness of one's own being: body, mind, emotions, spirit. It is awareness of as many parts or dimensions of oneself as one can see, observing the ways in which we can be pulled into the world, the ways in which we can react, the ways in which we attract, hold onto and identify with elements in the world, for good and for ill. Again, this is a non-judgmental knowing. But this self-knowledge is more than just information about oneself. It's also knowledge of one's capacities and the knowing of how to tap and express them. I may know, for instance, that I have a loving and compassionate heart, but how do I activate it? How do I bring it into expression? What in my life strengthens that expression, and what weakens or obstructs it? This is Deep Witnessing turned on oneself but for the purpose of awakening capacities and drawing forth the sacredness that we each embody.

**Blessing** — This is active, mindful participation in the life of the world in a way that enhances that life, its potentials and its possibilities. It is making mindful choices that guide actions. These choices can be based upon our Deep Witnessing and our Self-Knowledge, seeing what it is that seeks to unfold and how to blend with it and empower it. But it can also be initiating new actions, setting new flows into motion, creating what was not there before. Our options are not simply to "go with the flow" or "resist the flow." We also have the mindful option of creating a flow, of making our own unique input with a willingness to be responsible for consequences. There are times when resisting a flow is the appropriate and mindful action, there are times when blending with and enhancing an existing flow is the appropriate and mindful action, and there are times when being a generative, creative source, instilling and guiding a flow that wasn't there before, is the action of greatest blessing. We can be mindful Agents as well as mindful Supporters.

Here is a picture similar to one you've seen before back at the beginning of the book.

# THE PAPER TOWEL SELF

The Self

A Single Surface Area

Multiple Surface Areas--More "Absorbant"

Multiple Selves
Generate New Possibilities,
New Learning,
New Information,
And
Emergence

FIGURE 51

This time, instead of illustrating the Paper Towel Theory, it's illustrating the Paper Towel Self. It's a different title but the idea is precisely the same. There is a value to having different aspects of self—or if you wish, different selves—within us. The relationships between them and the different perspectives they offer can, like any relationship, generate new information and new learning and spur emergence.

The idea of the Mindful Self, the Soul Self, is not to eliminate all the other expressions of self but to integrate them into a coherent and whole incarnational system. Any particular part of us, maybe even a hungry ghost in the right circumstances, might have something important to offer, be able to make a vital connection of understanding and engagement with the world, or give us insights. It can be a potential ally and partner. But for this to happen, that part needs to be engaged and deployed, so to speak, in a mindful way. If it takes over and reacts or shapes our action or decision, this may or may not be appropriate or result in positive consequences. If it takes over, it is most likely not acting with mindfulness and it certainly doesn't possess freedom. It can't bring in perspectives and actions that transcend the situation; it can only act as it is structured to do so.

Mindfulness is not simply awareness. It's also enhances the capacity to connect holopoietically both within oneself and within the world. By enabling one's consciousness to transcend the automatic expression of structure, it opens options that might otherwise not be available. Such options might be subjective, elements of our own being and energy field, or they might be objective, possible new opportunities in the world.

Put another way, if I'm mindful in my engagement with the world, the world becomes more mindful, too. In this sense, mindfulness might be seen as an enabler or as a multiplier, enhancing possibilities within ourselves and within the world. It doesn't just "go with the flow," though it increases our ability to do just that with harmonious results; it also potentially opens up new channels and vectors for that "flow," for the impulses of incarnation and unfoldment that are within us and around us in the world.

In Incarnational Spirituality, mindfulness is much more than a contemplative practice, though it includes that. It is a mode of action, a type of "agency," if you will, a way of forming connections and participating through partnership in the ongoing unfoldment of life. And it opens channels through which a person can become more generative and more contributory to that unfoldment.

We have to be careful about romanticizing the idea of "flow" in the world or that the world is unfolding as it should or in the best way possible. Just as we can function in limited ways, bound by the structures of habit and the volitional hijackings of "hungry ghosts," the same is true for other beings and processes in the world.

It is a delusion for me to feel I always know best, but it's also delusion for me to think that the world always knows best. The fact is, we're all partners in learning, exploration, experimentation, growth, and discovery.

Humankind likes to think that it is the pinnacle of planetary evolution and that with our self-consciousness, we're in a position to "manage" the planet, shaping things according to our designs and believing we know what's good for the whole. This sets up false and disruptive relationships with the world, with dire consequences all the way around.

But it's equally true that we cannot assign all wisdom to nature or the "flow of things" or to the world (or even to "higher levels of consciousness"), seeing our role as simply learning how to "blend with what is." This can have disruptive consequences, too. Generally speaking, we come into incarnation both to shape and to be shaped, to blend and to stand out. The world has its plans and we have ours; how these blend and their mutual interactions are negotiated is what incarnation is about.

The metaphor I like here is wood carving. If I am going to carve something beautiful out of a piece of wood, I need to know the wood. I need to know how to work with its structure, how to cut with the grain, for example, and how to bring out its highlights and beauty. At the same time, I need to know my tools and what they can do and when one tool is more appropriate than another; and I need to know my own skills, what my strengths are and what my limits are, what I know how to do and what I don't yet know how to do. And I need to approach the wood with honor for myself and for the wood, with love for both of us, as partners in the artistic project.

But I cannot assume that the wood knows what it wants to be. It may not. I cannot assume that there already is a form within the wood waiting for me to release through my tools and skills; there may be, but it may also be that the wood itself doesn't yet know what it can be or is interested is discovering and delighting with me in what I creatively shape from it. My creativity and vision may be just the important force I need to attune to in the moment in working with the wood.

Mindfulness of self and other is the tool I need to find this partnership. Does the wood know best what it wishes to be? Maybe. Maybe not. Do I know best what the wood should be? Maybe. Maybe not. Mindfulness and loving partnership encourage the dialog through which we can both discover the answers.

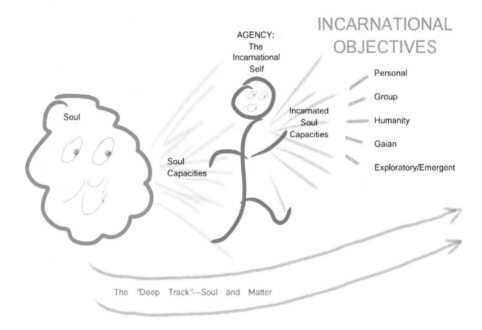

FIGURE 52

Each of us comes into incarnate life, as this picture suggests, with a variety of objectives: things we'd like to learn and accomplish. These objectives may be personal related to our own development; they may relate to our soul group, allowing us to contribute to the learning and development of others with whom we have deep affiliations. There may be objectives related to humanity as a collective or certain parts of humanity such as a particular race or culture or ethnic group. Some objectives may pertain to Gaia.

At the same time, we are always engaged in generating new learning and new information, some people more than others. This is the exploratory side of incarnation, the work that leads to emergent qualities and capacities.

We all participate to some degree in all five objectives if only by being part of larger wholes such as humanity or the planet itself, even if some of these objectives are not major ones in our life planning. At the same time, underneath it all, is what I think of as the "Deep Track" of our incarnations, the part of our incarnation that's part of the cosmic circulation I wrote about in the first chapter or that's involved in the ongoing project of blending soul and matter which I wrote about last chapter or so.

In this process, our incarnational self acts as the Agent. It receives the soul capacities from the soul (Embodied Soul and beyond) and translates them into conscious awareness, qualities, choices, decisions, actions, and so on. We incarnate these soul qualities, expressing love, freedom, will, holopoiesis, and so forth as best we can in our everyday lives in order to meet our incarnational objectives.

But this translation of capacities from soul to incarnate state is not without its distortions and failures. As the old saying goes, betwixt the cup and the lip there's many a slip. Whether it's forgetfulness, habits, hungry ghosts, incoherency in our incarnational system, internal conflicts, and so on, both the understanding and application of our soul capacities and qualities may be less than perfect AND we may fail to adequately meet our incarnational objectives.

We may be incarnational agents, but we're not necessarily aware and competent ones.

Mindfulness as I've described it is one of the correctives to ensure that the connections between soul, self and world work as best they can. But it's not the only tool we have. Just as important is imagination and the power of self-definition, a kind of internal shape-shifting. But before I pursue this topic, there are a couple of other concepts I need to introduce first. These are Self-Light and Sovereignty.

### SELF-LIGHT

The idea of "Light" is ubiquitous in spiritual writings and teachings. It is the radiance we associate with a spiritual presence. To some degree we may think of it as a spiritual energy, though in fact whether it is anything like a physical or subtle energy is a question. The idea of "Light" may simply be a metaphor for an experience of Presence, the actual quality of which is difficult to discern in its true nature. Light may be the way we experience a differential, such as a differential of subtle energy or presence or complexity. Thus, when John first appeared to me, he was surrounded with a nimbus of Light and was radiant. But as I learned to adapt to and blend with his energy and as I was inwardly able to meet him closer to his native level of existence, this Light diminished. His presence was every bit as potent as before, but it didn't manifest as a clairvoyantly visible radiance.

The fact is, I don't really know what "Light" is as a substance, but I am sure it is not the same as what we call light on a physical level, although it has similarities. Likewise, from an experiential point of view, Light affects me differently than do subtle energies. Light is more penetrating and touches me at the deepest levels, providing uplift and nourishment, whereas subtle energies interact with my own personal subtle energy field in a variety of ways. I suppose metaphorically it's the difference between sunlight which plays against my skin and warms my body and Julie's love for me which warms and nourishes my heart. Subtle energies affect me from the outside in; Light seems to affect me from the inside out.

Subtle energies can certainly be stimulating, but Light heightens and empowers in a different way. It helps me to be more of who I am, or more in touch with who I am. It connects me to essence, whether it's the essence of the Sacred or the essence of myself and my soul. I can get "high" and ecstatic from the impact of subtle energies, but Light has a different effect altogether, one that deepens and opens out into a serene and awesomely peaceful spaciousness. Light, it seems to me, is the touch of beingness rather than the touch of a particular energy, and in that touch, it nourishes the quality of being.

Having said that, not all Light is the same any more than all beingness is the same. John's beingness as a subtle being operating from the soul level was different from my beingness as an incarnate person. He was not necessarily more highly evolved or more spiritual, but he existed in a wholly different dimension of reality. The impact of that difference is, I think, what I experienced as his Light, at least at first. The quality of his being, existing as he did as a multi-dimensional presence as compared to my three-dimensional one, was a lot to take on at first. Later, as I said, as I learned how to be in his presence and hold his energy in mine, the phenomenon of his radiance diminished but the quality of his beingness did not. So the impact or emanation of his presence—his Light—remained, but it didn't take the form of "Light" or a clairvoyantly visible radiance. This was an important teaching for me: Light didn't have to manifest as radiance in order to be present.

For John, Light was an expression of the generative nature of all beingness, arising in part from the internal process with a being that gave it existence in the first place and in part from the nature and quality of its interaction and connections with its particular environment (and in this context, the Sacred would be considered the primal, universal environment to which all beings are connected and with which all beings interact in one manner or another). It is, in a sense, the product of self-expression. All Light is Self-Light, whether it's the Light emanating from the Primal Self of the Sacred, the Generative Mystery whose self-expression brings creation into being in the first place, or the Light emanating from the Self of a solar angel or a planetary angel, or Gaia, or a being like John or an incarnate human being.

What I hope I've shown in the text so far is that the phenomenon of Self emerges from relationship, so the "self" that is being expressed in "self-expression" doesn't exist in a vacuum but in engagement with a particular environment. This is true for the soul and it's true for the incarnate person. It's just that the relationship between soul and physical matter that generates the incarnate self (the "amalgam" or the "alloy") is dramatic and unusually extreme. The differential between soul and matter is a large one, which on the one hand makes incarnation challenging but on the other hand generates a particularly powerful manifestation of selfhood.

Note that a person's "I" or core identity is not synonymous with a person's "self," which is a construct or a phenomenon of incarnation. Does this mean our self disappears when we die? No, it persists into the "third act" of incarnation because it is held by our Embodied Soul. In that sense, our everyday self is a particular shape given to our Embodied Soul by its interaction with matter and the incarnate state. But while we continue to grow and develop in the post-mortem worlds and beyond, we don't continue to generate an incarnate self in the way we have while in the body and in engagement with matter. Eventually this self dissolves or is absorbed back into the Soul, all the information, learning and wisdom it contains becoming part of the relatively eternal part of who we are. Indeed, a major function of the post-mortem worlds is to enable this shift of consciousness from the incarnate self to the Embodied Soul and thence to the Soul itself.

Understanding the relational nature of the Self is important in this discussion of Self-Light. If Light is a generative product of self-expression (or, if you wish, of Identity expression through the instrumentality of a field of relationship with a particular environment, such field of relationship being what we normally experience as our "self"), then the nature of this Light partakes of the nature of the environment that participates in its emergence.

Here we come to the heart of the matter and why the idea of Self-Light is important. Let me tell a story from my book, *Apprenticed to Spirit*. I was seventeen. I had just graduated from high school and I was on my way to college in the fall. I was visiting a friend of my parents, and she asked me what my plans were for my future. Here's what I wrote in my book:

> My stock answer was, "Well, I plan to do research in molecular biology and genetics." That usually was enough to satisfy the questioner and shift the conversation to other topics. But this time something very different happened.
>
> There were no bells or whistles. There was no out-of-body flight and no sensations of entering an altered state of consciousness. There was nothing as dramatic as what happened when I was seven. I only saw a human figure appear in front of me.
>
> This was not a specific person but a generic individual, almost like seeing a department store mannequin. It was not a being of Light in the way I was used to seeing, but it seemed sculpted from Light that glowed from within itself. It definitely appeared solid and physical,

even though radiant with Light.

It seemed bursting with meaning, so much so that if information were heat and light, it was like standing in front of a furnace. I felt overwhelmed by the insights this figure contained and could not grasp them all. Almost fifty years later, I am still unpacking the information it had to offer.

But one thing stood out. This figure represented an incarnate person in the state of physical embodiment. It was not a spiritual or non-physical being. It was not an image of what a person might become if they left the physical plane or became some kind of ascended master. It was an image of the spiritual Light contained within and radiating from the act of individuation and personhood. It was the Light of being a person.

As I watched, the figure changed into a chalice and then it became a figure again. It did this three times altogether, as if emphasizing the relationship between this figure and a quality of holding. Afterwards, I thought of this figure as "the person who is also a chalice."

At the time, this vision, while interesting, didn't affect me much. I was on my way to college to become a molecular biologist, and I'd mapped out my future. Ha! Three years later I was in Los Angeles acting as a spiritual teacher and starting to work with a non-physical mentor I named John. So much for making plans!

When I began working with John, one of the first things he pointed out to me was that I didn't simply receive Light from higher levels of being the way a planet receives light from the sun. I generated such Light myself as an incarnate person. "This Light does not come from your soul, though it shares its own Light with the world as well," he said. "It comes from you, from David as an incarnate person. You could call it your Self-Light." When he told me this, I remembered my vision from three years earlier.

Self-Light was an important concept for John. It was not a subtle energy such as our thinking and feeling might produce. It was a spiritual emanation arising from the process of being an incarnate self, and like any manifestation of Light, it was a force for blessing. Just as we get hot when we exert ourselves doing physical work, Self-Light is the spiritual "heat" generated as our souls do the work of engagement and blending with the incarnate realm, the work that produces the "amalgam" of spirit and matter and creates an emergent incarnate self.

John said once, "Self-Light is the radiance of your expression of sacredness." He didn't mean by this any particular mystical or spiritual activity; he meant that the act of incarnation itself is an expression of our sacredness. And he also meant what I was referring to elsewhere about the expression of our soul capacities. "Doing soul" (i.e. expressing in some manner, however limited, the capacities of the soul) was for the John the equivalent of "doing sacred."

The fact that we generate such a spiritual force doesn't mean that we cannot or do not also draw upon and receive Light from other sources. It's not an either/or situation. But the fact that we are a source and not just a recipient is an important idea. Indeed, in many ways it is at the core of Incarnational Spirituality.

Self-Light was important to John—and is important to me—for two main reasons. One is practical and operational; the other is psychological

On the practical side, Self-Light represents a form of Light that is indigenous to the physical plane and the incarnate realm. Remember it is generated by the self-expression of the soul engaging specifically with the incarnate realm. This gives it a "flavor" or a "spin" that makes it particularly attuned to matter and to incarnate reality. It's as if our Self-Light, being in effect an "incarnational Light," speaks the "language" of this realm. It is born from and is part of this realm. This means that it can connect with matter and the phenomena of the incarnate world very easily.

Here's a simple metaphor. Imagine that you come up to me on the street and ask me for money for a meal and a cup of coffee. If I give you cash, you can immediately go to a restaurant and spend it. Cash is quickly accessible. But if I write you out a check or give you a money order, you have to first go to a bank and cash it before you can use it. A check doesn't connect as readily with life on the street as cash does.

Or let's look at this another way. The other evening, not long after my latest surgery when things hadn't quite settled down with my body, I was in pain and felt very restless, unable to relax. I could feel how tense my muscles were as my body attempted to cope with the aftereffects of surgery, anesthesia, the pain of the things that had been done, and so forth. I was aware of healing and comforting energies in our house, many of them sent my way by loving friends; I was aware as well of subtle beings who were there to help. But none of that good subtle energy was helping me to relax and in some instances, it was actually keeping me stimulated as I attempted to process the forces impacting my own subtle bodies. What helped was when Julie came over and just held me in her arms. The touch of another physical body was just what I needed. Subtle energies are nice but nothing quite replaces caring, loving arms!

Light is Light. But the Light from higher realms carries a different vibe. It's like a check, which is OK if transactions are from bank to bank but not as useful initially if you need cash on the street. Receiving a blessing that resonates in its vibe and structure with the realm in which you're living—like the physical arms that held me and let my body relax—can just be more accessible, at least at first. This doesn't mean at all that Light from higher realms is useless or cannot reach us (though sometimes the latter is true) or if it does reach us, that it cannot bless us in deep ways. As I say, it's not either/or but both/and. Having cash for some transactions and being able to write a check for others creates much more flexibility.

So on a practical level, Self-Light gives us a power to bless that is resonant with this realm (an idea I explore at length in my book Blessing: the Art and the Practice). It is, so to speak, the coin of the realm.

The second reason Self-Light is an important concept is psychological. It helps us see ourselves as generative sources and not just as passive recipients. The metaphor I often use for this is the difference between being a star, like our sun, and being a planet. The nuclear processes within a star generate heat and light; a planet, on the other hand, simply receives this heat and light, offering nothing of its own.

There are many kinds of stars, very bright ones and very dim ones, very hot ones and stars that are less hot. The amount of Self-Light any person radiates is unique to him or to her. It can be obscured by various factors, such as "hungry ghosts" that interfere with or obstruct our mindful self in its expression of soul qualities, or it can be enhanced by our mindfulness and our deliberate acts of blessing. We can be dim at one time and bright at another. But we are always generating Self-Light. We are always a source and not just a sponge, soaking up what comes from the outside.

I have already written that one of the imperatives of John and his colleagues was (and continues to be, even though John is no longer in the picture) to foster partnership between the personal and transpersonal dimensions. To this end they wanted to diminish our tendency to privilege the transpersonal and instead help us honor our human, incarnate self. Understanding our Self-Light and seeing ourselves as generative sources of spiritual influence are ways to accomplish this.

In particular, in approaching the subtle worlds and subtle beings with an attitude of partnership, it helps if we realize we have something to offer that is rich and important. We are not the poor relatives approaching a rich uncle for a handout. Instead, we bring to the potential partnership our Self-Light, a treasure in its own right. We come not as planets seeking the light of a sun but as a fellow star.

Appreciating this and having a felt sense of being a source and a star can be an enormous boost to our self-image and our sense of self. It can unleash potentials we may not have suspected. Being able to be in the world—to stand in the world—as a generative source of blessing and spiritual Light, not simply because we're attuned to transpersonal sources but because we are persons, individual incarnate selves, is a powerful experience, one that I'd like everyone to have. Then we truly touch our sacredness, and in so doing, we open to touch the sacredness in everyone and everything else.

SELF-LIGHT

FIGURE 53

## SOVEREIGNTY

Sovereignty is the other key concept in Incarnational Spirituality.

In my online dictionary, sovereignty is defined as "possessing supreme and independent power and authority in government." I define it simply as the capacity to be self-governing and the ability to make choices for oneself. In a way, it's the capacity to be mindful, to give expression to a mindful self rather than just expressing in automatic ways under the competing influences of various habits, hungry ghosts, and so forth.

But it's more than just that. Sovereignty is the name I give to our ability to be in touch with the qualities and capacities of soul. It is the link to our Embodied Soul, providing the integrative power that draws the incarnational system together. It is, in a manner of speaking, the organizational principle that enables coherence.

Sovereignty is the active expression of the incarnational impulse within us, particularly as it translates the spacious, multi-dimensional, highly energetic nature of the soul into the three-dimensional, particular, individuated nature of the incarnate self.

We experience Sovereignty as a personal state, but in fact it's a universal impulse. By this I mean that I cannot damage or disrupt your Sovereignty without doing the same to mine. My Sovereignty is not an excuse to attempt to dominate you; rather, I enhance my Sovereignty, my coherency, my wholeness, by enhancing yours. To violate another's Sovereignty—or one's own, for that matter—is to risk making this impulse incoherent, causing the incarnational system to lose its integrity and risk a systemic breakdown into imbalance.

In December of 1963, the Rev. Dr. Martin Luther King, Jr. gave a talk at Western Michigan University. Its topic was "social justice and the emerging new age." In it he said:

> "All I'm saying is simply this, that all life is interrelated, that somehow we're caught in an inescapable network of mutuality tied in a single garment of destiny. Whatever affects one directly affects all indirectly. For some strange reason, I can never be what I ought to be until you are what you ought to be. You can never be what you ought to be until I am what I ought to be. This is the interrelated structure of reality."

This is a perfect expression of the nature of Sovereignty as well. I am not fully free to be self-governing unless you are equally free in the same way. All Sovereignty, like all life, is interrelated and interdependent. It is because of the relational nature of the self. If I diminish that to which my self is relating and connecting, I diminish my self in the process.

The Standing Exercise is about experiencing your Sovereignty

### THE TOOL OF IMAGINATION

Earlier I wrote, "Mindfulness as I've described it is one of the correctives to ensure that the connections between soul, self and world work as best they can. But it's not the only tool we have. Just as important is imagination and the power of self-definition, a kind of internal shape-shifting." Having discussed Self-Light and Sovereignty, I want to pursue this thought now.

Here is a new picture of the Incarnate Self:

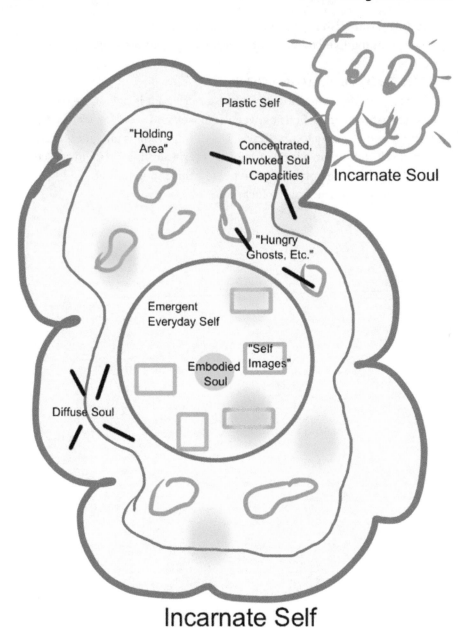

FIGURE 54

In this picture we see several things. First, and most important, we see that the presence of the Embodied Soul—really, the presence of Soul in general—is diffused through us. It is our life-force and the presence of Sovereignty, connecting all our parts together. The capacities of soul—identity, boundary, the power to connect, the power to learn and develop, love, freedom, will, holopoiesis, and so forth—are diffused throughout us, available to all the parts within us.

The dark golden circle at the center labeled "Embodied Soul" isn't intended to say that the Embodied Soul is at our center as much as to say, "Here is where it's influence and capacities are most highly concentrated." But as an active presence, it is diffused throughout our being.

Here we see three "layers" of self. First is the "plastic self," the part of us that is constantly changing, growing, adapting, trying on new self-images, being shaped by the world around it, and so on. Then there is a "holding area," metaphorically speaking. This is where various ideas, images, 'hungry ghosts," etc. reside as "floating complexes" which circumstances might or might not activate.

If they are activated, they will shape the plastic self accordingly as it becomes an instrument for their expression.

Thus a floating idea might be one implanted by an advertiser, MacDonald's, say. Then when I'm driving down the street and I see the Golden Arches, this idea gets activated and shapes my plastic self with its vector. I get a "Big Mac attack" and find myself suddenly turning into the drive-through lane of the fast food restaurant! There is nothing mindful about this!

Then there's my Emergent Everyday Self, which is more highly structured and contains those ideas, feelings, habits, and self-images that I have cultivated or accepted over the years and made part of me. This is where my sense of self usually resides. When I describe who I am, I usually describe the contents of this part of me. This is where my capacity to be mindful resides; it's where my Sovereignty is.

Note, however, that here and there are darker golden patches, some of which surround particular "organelles" or psychic structures both in the "holding area" and in the Everyday Self area. These are where soul capacities are crystallizing around specific ideas, feelings, habits, and behaviors, i.e. internal, subjective structures.

I might, for instance, see an inspiring movie that fills me with loving thoughts and feelings. They act as points around which soul gathers; I don't necessarily take them up into myself as a regular part of me, but in the moment, they are focal points of soul. So, for instance, I come out of the movie feeling warm and loving and meet a homeless person asking me for some money. Ordinarily, I might ignore this request, but now, under the influence of this inspiration, I happily share some of my cash.

There may also be self-images I hold or regular activities (such as meditation)

I perform that gather and focus an area of "concentrated soul." For instance, when I think of myself as a spiritual teacher, I may be more consciously in touch with a "spiritual part of me" than when I think of myself as someone who loves to play games.

In this context, the object of the incarnational exercise is to enlarge and deepen these areas of concentrated soul so that over the course of our lives, the diffuse soul within us becomes less and less diffused and more and more the mindful, operative presence in our lives, compelling the hungry ghosts and other psychic elements within us either to dissolve into soul or align themselves with it in such a way that they express our soul qualities and capacities.

By the way, I added the Incarnational Soul to remind us that it's present in our lives, too, acting "from the outside," as it were as a "high self" and source of inspiration and help.

One way to understand this is to think of the Embodied Soul as the part of our Soul that falls asleep in the realm of matter and awakens only in part as the conscious, everyday self. As in a fairy tale, our task as the everyday self is to find and awaken (with a loving kiss, of course!) the sleeping beauty within us.

Our task is to awaken soul and draw it out, enabling it to be less diffused and more concentrated and present in our thoughts, feelings and activities. And remember, this doesn't mean only thinking "spiritual" thoughts or having "spiritual" feelings. Soul isn't differentiated in that way; that can lead us back into privileging transpersonal or transcendent and mystical thinking.

Rather soul gathers and concentrates where its capacities are invoked and employed. We become soul by doing soul; we connect with it by performing its functions. And those functions are those I've been describing. When we act lovingly and holopoietically within ourselves and in relationship to our world, we are doing soul. As we do, soul becomes more awake, less diffuse, more concentrated.

This may or may not feel like a transcendental contact. Most likely it won't. Awakening and concentrating the Embodied Soul isn't the same as contacting the Incarnational Soul (or even the Planetary Soul or beyond), which definitely can feel like a transpersonal experience. The deceptive thing about the Embodied Soul is that it doesn't feel like what we've been told soul should feel like, when our only image of soul is that of a transpersonal, transcendent entity. What it feels like is like being more of who we are, but in a spacious, earthy, loving, whole way. But as it is part of an amalgam, it still feels down to earth, connected to the earth, a Presence that is here in this realm, not "out there" in some higher realm among the stars.

So how do we awaken the sleeping beauty within us? How do we gather and concentrate the presence of Soul so that it's not just there in patches (though that's a good place to start) but more fully active and present throughout all aspects of our lives?

How do we go from this to this?

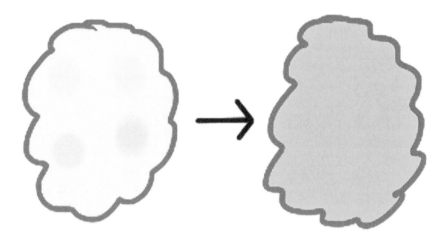

FIGURE 55

There are four techniques that I use. They are:

- Mindfulness
- Imagination
- Blessing Inward
- Blessing Forward

First, a caveat. We are complex beings with physical, psychological, energetic, and spiritual dimensions. To achieve personal wholeness and integration, to deal with the "hungry ghosts," to foster coherency within ourselves and our incarnational system, may require work at each of these four levels. For example, diet and exercise and adequate rest and sleep may be important to bring wholeness to our physical bodies; sometimes we may need medical intervention and help. Likewise, we may find that some kind of psychological therapy is important (I'm particularly impressed with the new "somatic" therapies that incorporate neurobiology and the body into the psychological therapeutic process; they seem very "incarnational" to me in the way they use the body as ally in dealing with the unintegrated "hungry ghosts" of trauma and other psychological dysfunctions). Likewise a spiritual practice that puts one in touch with his or her Interiority and sacredness through prayer, meditation, contemplation, and so forth can play a major role in achieving inner and outer balance, coherency, harmony and wholeness.

What I'm offering here is neither physical, psychological, nor contemplative in the usual spiritual or mystical sense. It is a subtle energy approach based on a clairvoyant understanding of the energetic aspects of incarnation. It is a form of "energy hygiene." It complements all other forms of inner and outer work, whether through diet and exercise, therapy, or spiritual practice and meditation. It is most certainly not a substitute for any of them, nor is it intended to stand alone. Each of us needs to discover and work out our own holopoietic incarnational practice (a term I prefer to "spiritual practice") addressing the different elements of our total incarnational system from sacred to soul to subtle bodies to physical body to our relationships. Our life in the world—where the world has transcendent, subtle energetic, and physical environments—is our incarnational practice.

We may find many different tools that help us individually. I have good friends who swear by astrology, for example, as a means of gaining insight into the inner structure of their incarnations. This isn't a tool that I use, though. One of the most helpful tools for me over the years (I first learned it when I was a teenager) has been Personology, a particular approach to assessing and understanding the physical structure of the body and how that structure and its traits influence how we physically perceive and respond to the environment. Personology gives me a basic understanding of my "default personality," the way I'm likely to express if I don't exercise conscious and mindful direction otherwise. It has been an invaluable and consistently accurate and useful source of information for me in bringing wholeness and balance into my life. (Unfortunately, the Interstate College of Personology and its four year program in which my wife Julie was trained years ago no longer exists, and information about this interesting and helpful approach is not easy to come by these days; Julie and I and others in Lorian are hoping to change this situation by reformulating and representing Personology within an Incarnational Spirituality context.)

Whatever approaches you find helpful, make use of them for as long as they serve you. Just keep in mind that you are a complex and whole system, not just one thing or another. And keep this in mind, too, as we proceed. I will be focusing exclusively here on the subtle energy aspects, but we need to remember that we are much more than just this.

Continuing on, then, I've already discussed Mindfulness, so let's go on to Imagination.

What I particularly have in mind here is our ability to craft a self-image and to imagine who we are. We all have self-images, and they are built up from a number of sources. They may come from the felt sense of who we are based on experience and memory. They may be based on what other's have said about us or told us or from ideas drawn from our culture (if, for example, I've been taught that I start out life in a sinful state due to the transgressions of ancient ancestors, then part of my self-image will be that I am fundamentally sinful). Self-images can be built from empirical data (my body image as having a head, two arms, and two legs, for instance) and rational thought, but they can also emerge from feelings which may be irrational and not based in fact but which are powerful within us nonetheless. Many feelings of a lack of self-worth are not logical but are compelling nonetheless.

A self-image is essentially a thought-form in which we are investing energy; like any thought form, it shapes, patterns and configures the energy that flows around it or through it, much as a boulder in a river shapes the water that flows over and around it. Psychologically, a positive self image can uplift and inspire us while a negative one can depress and diminish us. But as a phenomenon of subtle energy, our self-image affects and shapes how we form energetic connections with the world around us as well as the quality and amount of subtle energy that is normally available to us. You could say it is a "flow regulator."

My self-image can affect what I believe I'm capable of and the capacities that I develop and express. You will remember that one of the "veils" I wrote about earlier was labeled "the Veil of AAB," meaning Attention, Attitude and Belief. I could also have called this the "Veil of Self-Image." Our self-image shapes our beliefs about ourself and our world and shapes our attitudes as well; it can also affect the quality and kind of attention we give to the world around us and to ourselves.

Obviously, self-image is a vital and important part of our incarnational tool box. Imagination gives us an ability to craft it to our advantage.

There is nothing permanent about a self-image. We all experience how it changes through our lives. It's a way we have of defining ourselves to ourselves, but that definition can evolve and change over the years.

With the power of imagination—that is, the power of conceiving and forming images—we can craft this self-definition in deliberate and mindful ways. In fact, this capacity is at the heart of a plethora of self-help books that tell us how thinking and believing can change our lives. But we have neuroscience now to back this up, as modern brain studies have conclusively demonstrated the plasticity of the brain and how changing the pattern of our thinking can reflect in measurable alterations in brain structure and function.

Part of the challenge lies in a limited view of what imagination is. Culturally, we think of it primarily in a context of make-believe and fantasy; it's the faculty we use to "make things up" that aren't real. A sensible, realistic, "down to earth" person relies on empirical observation and rational thought, not on flights of fancy and imagination.

I remember when ROC (Robert Ogilvie Crombie) would give lectures at Findhorn on his contact and experiences with the non-physical realms and in particular with Pan and the nature spirits, he would preface his remarks by claiming how unimaginative he was. So biased was the culture of the time against imagination that he felt compelled to affirm that he didn't have an imaginative bone in his body and therefore was incapable of making up the contacts that he had. (By the way, if you'd like to read about his remarkable encounters with the subtle worlds, Lorian publishes his private journals: The *Occult Diaries of R. Ogilvie Crombie*; his book *Meeting Fairies* published by Findhorn Press is also excellent—shameless editorial plug!)

Yet imagination lies at the heart of human culture and advancement. Our capacity to see not simply what is but what could be, to envision the possible, is the engine that drives our evolution. The mindful cultivation of the power of imagination is at the heart of not only the arts and sciences but also of esoteric magic and the capacity to shape and work with subtle energies. (As another aside, Robert Moss's book *The Three "Only" Things* is an excellent read on the essential nature of imagination in our lives.)

My purpose here, though, is not to convince you that imagination is important or to point out how our culture tends to discount and dismiss it. My guess is that you already know these things. What I want to discuss is how to use imagination to further your incarnational process.

Incarnational Spirituality is all about having a particular understanding and vision of who we are as incarnate persons. In other words, it's about having a particular self-image.

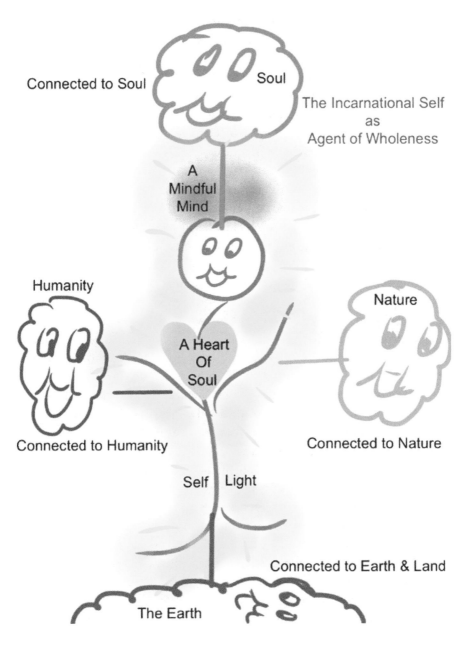

Connected to Soul

Soul

The Incarnational Self
as
Agent of Wholeness

A
Mindful
Mind

Humanity

Nature

A Heart
Of
Soul

Connected to Humanity

Connected to Nature

Self   Light

Connected to Earth & Land

The Earth

FIGURE 56

I think of this as having an image of ourselves as "incarnation agents," individuals who foster and empower the incarnational process and wholeness in themselves and in the world around them. My self-image is suggested by this picture.

As in the Presence Exercise, we are persons who are connected to the world, to nature and to the land around us. We are connected to humanity. We are connected to our own soul and its capacities and to the subtle worlds in general. We have a loving "mindful mind" and a loving "heart of Soul" which empower our connections with blessing. And we are generative sources of spiritual presence: our Self-Light. And we possess the sovereignty of our own unique incarnational systems, our own "amalgam selves." We are spiritual stars upon the earth, each of us unique and sacred, each of us a co-incarnate for each other and for all life.

Everything that Incarnational Spirituality teaches introduces, clarifies and supports this particular vision of the individual. It is the incarnational self-image, if you wish. Of course, each of us fleshes this image out and expresses it in our own unique ways with the texture of our particular autobiographies and soul's intent.

From the beginning of my work with John, it was this image that he and his colleagues wanted me to understand and to embody as much as I was able. It was this image that first appeared to me when I was seventeen and about to enter college, as I described earlier. It's why the idea of Self-Light is important. It's why the idea of Sovereignty is important. It's at the heart of the Standing Exercise, the Lap Exercise, and the Self-Light Exercise.

The power of this incarnational self-image for me is not that it simply describes who I am; I fall short of fully embodying all that this image represents. It's that it indicates the potential of what I can be. It offers a vision for moving forward and for guiding my practice.

Imagination is a way of seeing potential which might not be obvious on the surface and then taking steps to enliven and foster that potential. The fact is that in our culture, there are many voices that try to convince us we're planets and not stars, and rather dark planets at that. There are many voices that deny our sacredness, our spirit, our ability to create wholeness. In fact one of the main images projected upon us by Western culture certainly is that we are all consumers, not producers, not generative sources.

It's our holopoietic, loving, mindful generative self that the earth longs for and which our souls seek to manifest in this world. This is a self-image worth understanding, worth embodying, worth working for. And when we do, we have many allies ready and willing to help us turn it from image into reality.

After Mindfulness and Imagination, the third technique I call Blessing Inward.

This is a straight-forward practice, but to fully appreciate it, I think I need to offer some background. Remember that in IS, there is no "lower" or "false" self, no single part of us that embodies resistance to our spirit and soul or to our wholeness or generally to being a "good person." What we have is a system of interactive elements, and it's possible for the system itself to be incoherent and less than holistically integrated. There can be competing "vectors" within us, and any of them in the moment can be the focus of embodiment, the lens through which we express our will and life. So while there is no "false self" as such, there can be "false moments" when we are not expressing our wholeness in any mindful way.

There are core elements within us, those that reflect, embody and express the Embodied Soul and the Soul's Intent. And we have the power of mindfulness, of being aware and deliberate in what we choose to think and feel, say and do. But we also have unintegrated and disassociated energetic material that can arise from within ourselves based on our experiences in life (trauma can produce such material) or which we can take on from the subtle energy environment in which we live. Such "free ions" of subtle energy can come from the land, from nature, from specific other people whom we meet, or from the collective field of humanity. They can come from subtle world sources. The primary characteristic of all such material is that it is energetically disconnected. It has not been successfully or sufficiently integrated into a larger system of wholeness.

The primary "larger system of wholeness" in us is the Embodied Soul and its Emergent Self, in short, our identity. But subsidiary and smaller and comparatively incomplete complexes can form to which certain kinds of material become attached rather than blending with the core identity. So, for instance, if there's an unintegrated, disassociated complex in me that arose from a prior experience (perhaps as a child) of rejection or suffering and which holds subtle energetic elements of anger and fear, let's say, if I encounter such subtle energies of fear and anger in my environment, they may attach themselves to (become identified with) this inner complex rather than becoming engaged and transmuted by the core elements that embody the capacities of soul. So this disassociated complex—this hungry ghost—might be just a single thought or feeling—a "meme" in the words of the evolutionary biologist Richard Dawkins—or it might be a complex of thoughts and feelings that has the power in the moment to be activated by circumstances and act on my behalf. In effect in that moment it is my self, even though I possess other potentials of self that would be less hurtful (and hurting) and less disassociated energetically.

So there's a core system of wholeness in us but also, potentially, clusters of disconnected and unintegrated energies that are nonetheless volitional and possessing vectors and therefore able to reflexively or automatically express given the opportunity.

From the standpoint of energy hygiene, one way to deal with this is to strengthen the core system so that it's power is enhanced to reach out within the incarnational system and provide holistic and loving connectedness and integration.

Here is one of my symbolic pictures:

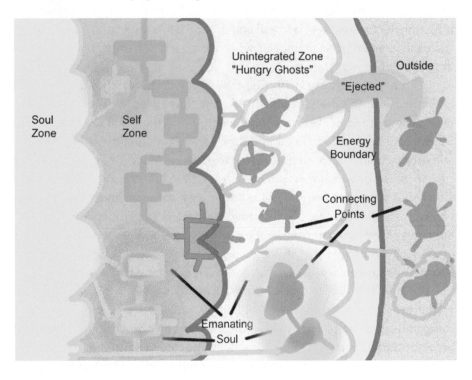

FIGURE 57

In this picture we have four "zones" and the "outside," the world environment that surrounds a person. These four zones are the Energy Boundary (like the cell wall or like our physical skin) that separates the "I" from the "Not-I;" the presence of unintegrated material—the "hungry ghosts" hungry for expression, fulfillment of their volitional vectors or connection with a larger whole; the (Emergent) Self, and the Soul which carries the soul capacities. Of course, we are not divided up so neatly into these zones—the situation in our energy field can be much more diffused and blended than this—but this is just a representation to illustrate the players and the process.

The red blobs are the unintegrated energy packets, memes, thought forms, etc. Each has the capacity to connect and seeks that connection. This capacity is represented by the "connecting points." We see them "floating" in the outside environment waiting to be picked up, so to speak, and we see them "floating" within the individual's field of self; when they are unintegrated and disconnected, they collectively form the "zone of hungry ghosts."

(By the way, as a point of interest, it is possible to see these disconnected bits in a person's aura, so this drawing, while mainly symbolic, is not entirely fanciful.)

When these bits are wholly disconnected, they are red in color. When they become accepted and connected and part of our Emergent Self, they become green. And if they are connected to the soul presence within us, they become gold.

You will notice that what defines the "Self Zone" is that all the bits are in fact connected and part of the self, part of the energetic and psychic structure of who we are. Note that this diagram doesn't distinguish here between "good bits" and "bad bits," only between the states of being connected and integrated and being disassociated, disconnected and unintegrated. It is quite possible to connect and integrate negative elements of hatred, anger, fear, suspicion, and the like, which, of course, would produce an emergent self that embodies and manifests such qualities and their consequent behaviors.

The operative principle of connection here is primarily resonance, like attracting like. Connection can, of course take place through an act of will and desire when we encounter thoughts and feelings in the environment (or arising in ourselves) that we approve of or wish to make part of our lives.

In this picture, we see several things happening. From the top down, we see one of the DUBs (Disconnected, Unintegrated Blobs—a little known esoteric term—Archivist Dave) being rejected by the Emergent Self. The self is saying, "No, you're not part of me," and the DUB's energy is ejected back into the outside.

Just below it, however, a DUB is being accepted and drawn deeper into the self. And below that we see a DUB that is in the process of being accepted and integrated into the structure of the self (obviously in this case, the individual is accepting the idea of Self-Light, previously held as a disconnected idea but now being accepted and integrated into his self-image!).

The long blue line with the arrows suggests that some energetic bit—a stray meme, perhaps—that the individual has become aware of in his or her surroundings is being attached and drawn directly into the structure of the self; no interim period of "floating disconnectedly" for it.

Finally, the golden lines are elements that are being directly linked to the soul; these could be spiritual ideas, feelings of love and wholeness, the Incarnational Spirituality cosmology—who knows. But in the process, the soul is permeating the self more fully, and where it connects, that psychic and energetic element becomes itself a radiant expression of soul capacities. Note that this can take place both with structures that are already part of the self and with disconnected bits. For example, I read a bit of inspirational poetry and both the ideas the poem expresses and the ways it does so fill me with a wave of love and insight that connects me to my own soul presence. In that moment, that disconnected bit of poetry takes on an emanation of soul and is connected directly to my soul presence and not just to the concrete mind or feelings of the everyday self. Whether it becomes part of me or whether it's just a momentary bit of inspiration that I later forget is not shown here.

If I were fully integrated with and attuned to my soul presence, all the green bits in the Self Zone" and even that Zone itself would be golden, and chances are the Unintegrated Zone would become "golden," too.

This process of connecting the various parts of me to the holopoietic, integrative, loving presence of soul is what I mean by "Blessing Inward."

So what is Blessing Inward? Basically, it's a practice of blessing yourself which can take different forms but an essential part of it is enhancing the presence of soul within yourself. In my drawing of 21:32, it's a process of enhancing and expanding the "patches of soul" so that its presence becomes more dominant within you.

Now here it's important not to get too caught up in images of what this means from other spiritual and esoteric traditions. You're not turning yourself into a saint, necessarily, nor trying to have mystical or transcendent experiences. Those are nice to have, of course, but they come out of a different process entirely. Generally they arise from contact with your transpersonal self, your Incarnational Soul (or High Self) or the Planetary Soul or beyond. In Blessing Inward, you're not seeking a transpersonal contact. Rather you are connecting with, awakening, heightening, and drawing forth in a more concentrated way the diffuse presence of the Embodied Soul. Blessing Inward is contacting the part of your soul that is sharing earthly incarnation with you, the part that is you as an incarnate entity.

(I should add here that because soul is soul is soul, it's possible that in connecting with your Embodied Soul, you may find yourself coming into contact with the higher levels and manifestations of soul as well; you may slip into a transpersonal, mystical, transcendent experience without intending to. That's OK. Nothing wrong with that, as long as you keep the original intent in mind. It's just that you don't enter this practice with a transpersonal contact in mind.)

In a way, the three exercises of Standing, Lap, and Presence lead into Blessing Inward. Each of these can be a way of coming into touch with the felt sense of the Presence that is your Embodied Soul.

Here is another thought: what you are doing in this practice is a kind of "self-mysticism." You are seeking to acknowledge, honor and foster the sacredness of your incarnate life, what at other times I've called our "ordinary sacredness." It's a mystical approach, if you wish to see it this way, towards your ordinary incarnate self.

This is another reason why understanding the presence and reality of Self-Light is important. If you have a felt sense of being a source of spiritual presence as an incarnate self, that you are every bit as spiritual in your earthly form as you are in your transpersonal forms, then it's very much easier to expect to find sacredness and soul in the midst of your everyday self. It's the soul in you that experiences your ups and downs, your positive days and your negative ones, your triumphs and your failures; it is completely and joyously human: it's the soul that can have a bad hair day and still be a source of blessing and love. It's the soul of a star within you.

Here is where imaginatively crafting a self-image that incorporates Self-Light and Sovereignty can be a huge help in Blessing Inward. You may not feel any less human or more "spiritual" in conventional terms, but having a vision of yourself as a generative source, as a presence of Light in the world not because you can channel it from higher levels but simply and wondrously because you're an incarnate self is amazingly empowering. In the clarity of such a vision, such a self-image, reaching into your humanity, your selfhood and finding there a presence of embodied soul becomes the most natural thing in the world to do.

The practice itself is deceptively simple. It's object is to occupy soul, so to speak, to be in this presence within you and heighten it through the simple yet profound process of giving it your attention and intention. And the result is to change the internal energetic "chemistry" of your incarnational field, enhancing connection, integration, coherency, and wholeness. This is most definitely a holopoietic practice.

Here the biologist in me thinks of another metaphor. This process doesn't "attack" or do battle with the DUBs that you may have in your field. Rather it changes the vibe within you from one in which disconnection is possible to one in which connection and transformation become the order of the day. Any disassocated bits of energy that cannot handle this simply dissolve or leave. In this sense, it's like changing the pH or acid balance of a solution, making it increasingly uncomfortable and inhospitable for certain kinds of microorganisms that then leave or die.

(Remember this is an energetic process, not a psychological one. It may well have psychological affects, bringing healing, but it may also simply complement other therapeutic practices with which you may be engaging; also some DUBS have over time become powerful complexes, cysts of energy that take time to transform and dissolve, particularly if we've been feeding them energy through our thinking and feeling over the years. But I would never underestimate the power of soul to transform, heal  and make whole our internal environment with consequent healing in other areas of our lives.)

Here's how I do this practice. You may (and should) find your own approach. At least if it's identical to what I do, be sure that you're making it your own, understanding and experiencing the steps and inhabiting them in your own unique way. There are no cookie cutter approaches in Incarnational Spirituality!

- I begin by honoring and appreciating my self as an individual person and as an incarnate human being. I might start this process using the Standing Exercise or the Presence Exercise, but neither is necessary. What I really want here is the felt sense of approaching myself with love and honor.

- Next I work my way inward. My conscious, everyday mind is all I need as I draw upon its ability to choose to do this, to give this process attention and intention. This is important. I'm not doing it because "I have to" or because someone (like me or some book I read or class I took) told me I should do it. I'm doing it because I want to, because hanging out with myself is a joy and a pleasure, even a privilege. It's the same spirit in which I might seek out the company of a loved one. There is intention, not compulsion. I am acting in the soul quality of freedom, freely choosing to do this practice.

- I imagine myself stepping into a spacious room within myself. In this room are the other partners in my incarnational system. They are here because I'm here. This is an important part of my self-image here: I am the incarnate nexus that draws these partners, the elements of the Presence Exercise for instance, together. My choice to be incarnated has drawn them together into an incarnational system. Realizing this, I feel love for them and gratitude. They may or may not work together with all the coherency and wholeness I would wish, but I have the power to foster such wholeness. In fact, that's why I'm doing this practice. All are connected through soul, so it's soul that I'm awakening and heightening through my attention, my intention and most powerfully, my love. And my partners return that love for through my choice to be incarnated, I'm giving them an opportunity to be together, to work together, and in the process bring something new and emergent into being.

- Standing in this spacious, imaginary inner space, I give my attention to soul which is all around me, the very atmosphere and structure of this space though it may be diffuse. And here is the important secret behind Blessing Inward. I don't invoke soul by calling out to something separate from me. I inhabit it and awaken it by being it. I think of the capacities of soul, all capacities that I can express as a conscious, everyday self. I don't have to be a saint, a master, an adept, a spiritual Olympian, to be soul. I become soul by doing soul. I become soul by loving, by standing in my whole identity, by knowing and honoring my boundaries, by engaging in connection and relationship with the world, by opening myself to growth and emergence, by appreciating and expressing when appropriate and necessary my freedom and my will. I become soul by being holopoietic, doing whatever I can to create wholeness.

- For me, the key touch point into soul and into doing this practice is love. So I occupy this inner space with love and in love. I eschew entering into combat or antagonism with any part of me. My purpose is not to be adversarial. My purpose is to act in a soulful, loving way within myself, towards myself, towards all parts of me. So at this point, I imagine my love radiating out from me and filling this space. I love the part of me connected to the world, I love the part of me connected to humanity, I love the part of me connected to the transpersonal and the subtle worlds, I love the part of me connected to my personality and my body. And I love all the disconnected hungry ghosts that may be there. Whatever my faults and flaws, my strengths and accomplishments, I simply love the space in which they exist in me. This is a gentle exercise. I'm not trying to make anything happen; rather I'm giving attention to being something, to doing love and being soul. In this process, I may think of how the sacred accepts, honors and loves me unconditionally, and I want to have that same love to all the parts of me.

- As I stand in this love, I can call to mind whatever I wish about myself that either pleases me or bothers me. If there are parts of me that need healing, whether they are physical or psychological, I call them forth, but—and this is very important—not with the intent to heal them. My intent is simply to love and connect with them. I am inclusiveness personified, demanding only that whatever stays in my field participate in this presence of soul, i.e. that it, too, becomes soul-filled and expressive of the capacities of soul as best it can. By simply being a presence, I am heightening that presence, bringing blessing to all parts of me and to my incarnational system as a whole.

- I do this for as long as feel comfortable. There is no strain about it. It could be for a long time or a very short time. The point is not duration but attentiveness and strength of intent. I am the conscious, mindful agency of soul in the midst of my incarnational system. I am the conscious, mindful agency of holopoiesis within me, and however long I hold this space, it is enough. When I am finished, I simply give thanks to all parts of me and resume my outer life, knowing I can reenter this inner space with attention and intention any time I wish, for as long as I wish.

This for me is the process of Blessing Inward. It is a simple yet profound act of acceptance and love for one's incarnate self, and in the process the self-image of oneself as an incarnational agent and a presence of sacredness and blessing in the world grows. The "sacred pH" of the living solution of my life alters, and overtime transformation happens.

Again, I want to emphasize this practice doesn't necessarily lead to any bells and whistles of transpersonal or transcendent experience. That's not its objective. It's purpose is to honor the incarnational self and heighten the Embodied Soul, not necessarily its transpersonal counterparts. It may not make me more "spiritual" in the conventional way we think of this, but it will make me more whole as a person. It is the practice of Incarnational Spirituality at its best.

The final technique I call Blessing Forward.

Blessing Forward serves three purposes using the same principle: we manifest and heighten soul by doing what soul does. This is the principle you used in Blessing Inward, but here your attention and intention is turned outward.

The first purpose it serves is the most obvious one of bringing your Self-Light and blessings out into the world around you. It's a form of service.

The second purpose is to heighten soul within you and enhance your own wholeness.

The third purpose is to enhance your incarnational process by fostering, nourishing and inhabiting your larger incarnational field.

I don't have anything special to say about the first purpose. Obviously anything you do that brings blessing into your environment is going to help those who share than environment with you. If you'd like to explore this side more, then I suggest my book *Blessing: The Art and the Practice.*

The second purpose is more inward and is based on a very simple principle: the way to develop a muscle is to exercise it. The way to develop the presence of soul within you is to exercise the capacities of soul in your life.

Your soul and mine are profoundly relational critters. Soul expresses and develops through relationship and blending with other souls; the incarnational principle of connection, engagement and relationship is an expression of this.

So when we express our soul capacities forward into the world, loving and honoring the presence of freedom, of will, of identity, boundary, connection, emergence, sovereignty, and Self-Light in others and generally in the world around us—when we are agents fostering and supporting the incarnational processes in the world around us—we cannot help but heighten the connective tissue and holopoietic presence of soul within ourselves. In this sense, it is a complement to Blessing Inward, accomplishing much the same thing.

Here is a picture (of course!):

## Blessing Forward

FIGURE 58

This picture illustrates the principles. My Self-Light is a form of Light that specializes in connectivity within the incarnate realm for it emerges from this realm. When I extend the energy, blessing and presence of my Self-Light out into my world towards a person or thing or a setting within nature, it sets up a connective vibe along which the deeper presence and blessing of the soul can flow. Self-Light becomes the channel for "Blessing Light."

In effect, as the soul reaches out into the world it does so by overflowing within ourselves. We are not simply a channel, like a tube, through which transpersonal energies and blessings pass. That can happen, for sure, but that is not what this practice is about. Like Blessing Inward, here our attention is on blessing from our own Embodied Soul, from "earthly soul," so to speak, and our Self-Light is one manifestation of this earthly soul.

By seeing ourselves as a source of blessing, a source of incarnational Light, we give further power to our self-image as an incarnational agent and in the process we heighten the presence of Embodied Soul within us.

Often this technique can be more powerful for us than Blessing Inward; I may find it easier to love and bless something outside myself such as another person or an object or some part of nature than I do loving and blessing myself. Having an outer focus gives something concrete for my attention and intention to work with. But since doing soul enhances being soul, if I truly Bless Forward, I will simultaneously Bless Inward.

Pretty cool, eh?

The third purpose of Blessing Forward is illustrated by this picture:

# THE INCARNATIONAL FIELDS

FIGURE 59

As I've suggested throughout this text, incarnation is a process of creating and inhabiting fields of energy and presence. At the beginning, as we've seen, the soul creates a unique and focused field to begin the incarnational process. This field is the Incarnational Soul. It in turn creates a specific incarnational field embracing physical body and its subtle body counterparts, and this becomes what we might call the "Field of Self."

Each of these fields is filled with the life and capacities of the Soul. Each of these fields holds some degree of the Soul's energy.

But there's a third field that we've haven't really discussed yet, in part because it's very fluid and conditional. I call it the "Relational Field" and its formed through our relationships with others and with the world around us. The main structures of this field develop over time with those people and places (and creatures as well) with whom we're involved in a deep and lasting way, such as parents, siblings, the land where we were born, the land where we live, the place where we work, a pet we may have had for many years, and so on. The longer and deeper and more loving the relationship with these others may be, the more permanently they become part of our relational field, whereas others whom we may meet and relate to only for a few minutes or hours may create very temporary fields that collapse and dissolve when the relationship ends.

Part of the impact we feel when someone with whom we've developed a lasting and loving relationship dies is due to the rupture and alteration in this relational field and its energy structure.

The fact is that our Soul—the Planetary Soul, in this case, but it's true to a lesser degree for the Incarnational Soul as well—has so much presence and energy to offer, more than our individual Field of Self may be able to hold. The fields we create with others then become means to receive and hold this additional energy and presence. In effect, we incarnate soul into the field of relationships we form with others and with the world. This relational field is every bit as much a body of incarnation as the physical body or the field of self.

The strength and holding power of this field is not necessarily dependent on quantity, i.e. it's stronger the more relationships we have. It's dependent on the quality of the relationship, its depth, the degree of blending and resonance it manifests, the love or mutual support, the duration, and so forth. Having one deep, good friend can create a more powerful relational field than having a hundred casual acquaintances.

The third purpose of Blessing Forward, then, is to bless our relationships and the connections we form with the world around us. In so doing we bless our own relational field and heighten the presence of soul within it.

There is an important exercise or practice in Incarnational Spirituality called the Grail Space Exercise. I include it in the exercises for this chapter. Creating Grail Space is a form of Blessing Forward. It is a way of extending and connecting our own Self-Light and personal field of incarnational energy with the Light and incarnational energy of our immediate environment. It's purpose is to create a temporary relational field, a "Grail," that can serve in the moment and in that place as a way to hold more subtle energies than we might do otherwise. It's a powerful tool that's especially used in Subtle Activism and in working with the subtle worlds. It was one of the first practices John taught me to help me receive and hold some of the intense and complex energies I felt from subtle beings he asked me to contact as part of my training.

In this context, though, Grail Space might be seen as another way of Blessing Forward and enhancing the soul resonance within our relational field and within ourselves as well.

### BALANCING RELATIONS: SYSTEM, SOVEREIGNTY AND SELF

So much of the incarnational process can be discussed in terms of connections, relationships, holding, and balance. Personality holds soul, body holds self, self holds sovereignty, and so forth. There is nothing passive about this holding and the process of balancing our various connections and relationships. It's very dynamic and constantly changing, sometimes slowly and sometimes very quickly. A permanent relationship in our life may change slowly as it matures and deepens, but a person we meet briefly on the street forms a quicksilver relationship that is energetically there one minute and gone the next. Our incarnational energy field accommodates and responds to both.

As I said earlier in the text, we live in a sea of information and influence that comes to us from all directions. Our incarnational system and the field it generates is under constant stimulation. Much of this information just "bounces off" and is ignored; much is registered; and some is taken in to become part of us in one way or another, perhaps as a "hungry ghost," perhaps as a more integrated and permanent part of us.

Here is a picture illustrating this. I suggest some of the kinds and sources of information and influence to which we relate, and I organize them along the lines of the Presence Exercise into categories such as "Humanity," "Transpersonal," "World," and "Personal." You can see in the picture some of the sources of influence and information that can flow in to our incarnational systems through the connections we have with these broad categories. Of course, this is just a small sampling of the many influences and sources of information to which we can be exposed in the course of our life — or even of a single day. It's meant to be suggestive, not descriptive.

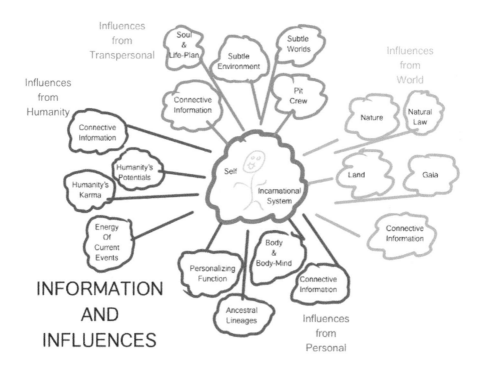

Influences
from
Transpersonal

Influences
from
Humanity

Influences
from
World

Soul
&
Life-Plan

Subtle
Worlds

Subtle
Environment

Connective
Information

Pit
Crew

Nature

Natural
Law

Connective
Information

Humanity's
Potentials

Self

Land

Gaia

Humanity's
Karma

Incarnational
System

Energy
Of
Current
Events

Body
&
Body-Mind

Connective
Information

Personalizing
Function

Connective
Information

**INFORMATION**

**AND**

**INFLUENCES**

Ancestral
Lineages

Influences
from
Personal

FIGURE 60

These categories, however, are not simply made up. They do represent actual differences in subtle energy frequencies, like differences in the broadcast frequencies of different radio or television stations. On any particular station, I may get a wide variety of information, such as news, music, conversation, and so on, but it's all coming over the particular frequency assigned to that radio station. And each station is identified by the kind of material it mainly broadcasts, such as music (Top Ten, Rock and Roll, Golden Oldies, etc.), Talk Radio, all news, and so forth.

So there is a vibrational difference that I feel between the subtle energies carrying information from a natural source such as a forest or a stone or a particular landscape and those carrying information from a city or a neighborhood or the collective field of humanity in general. There is a difference between a transpersonal vibe coming from a being like John and a vibe coming from my body.

There can be overlap between these. A music station may also broadcast news at the top of the hour while a news station might play a piece of music. I can pick up anger from the land or from a human being; the carrier vibe is different but the anger and its effect in my energy field is more or less the same.

Even though many sources are in fact involved, the commonality within particular categories allows me to identify four major "radio stations" within us: those attuned to transpersonal sources, those attuned to Gaian, world and natural sources, those attuned to sources within Humanity, and those attuned to those forces involved in giving me a particular embodied identity, which I call the personalizing forces. In the Presence exercise I refer to these "radio stations" (really "radio receivers" might be a better description) as "selves," as in our "World Self" or our "Humanity Self" and so on.

Calling these "selves" isn't entirely fanciful either. Remember that we are dealing with living, sentient energies. There is an active awareness here that is part of our incarnational field, a part of our overall incarnational consciousness attuned to particular frequencies. Also there is a long and useful tradition in psychology in personifying certain inner phenomena and then communicating with them as actual "others" who are also part of us. This has a very long history in the esoteric and clairvoyant traditions as well. What constitutes a consciousness or being that can communicate with us is often a good deal more broad based and surprising than our limited definitions of "organism" here in the physical world may lead us to expect. To call these elements within us "selves" is much more than just a useful metaphor.

We might picture these inner, component selves as akin to nerve synapses connecting our incarnational field with the larger world beyond us. In this picture we look at one of these selves in particular, the one that is attuned to and thus connects us to information and influences coming from other human beings and from the collective field of humanity in general. This connective "synapse" or "radio receiver" or "connector" is what I call in the Presence exercise our "Humanity Self."

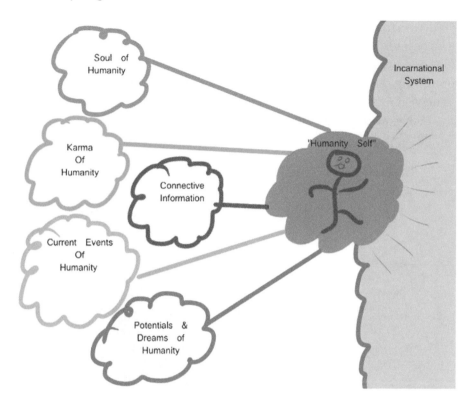

FIGURE 61

Here we see this Self receiving information and influence from a variety of sources within humanity.  These might include the Soul of Humanity, Human Collective Karma, subtle energies of human thinking and feeling unleashed by current events such as wars or political campaigns or natural disasters, and subtle energies arising from the potentials and dreams seeking emergence and fulfillment within humanity.  At the same time, there is specialized information that organizes and maintains our incarnational connection to Humanity, such information as "what it means to be a human being."

(Note that each of the four Selves or "synapses" here are receptor sites for the particular connective information required for the incarnational field to be part of the larger environment represented by that Self; thus there is connective information that keeps us in touch with the transpersonal and subtle worlds, connective information that makes us part of Gaia and the natural world, and so forth.  This "connective tissue," as we saw earlier, is what is formed in Act I of the incarnational process , bringing the incarnational system into being in the first place.)

In this picture, the Humanity Self is receiving information, energy and influences from all the sources to which it is attuned, processing it, and passing it on as information and energy into the Incarnational System where it will be further processed. This is much like a physical sensory organ receiving and processing sensory information from the environment and then passing it on as nerve impulses to the brain where it is further processed and evaluated.

In this picture all is well.

But now, look at this:

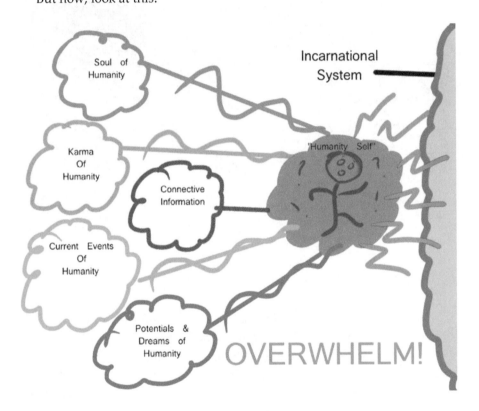

FIGURE 62

In this picture something has happened. Information, subtle energies, and other kinds of influences from one or more sources within the human collective are overstimulating and overwhelming the Humanity Self. Here's an example: When the World Trade towers were attacked and fell on 9/11, a wave of fear rippled through the collective field of the United States. People living in the most out of the way places in the heart of the country still felt anxious that they might be attacked by terrorists. I felt it here in my little town in the foothills of the mountains east of Seattle; in fact, I had a vivid dream that Osama bin Laden was leading a horde of ravaging Arabs down the streets of our neighborhood, and woke up fearful and ready to flee! The majority of Americans were safe from any terrorist threat but yet many people were irrationally afraid that they were in harm's way.

The reason is that people were picking up on and internalizing and identifying with a subtle energy of fear that was resonating through the collective American psyche, like a wave sloshing back and forth in a bathtub. Their "Humanity Selves" were picking up on and passing on into their Incarnational Systems a powerful and overwhelming fear vibration with which they were then identifying on a personal level. But even if you don't identify with such energies, they can still have an effect. Feeling the subtle energies of fear or anger or hatred is not pleasant.

There are centering and integrative forces within us that dampen down and alchemize many of the potentially unbalancing energies and influences we encounter during the day (and of which we usually remain unconscious). But sometimes they are overwhelmed, too, and that is when the superhero of integration, balance and calm comes to the rescue: You as your conscious, mindful everyday self standing in sovereignty.

Let's explore this concept of sovereignty and standing in sovereignty a bit more. Here is a picture:

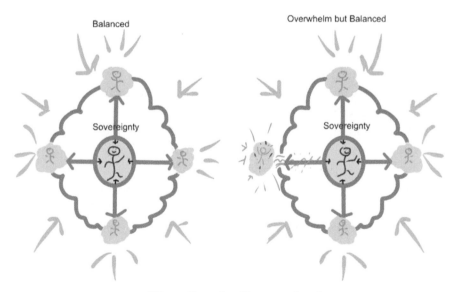

## Standing In Sovereignty

FIGURE 63

Here we see an incarnational system and field with its four major "synapses" or "selves." The crucial thing to understand about these is that they are connective and receptive functions, not integrative ones. They draw attention to themselves, saying in effect, "Pay attention! Here's what I'm sensing and receiving from the Transpersonal Realms (or from the Human World or from Nature, or from your body and your personality, depending on the nature of the "synaptic self)." They provide and maintain connections with the larger world and pass information and energy through from that world into the interior of the incarnational field.

Sovereignty is the organizing force within the incarnational system that connects these four "Selves" together with the Embodied Soul and Emergent Self and creates the space for self-governance and mindfulness. It is an incarnational emanation from the Embodied Soul, a kind of soul quality in itself like love or freedom. In the picture, Sovereignty is the golden center.

The little figure within this golden center is You, the conscious, mindful, everyday self, standing in that space of Sovereignty. Note that the arrows point towards the "synaptic selves," indicating that they each pull attention and balance in their own particular direction; they are not in themselves balancing agents. But within the sphere of Sovereignty, the arrows of power and influence point to you. You, though your mindful presence and attention to your own internal spaces and your own life and through standing in that felt sense of your generative, star-like self, are empowering the integrative effect of sovereignty within you. (This is one of the objectives of the Standing Exercise.)

So, harking back to my example of what happened in 9/11, a person might still receive all the fearful input from the collective field of thought, but, standing in Sovereignty, is able to affirm a spirit of calm and peace and wholeness that keeps his or her incarnational system in balance. The person still feels the energy of the fear, but is not thrown for a loop by it. Sovereignty exerts a holopoietic influence over that person's subjective world and incarnational field.

But what happens if the person cannot or does not make a conscious, mindful choice to stand in Sovereignty or to stand in peace and in an integrative spirit? Then we get something like this picture:

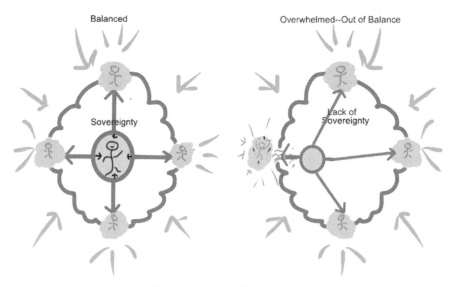

Standing In Sovereignty --2

FIGURE 64

Here, too, we see the subtle energy of information and influence coming from all directions but focused on the four "receiving stations." As above, some energy comes in from the human collective that is stressful, possibly overwhelming, perhaps fearful or angry (no doubt from the evening news!), but unlike in the picture above, there is no attention given to standing in Sovereignty in order to maintain integration and calm. Instead, the inner field over-responds to the stimulation, unbalancing the incarnational system.

The result of this could be fear spreading throughout the person, perhaps without him or her consciously knowing why. The imbalance could give more power to hungry ghosts, particularly if they resonate with the information or influence coming in. If the person, for instance, has fearful hungry ghosts anyway, they could be given greater power and influence in how the person reacts and behaves in the moment. Mindfulness is lost. In that moment, the individual becomes an expression not of his or her Emergent Self or Embodied Soul but of some fragment of self or volitional energy either taken in from the outside or arising from subjective factors within.

Within the soul lie all the capacities and energy needed to keep ourselves in balance and harmony; it is the holopoietic source in our lives. But the soul cannot always compete with subjective elements of mind and emotion—the hungry ghosts and other inner voices—particularly when we are vibrating to turbulence from the environment (and adding our turbulence to it). In effect, when our everyday self decides to "go fishing" in the stream of consciousness and forgets to be mindful and present, the soul finds its ability to grasp the levers of power in our life blocked by the hungry ghosts.

Incoherency can result.

FIGURE 65

Who's To Blame?

As I've written before in this text, when the incarnational system goes "Boom!" with incoherency and we behave in violent, hurtful, or simply selfish and negative ways, the blame traditionally goes to the personality or the "lower self." The result can be the development of an adversarial relationship between parts of ourselves seen in a binary relationship: the "good self" and the "bad self."

# THE BINARY BATTLE

Low Self
Bad Self

High Self
Good Self

FIGURE 66

But in Incarnational Spirituality such a binary perspective is seen as both counterproductive and inaccurate. While it is certainly possible for powerful and complex habit patterns to develop that promote negative or positive behavior, there is more going on that just a simple struggle for control by a Low Self or a High Self.

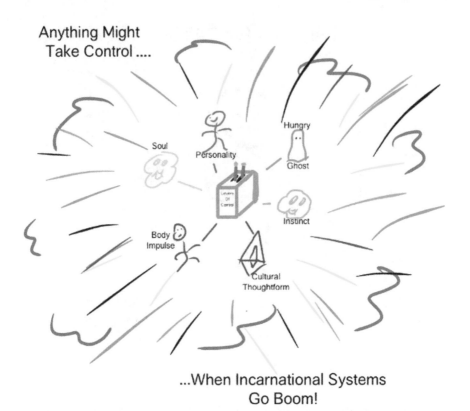

FIGURE 67

When incoherency results because our incarnational center doesn't hold and the system temporarily goes "boom!," a vacuum is created. In the moment, anything might take control and provide the motivation or impulse for our behavior. The "Levers of Control" might be seized by the Soul if we're fortunate or even by the personality, but they could also be used by an instinctive response, a hungry ghost, a body impulse, a cultural thoughtform, or some other emotional or mental manifestation such as a reflex of fear or anger.

Usually the personal self is the one blamed for this turn of events. The important idea here in Incarnational Spirituality is that the culprit or culprits responsible for this incoherence and loss of integration and wholeness might lie elsewhere.

The Incarnational System Goes BOOM!

And the culprit is....?

Transpersonal Self

Humanity Self

World Self

Personal Self
(The Usual Suspect)

FIGURE 68

The fact is that we are not binary creatures but systemic ones. We do not have only two poles to our beingness; we are multi-polar. As a consequence, incoherency can be triggered at various points within our incarnational system not only or simply by or within the personal self.

For instance, as with my example of 9/11, energetic impulses, feelings, and thoughts may impact us from the psyche of humanity and its collective energy field. We may feel temporarily overwhelmed or, because of elements within us already, we may identify and take on such collective impulses, treating them as if they were our own. We know that body instincts and needs can be very powerful, and the same is true for energetic impulses from the world of nature and from the land.

What may seem strange to contemplate is that incoherency could result from something coming from the Incarnational Soul or from other subtle world or transpersonal sources, but the fact is that transpersonal beings, including at times the soul itself in its transpersonal (not Embodied) state, do not always understand the "carrying capacity" of the incarnate human self and can bring more energy to bear on the incarnational field and system than it can hold and integrate in the moment. Incarnation is a skill that souls learn, and at times the level of skill doesn't quite match the needs or circumstances in which the incarnate self finds itself. Though the physical world seems solid and dense to us, in fact it's quite fluid in its way energetically because a variety of different variables—mental, emotional, physical, energetic, relational, environmental, and collective—can come into play within and around the incarnate self at any given time. As one of my inner colleagues once said, "Incarnation is like building a house of toothpicks while standing in a flowing river."

In other words, the soul can make mistakes.

Such mistakes are not born of negativity or what we might think of as "evil" influences; in fact many of the impulses or energies that come from Humanity or from the World or even the body and the forces of personalization do not have to be "negative" per se to be destabilizing. They simply need to be more that we can hold or integrate in the moment. The transpersonal soul—the soul in its Incarnational or even its Planetary or Cosmic aspects—can misjudge what its incarnational field can handle energetically or informationally under particular circumstances. It might try to communicate information but lack the fluency in "incarnation-speak" that allows the incarnate mind to grasp and understand what is being transmitted, leading to misunderstandings or misinterpretations.

When things go wrong, then, we need to think systemically, not in a binary way. It's not a part of us that has gone bad or that is inherently clumsy or evil, but a system that has become incoherent and in that incoherency is behaving badly and without mindful, loving or holopoietic direction.

The good news is that as we pay attention to our incarnational system and practice coherency, integration, and inner wholeness, we develop our holopoietic presence from the ground up, so to speak, building in a habit, if you will, of balance. The incarnational system can definitely be strengthened. It can learn and it can become resilient in ways that maintain wholeness even when experiencing powerful impulses of energy from the environment.

What makes this learning possible is YOU.

### THE CONSCIOUS, EVERYDAY SELF

In Incarnational Spirituality, the transpersonal levels of consciousness and life are important, but the real hero of the three-act play is the personal, everyday self, the part of us with which we most readily and often identify. You as the conscious self are the linchpin upon which everything else depends.

This may seem overly optimistic when we consider all the unconscious forces both in our psyche and in the world around us in the form of various subtle energies that act upon us and in turn prompt and determine our own reactions. The conscious mind can feel dwarfed when compared to what is below the surface of our everyday awareness.

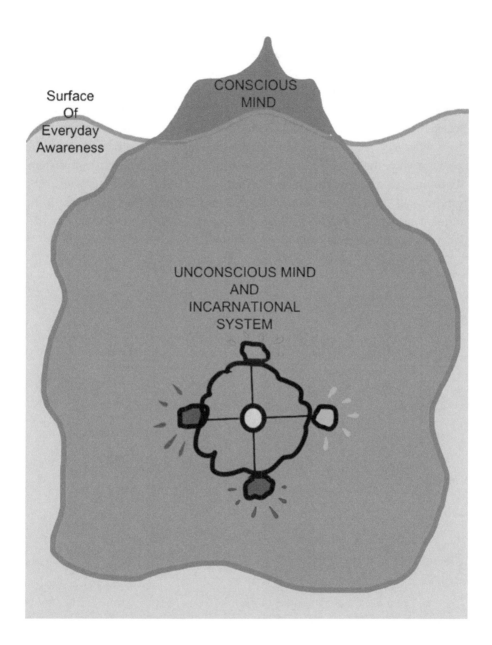

FIGURE 69

When a large ocean vessel such as a cruise ship or an aircraft carrier wants to turn, it will use its rudder to do so, but as you can imagine, the rudder itself on such a vessel is very large and is being acted upon by powerful hydraulic forces from the flow of the water around it. Normally such forces will create resistance to the rudder's movement so that it would take a great deal of force to get the rudder itself to change position. However, inset into the control surface of such rudders is a trim tab, a kind of "rudder for the rudder." Being smaller, it takes much less power to move it, and when it is moved, it alters the flow of water around the rudder itself so that now the hydraulic forces of the surrounding water flow exert pressure on the rudder to move in the desired direction. Because of the trim tab, a small change can result in a large effect, enabling ships with great mass to turn more easily than they might otherwise.

In a way, the conscious mind is a trim tab for the incarnational system. There may be a great deal going on under the surface, but the power of the mindful self to provide intention and attention and to make choices in the moment can set a holopoietic change in motion. The direction can be towards coherency rather than the other way around.

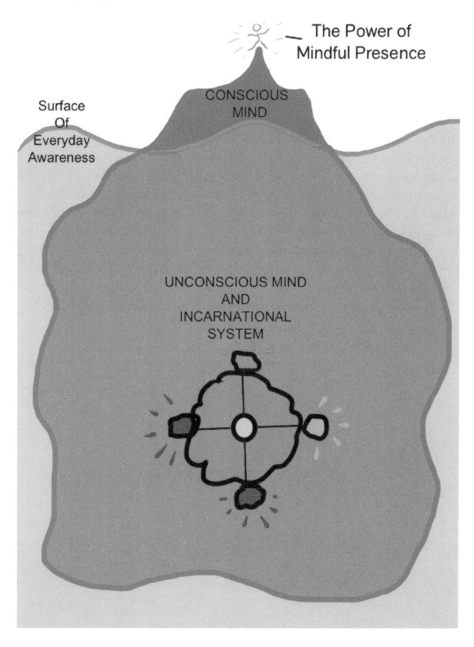

FIGURE 70

In our everyday, incarnate self, we have the power of mindful presence in all the ways I described earlier. We do not have to be at the mercy of our own depths or of the forces in the subtle environments around us. There are moments and circumstances when we can be overwhelmed, of course, and things that we do that diminish our conscious capacities for mindfulness and presence, such as drugs of various kinds (including alcohol) or other forms of addictive behavior, make us more vulnerable to incoherency. Habits of inattention and the surrender of our sovereignty to other forces can be hard to break. But this doesn't diminish the inherent power of the conscious self, though decision-making, mindful awareness, attention and intention, to be a trim tab for the incarnational system and set the course for integration and wholeness.

Furthermore, the conscious, everyday, incarnate self is the Embodied Soul in action as an Emergent Self. By doing soul—by choosing to embody and express the qualities of soul as I previously discussed—the conscious self becomes soul in action. We can in the power of our mindful presence form the link between our conscious mind and heart and the presence of soul within us and around us. We can form the golden link to the resources of our holopoietic center, releasing the holopoietic power of soul within our incarnational system and making soul active in our lives. As we do this, we truly stand in our sovereignty and build habits of coherency and wholeness in the deep incarnational system.

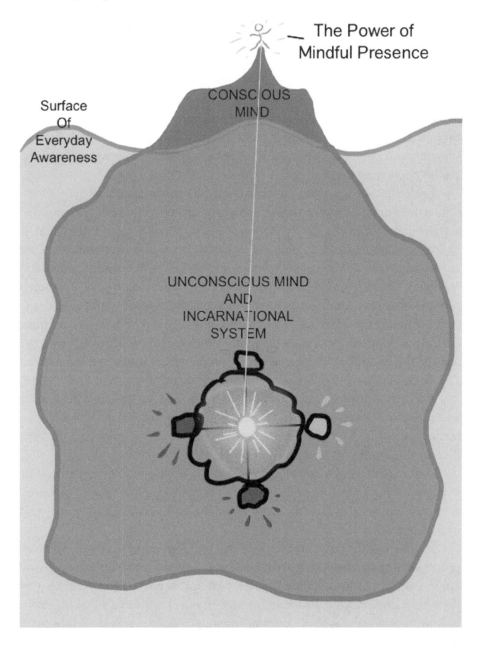

The Power of
Mindful Presence

Surface
Of
Everyday
Awareness

CONSCIOUS
MIND

UNCONSCIOUS MIND
AND
INCARNATIONAL
SYSTEM

FIGURE 71

## STANDING IN SOVEREIGNTY

The idea of "standing in Sovereignty" is key to the practice of Incarnational Spirituality. It is a key to the partnership cosmology and practice that is the context for IS. When we are in our Sovereignty, we can be strong, loving partners for others whether they are physical or non-physical beings, and in these partnerships we can create the fields that promote incarnational processes.

The Standing Exercise is an illustration of one way to go about standing in Sovereignty. However, such an exercise—or for that matter, the idea of "standing in Sovereignty" itself—is not a panacea. It's not a magical phrase. Standing in Sovereignty is a dynamic, often improvisational process adapting to one's circumstances, sometimes requiring us to step forward and take charge, sometimes requiring us to step back and to be receptive but always maintaining our holopoietic center.

Sovereignty is not willful control over the environment and over others. Rather it is mindful awareness of one's sacredness and of the presence and activity of sacredness in the environment and within others. It is the capacity to foster and nourish this sacredness. It is both attention and intention directed to fostering and maintaining the capacity for freedom and choice for oneself and for others, the kind of freedom that can allow a person to do soul. The object of the exercise is to embody as fully as one can the qualities and capacities of soul within the incarnate realm for the blessing of this world as well as for the blessing of one's own incarnational process and objectives. Sovereignty allows us to do this as mindful, improvisational, adaptive beings able to fulfill the four principles of incarnation: Identity, Boundary, Relationship, and Emergence.

Standing in Sovereignty is always an act of love. It is doing and being soul, and the soul is a presence of love. Standing in Sovereignty is an attitude, an inner posture that does not see an adversary within you but sees elements, some disassociated and thus hungry and needful in their disconnected ghostliness, that can be loved and drawn into a healing and wholeness-creating partnership. It doesn't look for culprits but for allies. It can recognize where coherency breaks down in the system and why and fix it through a loving alchemy and inclusiveness.

So when you "stand in Sovereignty," you are not simply standing in power or proclaiming your boundaries and your unique presence to the world around you. You are standing in love—love for all parts of yourself, love for the world around you, and love for others and the incarnational processes they are embodying as they, like you, attempt to build a sacred temple out of toothpicks while standing in a flowing river.

YOU as the conscious, intentional self can make the choices to be mindful and present in the moment and to "stand in Sovereignty." You as the conscious intentional self can decide to do soul and thus to become and be soul in the world. You can decide to practice an incarnational spirituality and allow its effects to permeate your life. You are the one who can deliberately open your heart and mind and tap into your generative capacities to bless and to be blessed.

You may stand on the tip of an iceberg, but you are the star!

THE CONSCIOUS SELF

FIGURE 72

## FINAL THOUGHTS: CONSCIOUSNESS,
## SELF AND THE INCARNATIONAL SYSTEM

The actual incarnational system is richer and more complex than what I have described (or drawn!) here. For instance, I am aware of connecting pathways and flows of subtle energy between the organs of our bodies and elements within nature, within the landscape, and within the subtle worlds...and for all I know with aspects of humanity and human culture. I have encountered what might be termed "angels" or "devas" of our various organs (like a deva of the eye or an angel of the stomach), and these beings might in turn be connected to particular minerals in the earth or plants growing in the local environment or even to a nearby lake or mountain. In one sense, the system we incarnate into and inhabit is really the planet itself.

But there are boundaries and there are distinct limits to how various connections impact us, though these limits are mutable and fluid, and there are certain broad categories of vibratory influence as I have described. The four-fold system I've presented here and which is the basis for the Presence exercise is a useful tool. It puts us in touch with the larger whole and with aspects of our own being in partnership with the beingness of Gaia for which we may have no words or no easily rendered descriptions.

I say this not to confuse you or to undermine what I've presented in this text but only to say that what I've described is like the old drawing of an atom, with the nucleus at the center and the electrons orbiting around it like small planets. It conveys the basics of the relationships and gets us started in engaging with the deeper structure of the atom. But the actual atom as revealed in quantum mechanics is far more complex than the miniature solar system that is its icon. So what I've been presenting you is an iconography of you as an incarnational system; further, it's a useful iconography, one that works as a means of connecting with and engaging the deep forces at work in our beingness. The Presence Exercise works; it's just not a perfectly accurate depiction of the reality it's representing. It's an icon. Now it's up to you to discover the "quantum mechanics" that underlie the images.

Earlier I used the image of an explosion for dramatic effect to illustrate an incarnational system that has become incoherent (also because I didn't know how to draw "incoherency!"). But, of course, unless a person actually dies, as I'll show in the next chapter on Act III, the incarnational systems doesn't actually explode or disintegrate. And even though one particular category of input, such as energies from the human collective or from the instincts of the body, may be the source that initiates the incoherency, there are other parts of the incarnational system that remain in balance and functioning quite well.

This is how it is in the body, too. I am having problems with my bladder and kidneys, for example, but my hands are working just fine. There's nothing wrong with my stomach or my heart or my lungs. My brain seems to be functioning alright. The fact that one part of the physical system is out of whack doesn't necessarily mean that the whole system has broken down.

This is true for the incarnational system as well, and it's one reason why our everyday consciousness can have a profound affect. Not only can it align in mindful ways with the presence of soul but also with the other incarnational connections that are functioning in balance and harmony.

We do this instinctively. For instance, if I find myself feeling jangled and out of sorts due to the human environment and energies of my workplace, I may find calm and restoration by taking a walk in woods or working in my garden. The subtle energies coming into my system through my "World Self" help to nourish my balance and wholeness.

In my case, because I work daily with subtle energies from non-physical dimensions, there are times when I begin to feel out of balance, not because I'm dealing with negative forces at all but just because contacting and holding and processing transpersonal forces is work. It takes energy and can be tiring. I find relief by turning my focus wholly into my personal self or through doing something physical.

In fact, there are times when my inner colleagues will say, "You need a break," and will shut me down, closing off the inner connections for a time (or maybe I do that to myself) at which point I "take a vacation" by doing something fun at a personal level.

At one point in my work some years ago, constant interaction with subtle beings would leave me feeling only partly in my body and thus a bit spacey. For a time I found the most restorative thing for me to do was to visit a local mall. I wouldn't go shopping, but just being in the buildings and visiting the shops and watching the people brought me back into balance. I didn't have the energy or desire to actually interact with anyone, but being in the presence of people going about their personal lives energized my "Humanity Self" and helped bring coherency back into my incarnational system.

As I say, we do things like this instinctively. When we feel low and trapped in our human thoughts and emotions, we may seek out nature or we may seek out the transpersonal by visiting places of high energy where we can find inspirational art or music or the soaring architecture of many religious structures. Too much meditation? Go to a movie, visit a comedy club, sit in a mall. Too much personal stuff? Try some meditation or walk in the woods or sit in a cathedral.

In short find the parts of you that are healthy, in balance, connected and attuned, and draw on them. That's something you can do, that's a choice you can make, that's attention you can foster, that's an intention you can provide—it's something mindful, deliberate and conscious that you can do to restore balance, indicating once more the power of the conscious mind and the personal self to make a difference.

# Chapter Five Exercises

### EXERCISE: SELF-LIGHT

There is a spiritual presence and radiance that is generated by the act of being a unique self, an individuation of sacredness. It is a Light that is born from the love and will behind your intent to manifest as an individual upon the earth, an intent that whatever its other specific characteristics may be reflects and expresses the primal will-to-be of the Generative Mystery. I call this your "Self-Light."

Discovering and coming to know your Self-Light—your own unique embodiment and radiance of spirit—is a life-long process, one that can bring great joy, wholeness, and peace. There are many ways this can be done. Here is one simple exercise:

Let your attention and consciousness move into what you experience as the center of your body. This might be your heart, it might be some other area. Feel yourself surrounded by the millions and millions of cells whose individual lives make up your life. Feel the power and wonder of those lives all blending and connecting to support your own. You are immersed in a community of life.

Feel the force and light of a presence that pervades this community, drawing it into unity, giving it one identity. This presence is you. It is the presence of your Self. It makes you one being, one identity. Its light fills all your cells and all the activities that unite them.

Let your attention and consciousness move more deeply into this presence, moving into a sphere of Light that radiates the energy which forms into your physical body. Just rest in this Light of your unique body and the Self that forms it. What does it feel like?

When you are ready, let your attention move more deeply into this Light, as if you are moving towards the source of this Self-Light. As you do so, you become aware of a deeper presence that holds and empowers your Self-Light. This is the Light of the Sacred, a Light that fosters all incarnation. You are an emergent form of this greater incarnational Light. Expressed through your individuality, this universal Light becomes your Self-Light.

When you are ready, let your awareness and attention move back from this deep Light into the radiance of your Self-Light. Feel the wonder and magic of being who you are, manifesting a unique identity and creative potential. Feel your connection to the Light that runs through all creation and the way you individuate it.

Let your Self-Light flow into your boundaries, supporting their integrity and power and nourishing the space they create that holds and protects your unique identity. Let your awareness return to your body. Feel your Self-Light permeating and uniting the presence of all your cells. Feel the wonder of your physical incarnation, of your mind and heart, your ability to think, feel, and to make choices. Feel the wonder of your spirit. Let yourself be surrounded by this Self-Light forming around you your personal aura of grace and blessing.

Standing in this Self-Light, go forth to meet your day.

This is another which people in previous classes have found very useful and helpful.

### EXERCISE: WHERE STARS MEET

Imagine a spiritual star at the center of the earth. It's a green star radiant with the power of planetary life. Imagine the light from this star rising up through the earth, surrounding you, bathing and nurturing the cells of your body and forming a chalice around you.

Imagine a spiritual star within the sun in the sky. It's a golden star radiant with the power of cosmic life. Imagine the light from this star descending from the heavens and pouring into the chalice of earthlight that surrounds you and fills your cells.

Where the green and golden lights of these two stars meet in you, a new star emerges, a radiant star of Self-Light, born of the blending of the individual and the universal, the planetary and the cosmic, the physical and the spiritual. This Self-Light surrounds you and fills you, radiating back down deep into the earth and out into space, connecting with the star below you and the star above you. You are a Chalice of Self-Light within a pillar of spiritual energy rising from the earth and descending from the cosmos.

Take a moment to feel the star of this Self-Light within and around you. It is your connection to the earth, your connection to the cosmos, your connection to your own unique and radiant Self. Take a deep breath, drawing this Light into and throughout your body; breathe out, sending this Light out into your world. Filled with this Light of Self, attuned to heaven and earth, go about your day as a star of blessing.

### EXERCISE: BEFRIENDING YOUR BODY ELEMENTAL

This is a simple exercise for attuning to and blessing your body elemental as an incarnational partner. Although you don't need to, it can help to do this exercise with a mirror in which you address your body elemental through your own eyes. Sometimes you can see the elemental looking back at you through your eyes and acknowledging your communication and your love. However if this feels "creepy" or you don't have a mirror handy, it's not necessary.

1.  Begin with the Standing Exercise, feeling the power within your body and honoring all that it offers you.

2.  Take a moment just to feel into your body, appreciating it without glamour or judgment. Think of how it offers you contact and connection with this realm without which you would be disembodied soul, unable to participate in the richness of the physical realm. Think of your body as your partner and ally. If you wish to move about, dance, touch yourself, or otherwise make the experience of your body a more physical one, feel free to do so.

3.  If there are dysfunctional or sore and painful places in your body, just acknowledge them and embrace them as part of your physical reality at this moment. Don't let them define who you are as a body, however, for there are other places in your body that are functioning just fine. Be sure to feel into them and acknowledge them as well.

4.  Attune to the cells of your body. Appreciate the community of trillions of separate lives that make it possible for you to have (and be) a body. Let your love flow to this cellular community.

5.  Attune to the ancientness of your body and to its evolutionary lineage extending from primal organic chemicals in the primeval seas of the world through the various forms your body has taken right up to what it is now in the present day. Feel the ancient wisdom that your body possesses.

6.  Feel the connection of your body to Nature itself, to the biosphere from which it emerges.

7.  Now, gathering all these feelings and attunements together, just feel yourself in the presence of this remarkable, wise, ancient organism that is your partner in life. As you do, let your attention go to that spirit of the body that holds it all together, that takes all its disparate energies, participants, lineages, and connections and turns them into a single organism, a wholeness. This is your Body Elemental, a part of Gaia that is with you always while you are embodied. Give love to this being and thank it for its service, its partnership, its caring for your body. Tell it whatever you'd like it to know, if anything. Invite it into a conscious partnership with you and ask it for its wisdom and advice as well.

8.  Take a moment of silence to intuit, feel, hear, or otherwise sense any message or communication that may come to you from this presence.

9.  When you feel complete, thank the Body Elemental for its service, thank your body itself, and take a moment to feel the oneness and partnership between the three of you who, in your trinity, from one embodied being.

## EXERCISE: THE MINDFUL BODY

This exercise isn't about being mindful of the body but rather experiencing mindfulness through the body and the body-mind. The body mind extends throughout the body but it has a focus within the gut (where, interestingly, nerve tissue identical to that within the brain has been discovered).

1.   Begin with the Standing Exercise, opening to your Sovereignty and Self-Light.

2.   Take a moment to feel your consciousness in your brain, in your head; this is where you usually experience yourself as "residing."

3.   Now let your awareness drop into your body. Let it move downward into the region of your solar plexus. Imagine that this is the seat of your brain and your awareness. Take a moment to center yourself in this place.

4.   With your physical eyes closed, imagine that you are expanding awareness out from your solar plexus into the environment around you. As if you had eyes and ears in your midriff, see how you perceive your environment from this perspective. Instead of having sensing organs at the top of a pole (in your head) imagine them now at your center and your perception and awareness unfolding out from you like a sphere. What does it feel like to be a mind at the center of your body?

5.   Feel the presence of your arms and legs, your hands and feet extending out from this sensory center. Your appendages extend your awareness outward, down towards the earth, out into the environment. They are like antennae drawing in sensation, feeling, and information to the mind of the body within your solar plexus. What is this like? What do you sense?

6.   Feel your whole body as a sensing organ and as a mind as well, with every part of you, including your head, receiving and processing subtle information, sensation, feeling, and thought. What is this body mindfulness like for you?

7.   With gratitude for your body, let your awareness rise back up the "pole," back up the spine to your head and brain where you usually experience it. When you feel centered there again, open your eyes and look around. What does this feel like? How is it different from feeling centered and aware in the middle of your body or in your body as a whole?

8.   Finish by doing the Standing Exercise again as a way of honoring your body and your wholeness.

This is a restatement of the practice I outlined earlier. Using this outline, feel free to find your own approach. At least if it's identical to what I present here, be sure that you're making it your own, understanding and experiencing the steps and inhabiting them in your own unique way. There are no cookie cutter approaches in Incarnational Spirituality!

## EXERCISE: BLESSING INWARD

1.  Begin by honoring and appreciating yourself as an individual person and as an incarnate human being. You might start this process using the Standing Exercise or the Presence Exercise, but neither is necessary. What you want here is the felt sense of approaching yourself with love and honor.

2.  Now work your way inward. You might begin by thinking about and honoring your body. Then honor and consider your heart, your feelings, and your mind, your intellect, and your thoughts. Then go more deeply into consideration of your subtle nature and then of your Interiority. Your conscious, everyday mind is all you need as you draw upon its ability to choose to do this, to give this process attention and intention. This is important. You're not doing this exercise because you have to or because someone (like David Spangler, or some book you read or class you took) told you you should do it. You're doing it because you want to, because hanging out with yourself is a joy and a pleasure, even a privilege. It's the same spirit in which you might seek out the company of a loved one. There is intention, not compulsion. You are acting in the soul quality of freedom, freely choosing to do this practice.

3.  Imagine yourself stepping into a spacious room within yourself. In this room are the other partners in your incarnational system. They are here because you're here. This is an important part of your self-image here: You are the incarnate nexus that draws these partners, the elements of the Presence Exercise for instance, together. Your choice to be incarnated has drawn them together into an incarnational system. Realizing this, you can feel love for them and gratitude. They may or may not work together with all the coherency and wholeness you would wish, but you have the power to foster such wholeness. In fact, that's why you're doing this practice. All are connected through soul, so it's soul that you're awakening and heightening through your attention, your intention and most powerfully, your love. And your partners return that love for through your choice to be incarnated, you're giving them an opportunity to be together, to work together, and in the process bring something new and emergent into being.

4.  Standing in this spacious, imaginary inner space, give your attention to soul which is all around you, the very atmosphere and structure of this space though it may be diffuse. And here is the important secret behind Blessing Inward. You don't invoke soul by calling out to something separate from you.

You inhabit it and awaken it by being it. Think of the capacities of soul, all capacities that you can express as a conscious, everyday self. You don't have to be a saint, a master, an adept, a spiritual Olympian, to be soul. You become soul by doing soul. You become soul by loving, by standing in your whole identity, by knowing and honoring your boundaries, by engaging in connection and relationship with the world, by opening yourself to growth and emergence, by appreciating and expressing when appropriate and necessary your freedom and your will. You become soul by being holopoietic, doing whatever you can to create wholeness.

5.    The key touch point into soul and into doing this practice is love. So occupy this inner space with love and in love. Avoid entering into combat or antagonism with any part of yourself. Your purpose is not to be judgmental or adversarial. Your purpose is to act in a soulful, loving way within yourself, towards yourself, towards all parts of you. So at this point, imagine your love radiating out and filling this space. Love the part of you connected to the world, love the part of you connected to humanity, love the part of you connected to the transpersonal and the subtle worlds, love the part of you connected to your personality and your body. And love all the disconnected hungry ghosts that may be there. Whatever your faults and flaws, your strengths and accomplishments, imply love the space in which they exist in you. This is a gentle exercise. You're not trying to make anything happen; rather you're giving attention to being something, to doing love and being soul. In this process, you may think of how the sacred accepts, honors and loves you unconditionally and express that same love to all the parts of you.

6.    As you stand in this love, call to mind whatever you wish about yourself that either pleases or bothers you. If there are parts of you that need healing, whether they are physical or psychological, call them forth, but—and this is very important—not with the intent to heal them and certainly not to judge them. Your intent is simply to love and connect with them. You are being a holopoietic force, inclusiveness personified, demanding only that whatever stays in your field participate in this presence of soul, i.e. that it, too, becomes soul-filled and expressive of the capacities of soul as best it can. By simply being a presence, you are heightening that presence, bringing blessing to all parts of yourself and to your incarnational system as a whole.

7.    Do this for as long as feel comfortable. There is no strain about it. It could be for a long time or a very short time. The point is not duration but attentiveness and strength of intent. You are the conscious, mindful agency of soul in the midst of your incarnational system. You are the conscious, mindful agency of holopoiesis within yourself, set into motion by your own choice, your attention and intention, and however long you hold this space, it is enough.

When you are finished, simply give thanks to all parts of you and resume your outer life, knowing you can reenter this inner space with attention and intention any time you wish, for as long as you wish.

## EXERCISE: GRAIL SPACE

I use the term "Grail Space" to mean any space that holds sacredness, just as in legend the Holy Grail held the transformative blood of Christ. Sacredness in this instance manifests as the incarnational consciousness and process that brings creation into being and sustains it in its unfoldment

We live in Grail Space. The entire cosmos is the primal Grail Space holding the sacredness of the Generative Mystery which I call the Sacred. But this primal Grail Space can be accentuated in local space at any time that we invoke the presence and flow of sacredness by honoring the incarnational process through which it manifests.

The practice of creating a local Grail space is one of standing in our own Self-Light and engaging the immediate environment around us and everything within it to evoke more fully the incarnational Light that flows from the primal Grail Space, i.e. from the Sacred itself. Fundamentally, this is a practice of extending love to everything around us. It is an act of honoring and relating to our environment in such a way that it responds energetically to our presence, awakening and expressing its own Grail capacities. It is the act of mutual holding that turns the environment, with ourselves in it, into a Grail in which sacredness may shine forth

The creation of Grail Space is a reciprocal act, not something we do to something else. It is an act of extending an invitation, allowing the environment to respond as fully as it can in the moment. Grail Space is born of relationship and mutual engagement based on honoring the sovereignty and identity of all involved

Creating Grail Space is really a simple process, but I break it down into a number of steps just so you can get a sense of the procedure. To read it, it can seem like a lot, but it's really a very fast, simple process. The main difference between this technique and simply sending love into your environment is the connection with the incarnational process and identity of everything about you in a partnership modality. You are joining with the Incarnational Light—the Light of Identity—within the things in your environment to create a mutually beneficial space or field into which sacredness may be invoked.

One way to think of this is as if everything in your environment is alive and a person and you are joining hands with them to form a great circle. This circle creates the Grail Space, and into it sacredness is invoked.

THE EXERCISE

1.  Begin by standing in your own Sovereignty, in the felt sense of your unique identity and your connection to your soul and to the sacred. If you wish, you can imagine this Sovereignty as a "spine" of Light within you, an axis around which your physical and subtle bodies develop and align.

2.  Imagine this spine of Light becoming brighter and brighter with the energy of your own incarnational process as it unfolds from the love within your Soul and within the Sacred of which it is a part. As this Light becomes brighter within you, it expands and enfolds you.

3.  Imagine yourself standing in an oval of Light emanating from your "spine" of Sovereignty and individuality, an oval that surrounds you on all sides, top and bottom, connecting you with the energies of the world. It forms and radiates from you as a personal Grail, an incarnational field holding sacredness.

4.  Take a moment to survey your immediate environment, taking note of all the things that are in it. Do so as a witness in a non-judgmental way, as if seeing these things for the first time with beginner's mind. You don't have to focus on each item separately but just take in the general arrangement, content and feel of the space around you.

5.  Everything in your immediate environment is an expression of the Sacred. Everything you see participates in the primal Grail Space. Everything has within itself a "spine" of incarnational intent and Light, its own form of Sovereignty and identity. Imagine yourself surrounded with a multitude of "grails of Light" emanating from everything in the space around you. In your heart, acknowledge and give honor to the presence of all these "spines" or "grails" of incarnational and sacred Light.

6.  Imagine your aura of Self-Light—your Grail of sacredness and incarnational Light—expanding into the room, joining in love with the myriad multitude of Lights all around you. Feel your Light augmenting and blending with the Lights around you, feel their Lights blending with an augmenting your own. You are forming a subtle partnership with your environment and everything seen and unseen within it. Feel this partnership turning your immediate, local environment into a Grail that you and all the things around you collaborate to create, a Grail you share.

7.  The felt sense of this field and the partnership and "circle" of reciprocal energy that generates it is the Grail Space. It is a field of collaborative partnership and support in the incarnational process with everything around you in your local space, a partnership that can receive and hold a Presence of sacredness.

8.  Standing in this Grail Space, acknowledge this Presence of sacredness

heightened in yourself and your environment. Imagine it being held in this space, and then overflowing into the larger world beyond, a source of energy, blessing, love, and life.

9.   Stay in this Grail Space as long as feels comfortable. When you feel tired or restless, simply draw your Self-Light back into yourself, giving thanks to your energy partners for their participation. Imagine their incarnational light moving back into themselves as well, knowing the environment you share will resonate with the Light and Presence you have collectively invoked for as long as it is able.

Stand in your Sovereignty, acknowledging your wholeness your integrity, your identity, and your connection to the Sacred. Then go about your daily affairs.

### EXERCISE: THE TOUCH OF LOVE
*This is a form of Blessing Forward.*

1.   Begin with the Standing exercise and feel the strength and integrity of your own presence. This is your unique contribution to the world. Feel into your Sovereignty and Self-Light. Along the axis of your Sovereignty, feel yourself connected to heaven and to earth.

2.   Feel this connection radiating within you as a felt sense of presence and love, a willingness to be here in this world, right now at this time, because you are a unique expression of sacredness. Experience it as a presence of blessing radiating through your body.

3.   Now let this presence of connectedness, Self-Light and blessing flow as if it were a liquid or an electric current down your arms, into your hands and into the tips of your fingers. Feel this energy alive and bursting at your fingertips. This is where your blessing presence lives at this moment, right in your fingertips. It gives you a loving touch.

4.   Now touch something. It can be anything. But as you touch it, imagine that you are using the power in your fingertips to hold it, support it, uplift it, and honor its sovereignty, its unique nature, its gift of being. You are touching its incarnation with your own, in honor of the incarnational process and spirit itself .You are creating for a moment a connection of shared presence in this world. You are partners in incarnation and from this blessing can emerge.

5.   When you feel complete (and it may only take a second), let go. If you wish, touch something else. Indeed, the presence of love in your fingers can become automatic with practice, intentionality, and mindfulness, allowing you to spread blessings wherever your fingers touch as you move through your day.

NOTE:   We touch each other's incarnations all the time.  The energies we project to each other, the way we think of each other, the feelings we surround others with, the looks we give, the tones of voice, the words we use:  all these are touches.  But are they touches that help us to incarnate and help the incarnation of another, or do they hinder and obstruct?  That is what only we can determine.

This incarnational touch of love can be practiced in a number of ways.  For example, you could step into your Sovereignty and Self-Light presence and let its power flow through your eyes.  Or you can listen through its influence.  Or this presence could fill your mouth, shaping and living in your speech.  It can live in every part of you, flow out of every part of you and everything you do so that as you go through your day, the world of incarnation is easier, brighter, more coherent and integrated than it might have been otherwise.

# CHAPTER 6 ACT III:  DEATH AND BEYOND

As I've said, incarnation is a play in three acts. We've looked at the first two acts, and now we come to the third one. I have to say off the bat that this is not an area in which I have much expertise. My work and research has been pretty focused on the incarnational process leading up to birth and then in the dynamics of our ordinary life. My experience with the realms after death, the post-mortem realms, is limited, and while I can access some general information about what happens and what those realms are like, it's not very detailed, I'm sorry to say. I have friends who are much more attuned to this area of working with the "dead" and more knowledgeable than I. And the theme of this text is "Partnering with Earth," after all. What happens when we're going "Up to Heaven" is really the topic for another text altogether! Still, our discussion of incarnation would not be complete without some mention of Act III.

Death is not the end of the incarnation, though it is the end of the physical side of it. There has always been great interest in whether or not our personality — our sense of ourselves as a unique, individual entity — survives the death of the body. Remembering at least two deaths in prior lives, I can state unequivocally that it does. But not always in ways we expect or imagine. Death is every bit as complex and transformative in its effects upon us as birth. It's rather like an explosion in that the incarnational system that has sustained and been part of us throughout our physical life now comes apart with different bits going in different directions.

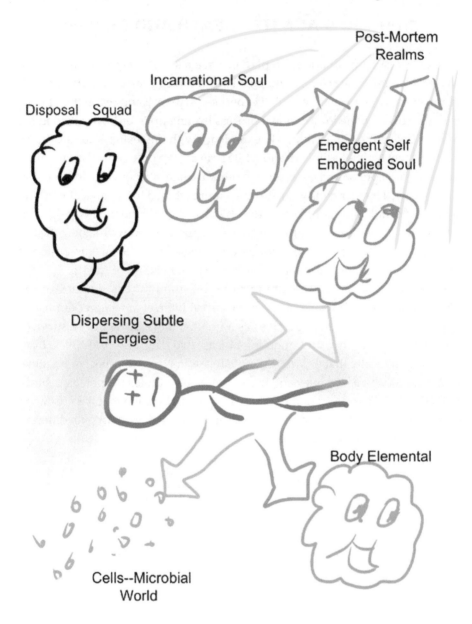

Post-Mortem
Realms

Incarnational Soul

Disposal   Squad

Emergent Self
Embodied Soul

Dispersing Subtle
Energies

Body Elemental

Cells--Microbial
World

FIGURE 73

To understand death from an energetic point of view, it's important to understand how complex a system we are while embodied. We have all the connections to humanity and to the earth and to Gaia that I've described, we are a focus for various kinds of subtle energies, we live in the midst of a hive community of trillions of cells with their individual energies and consciousness, we have a body elemental, subtle bodies, relational fields, and so on—and there are the subtle energies that bind and hold all this conglomeration together.

At death all this comes apart. The bonds are loosened and dissolve, sometimes slowly if the dying process is gradual and sometimes quickly and explosively if the death is sudden.

At the point of death, the incarnate person—the amalgam of Emergent Self and Embodied Soul—is freed from the body. Generally at that point three or four things can happen, but I'll get to that in a moment. The body, though, is still "alive." That is, it's constituent parts are still active up to a point. Functioning stops fairly swiftly, but the individual cells may continue living, depending on what and where they are in the body ecosystem. Soon, of course, they will all die as food and oxygen no long reach them. In effect, through decay they enter into the great pool of life that is the microbial world.

The body elemental leaves fairly quickly, carrying with it the impress of the body and self with which it was associated. This impress fades but qualities which the body elemental learned during the incarnation remain. In effect, the body elemental is an evolving entity, too. It returns to its elemental realm, of which I know next to nothing. But I believe from some things my inner colleagues have said from time to time that body elementals retain some basic memory or traces of the lives of which they were a part. This is not a memory of events per se but of qualities and of vibrational impressions. So, for instance, if a person in his or her life regularly meditated and drew transpersonal energies into his or her body, the contact with these energies would impress itself upon the body elemental, making it more than usually sensitive and awake to such higher forces.

At death as well, there is a "cloud" of subtle energies that begins to disperse. The etheric body may begin to break down immediately as part of this "cloud", although if it has a source of energy to sustain it, it may last for a time. It becomes an etheric shell, looking like the person who has deceased but not possessing any selfhood. It does, however, retain memory patterns which can be activated, so it can act in an automatic way along habit tracks; it can be a bit like one of those audioanimatronic robots of dead Presidents you see at places like Disneyland, able to mimic the real person and capable of limited interaction, depending on their programming, but not at all the real person. Such etheric corpses or shells are one of the explanations behind ghost sightings. Normally the etheric body is wholly dispersed after about three days, but again, if there is some source of energy sustaining it, like the electricity running the Abraham Lincoln robot at Disneyland, it can maintain some semblance of form and function for a longer time. Where would this energy come from? There are three likely places. One is from the deceased himself or herself if he or she has become earthbound.

One is from the human collective if the individual was very well known and loved (or hated, for that matter—energy is energy, after all). And the third is from close relatives or family who may feed energy to this etheric form in their reluctance to let the individual go. But the latter two cases are, I think, rare, and in any event, the natural processes of etheric decay will eventually win out. What is more likely is that the collective thinking and feeling—or that of relatives if held with sufficient intensity and will—may create a thought-form, an astral image, of the individual. Such a thought-form really has less to do with the individual himself or herself and more with how others saw that person and are projecting their own thoughts and feelings into the astral or imaginal realm. But this has nothing to do with the death process.

The cloud of subtle energies also include remnants of the immediate subtle fields that expressed the body-bound thinking and feeling of the individual as well as the subtle energy connections that made up the incarnational system, the connections to Gaia, nature, land, humanity, etc. All these energy connections are usually broken at death. Note that the deeper connections of the soul—the individual—with these things are not broken at all, but the actual energy structure of the incarnational system built up during the pre-birth, Act I stage is now broken and dispersed as it is no longer necessary. All connections that are essential and important and part of the life and consciousness of the individual are retained and held in the Emergent Self/Embodied Soul amalgam that is now moving on into the post-mortem realms; these are soul connections. It's their subtle energy counterparts that held the matrix of the physical incarnation that are released and which now disperse as the "cloud" of subtle energies.

In point of fact, there is a great deal of subtle energy that can be released at death, most of it connected to the individual and some of it related to the passing of a threshold (just as subtle energies are generated and released at birth). This is one reason why death sacrifice has been a tool to generate subtle forces for various purposes, often nefarious ones.

At death, a "disposal squad" usually shows up as well. These are the subtle world equivalent to decay bacteria; I'm not sure how to describe them. I think of them as part of the elemental kingdoms. Their function is to remove and absorb and clean up the "left over" or dispersing subtle forces and energies released when the incarnational system breaks apart and dissolves. In effect, they get rid of the "cloud" of dispersing subtle energies or those elements of the cloud that don't dissolve or transform on their own. These beings or elemental forces can be toxic to some degree, just as decay bacteria are. It's not that they're "negative" entities, only that they are "ingesting" and removing what is no longer needed, and their vibe has a "spin" to it that is opposite to the vibrational "spin" of living entities.

Because of this cloud of dispersing subtle forces, some of which can be negative depending on the nature of the death and the nature of the individual who just died (a hateful person leaves behind some not-very-nice subtle energies, for instance), and the presence and work of the "disposal squad," the place where a death occurs can feel energetically uncomfortable and even negative. Accentuating this is the fact that in many cultures there is such a fear of death and the energy of that fear, not to mention of grief and loss, gets projected into the situation as well. So there are reasons to be energetically careful around death and to practice good energy hygiene for personal cleansing and for cleansing the scene itself.

Of course, I'm speaking generally here. So much depends on the consciousness of the person who has died and those around him or her. The death process and the death scene can certainly be a place of great Light and love and blessing and peacefulness. Though there will still be a disposal squad and still subtle energies to be disposed of, all this can happen very swiftly and in great harmony. Welcoming, appreciating and loving what happens at death and immediately after creates an environment in which everyone can do their work and all the right processes can take place in harmony and with blessing. I should note here in passing that cremation is one way in which any and all potentially lingering or toxic subtle energies around a body can be quickly and powerfully cleansed and transmuted. Burial is a much longer process, though ultimately the presence of earth forces is just as cleansing as those of fire. They just work more slowly.

What may be problematic is the modern Western tendency to put corpses into hermetically sealed coffins that resist and slow down the decaying process. As long as the body exists, it can be a touch point for subtle forces that were associated with it and which now have had their natural process of dispersal and transformation obstructed and delayed.

This is just a broad description of what happens to the subtle energies and incarnational system of the individual at death. I'm sure there's much I'm missing here and details that I'm unaware of. As I said, this is not an area where I've done much research or work, so there's much more that I don't know than what I do. But having said that and having looked at the subtle energy side of things, what happens to the individual. In the picture above, the individual, who is the blend of Emergent Self and Embodied Soul (at this point, they are pretty much one and the same), is headed off to the Post-Mortem realms, the realms of Light, along with the Incarnational Soul whose job is nearing completion, too. What happens now?

POSSIBLE
STATES
AFTER
DEATH

Post-Mortem
Realms

Heading On--
"To Infinity
And Beyond!"

Curious or Helpful--
Staying Close for
A Time

Hanging On & Staying

"What
Happened?"

Lost
(But Help Is On The Way)

Earthbound

FIGURE 74

When I was ten years old or so, I was home alone one evening while my parents went out for a short time. I was sitting on a sofa in our living room reading when I saw movement out of the corner of my eye. Looking up, I saw a man and a woman coming down the hall from where our bedrooms were located. They were dressed well but looked disheveled, and their faces were wild. I thought that they were angry but later thinking back on it, I realized they were actually frightened and lost.

They came down the hall towards me and seemed focused on me, though I'm not sure they did actually see me. Startled and frightened, I jumped up and hid under a table. It had a tablecloth that came down to the floor on all sides, but the bottom of the cloth was a fringe of dangling threads that let me peer through them to see what was happening.

The couple were apparently speaking, as their mouths were open and moving, but I couldn't hear anything. They came into the living room, looking around in distress. At that moment, a shining figure appeared behind them, one of the "light beings" that I often saw in those days. At the time I just assumed they were angels. This being enfolded the couple in light, just as if it had surrounded them with wings or had opened a very wide cloak and wrapped it around them. It then looked right at me, smiled and said in words I heard in my mind, "I'm sorry they frightened you. They don't mean harm. They were just killed in an automobile accident, but didn't know they were dead. Unfortunately, we didn't locate them until just now. I'll take them where they can get help now." And with that they all disappeared.

I've never had an experience like that since, but it illustrates one of four possible things that can happen after death, particularly if the death was sudden, violent and unexpected. The individual may not realize at first that he or she is dead and may feel lost. But help is never far away in such instances to take the individual in hand and help them into the post-mortem realms.

Much more troublesome are those who for one reason or another are so attached to the physical plane that they refuse to move on, becoming "earthbound." Such an individual actively resists moving on and clings to the memory of its former physical existence.

From what I'm told, earthbound and lost souls are rarities, and both are the object of "rescue" missions mounted by both subtle world beings and physical individuals whose job it is to work with the dead from this side of things. Sometimes a person who is earthbound or lost is resistant to or even unaware of attempts to reach them from the subtle dimensions, but they can be reached by a physical person since their consciousness is still more attuned to this side of the veil than to the side on which they're now living.

Sometimes people are curious or wish to be comforting and helpful, particularly to loved ones who remain in physical incarnation. They can stay close to the incarnate world for a time, often with help from more experienced and capable subtle beings. They're not lost—they know full well they're dead and where they are and what has happened—and they're not earthbound—

they're fully capable of moving on—but they want to do what they can to ease the transition their death has caused for those whom they love and have left behind.

The majority of those who die, however, move on into the post-mortem realms. Even if they have a desire to remain and comfort loved ones still in incarnation, they may not be able to do so or those helping them "on the other side" deem it not a wise thing to do for everyone's sake. Each case is unique. Even if they do move on, it may then be possible for them to return at a later date.

An example of this was my father. I told his story back in 19:30. He had died suddenly of a heart attack and had immediately been whisked off to the post-mortem realms lest his obsession with "finishing his books" tie him to the physical realm. It was some months later that he appeared to me in a dream to explain what had happened. Since then he has been back to contact me several times.

My mother, on the other hand, had no such obsessions. She died in Ohio a year or so before my Dad, and minutes after her death, she appeared to me in my living room looking radiant, joyful, and absolutely splendid—and a good deal younger than the ninety years she had when she died.

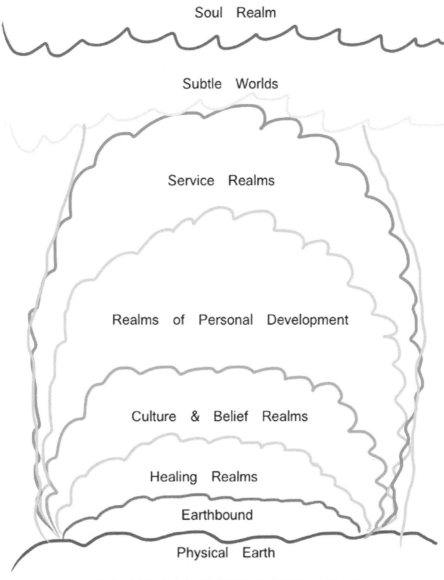

Soul   Realm

Subtle   Worlds

Service   Realms

Realms   of   Personal   Development

Culture   &   Belief   Realms

Healing   Realms

Earthbound

Physical   Earth

# POST-MORTEM REALMS

FIGURE 75

The picture above is a very simple diagram of some of the possible states and stages found in the post-mortem realms based on some limited personal experience of having visited these realms, information from inner colleagues, and insights from friends whose inner work takes them into contact with "the dead" and with these realms than my work has done. It's very simplified, but I believe accurate as far as it goes.

The post-mortem realms exist as a specific part of the inner worlds with the express purpose of enabling an incarnate person to re-enter the subtle worlds and regain full functioning in their multi-dimensional nature as souls. I think of it as the energetic equivalent to a hyperbaric decompression chamber that deep sea divers use when they return to the surface to avoid getting the bends. It is a series of realms designed to harvest the fruits of the incarnation, heal what might need to be healed, and bring the individual back into his or her full soul consciousness.

It doesn't always work like this. I understand that individuals for one reason or another may jump back into incarnation from some point within the post-mortem realms without ever fully completing the cycle; it would be like going from Act III in a play straight back into Act I or even in some circumstances Act II without taking some time off outside the theater. When this happens, the previous life has an even greater shaping influence on the new life than it ordinarily would have. But I am also given to understand that this is not the normal course of events. Perhaps there is an urgent need for the individual soul to reembody immediately for some reason or perhaps the individual is in an earthbound state that pulls him or her back into incarnation quickly because they don't want to be without a body. Again, there could be any number of different reasons as each case is individual and unique.

So moving upwards into increasingly higher or more complex and multidimensional energy states, we have the following:

Earthbound: This is the subtle energy realm closest to the earth plane. It might be in the etheric or the astral or close to them. This level can include both those who are truly earthbound and stuck and those who are temporarily lost and wandering close to the physical plane. The latter folks will receive help fairly quickly, but the former may languish in an earthbound state for a very long time depending entirely on their willingness to let go and to move on. This is NOT a realm of punishment. There are NO realms of punishment in the post-mortem realms. But there are realms that are punishing to those in them because they reflect the desire and will of that individual for self-punishment. The earthbound state can take two major forms. One, which I think is the more rare of the two, is that the individual is truly bound to the physical plane through obsessive attachment and emotion (which can include a fear of "moving on"). The other is that the individual is bound to certain attitudes and beliefs and in particular emotional and mental states that keep them bound to very limited and dark conditions. Someone deeply sunk into depression and self-loathing and carrying that attitude over into the post-mortem state may remain in that kind of funk and create an environment that reflects it. The person is not bound literally to the physical plane but he or she is bound to emotional or mental states originating in the physical state. They are never without help, but I'm told they can be so fearful or so self-absorbed that it's very difficult for help to reach them or for them to acknowledge or accept the presence of another. In some cases, they are just stubborn and refusing to believe they're dead or refusing to move on because they are bound to grievances they don't wish to release. This earthbound region generally reflects the realms of "stuckness" mirroring the stuck states of mind and feeling that we can get into.

- Healing Realms: These are areas, usually very temporary, that are akin to rest areas or hospitals for souls that have died after a long and debilitating illness or who arrive in the post-mortem realms damaged and wounded in some manner. They are not so damaged that they've become stuck, so they're not earthbound, but they need a time of recuperation. I'm told that many souls who arrive in this manner sleep through this stage while healing takes place, rather like a caterpillar in a cocoon, and then awaken refreshed and ready to move on.

- Culture and Belief Realms: A person may die with very strong expectations of what the afterlife will be like based on cultural or religious beliefs. They may also be very tied to a particular cultural, ethnic, or religious identity. To prevent shock and to ease them into the larger realities of soul life where such cultural, ethnic and religious beliefs don't matter or don't reflect the reality of things, a soul may find himself or herself after death in a realm created to perfectly model his or her expectations. Thus a Christian finds himself more or less in a Christian heaven or at least in a world that seems very familiar and earth-like, with houses and neighborhood, cities, churches and the like. The idea is to give the individual something familiar to stand on while learning how to adjust to non-physical reality.

- Realms of Personal Development: This is by far and away the largest section of the post-mortem realms. It is where most souls go either directly after death or after spending some time in the healing realms or in a culture or belief realm. This is where the individual can pursue the developmental arc of the incarnation, learning things they had wished to learn on earth, having experiences they may have wished for, expanding and developing themselves and regaining skills in navigating and expressing in non-physical reality. The purpose of this area is to round out the life, tie up loose ends, so to speak, and enable the soul to move on into the soul realms.

- Service Realms: Not all souls go here, but some do—perhaps many do, I don't know. This represents those individuals who use their proximity to incarnation as a connecting link back to incarnate humanity in order to give service. The incarnational self is still available to such a person; they haven't fully transited into a full soul consciousness. Consequently they can more easily return to earth and engage with incarnate consciousness. They can function as guides, teachers, helpers, and so forth. This is not to say that a being in the soul realm cannot do this as well; it's only to say that a person in the post-mortem realm is still technically and energetically in incarnation and thus has a certain "in" with planetary conditions that can be of benefit.

At some point, the individual fully moves on out of the post-mortem realms and into the subtle world and back into the soul level, thus completing fully the three-act arc of the incarnation. At that point, the individual is no longer incarnate but is completely and truly soul once again.

### THE INCARNATIONAL SOUL

One question that arises is the fate of the Incarnational Soul in the post-mortem realms. My picture in 25:1 shows both the Incarnational Soul and the Embodied Soul headed off for the post-mortem realms. This is only partly accurate. The post-mortem realms function to consolidate the blending of Emergent Self and the Embodied Soul; in this process, the Incarnational Soul may still play a part, but in fact much of its work is done. Without the influence of the body-mind and the physical plane in general pulling the Embodied Soul and the Emergent Self in one direction, the role of the Incarnational Soul as a "High Self" and counterweight to this influence is no longer needed, generally speaking. So, as I understand it, at death, the Incarnational Soul pretty much merges back into the Soul itself, that is, the Planetary Soul. The Soul itself more or less takes over the process of overlighting Act III and the resolution of the incarnational project.

However, I gather there are exceptions to this. If the individual is earthbound or the Embodied Soul has never really awakened or emerged as a force in the individual life, then the Incarnational Soul remains as an overlighting High Self. And there may be other exceptions as well, though I am unclear about this. One inner colleague mentioned to me once that if an individual moves back into incarnation early without fully returning to or merging with the Soul proper — that is, it incarnates not from the soul level but from somewhere within the post-mortem realms, then the Incarnational Soul continues and oversees this process. In such a case, you have a new incarnate self emerging with the new life but it has the same Incarnational Soul as in a previous life.

Also, I gather there are instances when an individual still within the post-mortem realms who wishes to perform some form of service to the people within the incarnate realm may retain or blend with the Incarnational Soul rather than the Planetary Soul because the former already has connections with the incarnate realm that can prove useful.

Again, I must emphasize that this has not been an area in which I have much experience, and most of my inner colleagues are also focused in other directions (and several of them have been out of incarnation themselves for a very long time and thus don't have recent experience with the post-mortem realms. So all I can do is offer some broad-brush strokes of insight and information with one sure bit of knowledge: we will all be researching and experiencing this at first hand for ourselves eventually! And I have no doubt the reality will be delightfully more wondrous and powerful than anything I'm able to describe.

There is one more thing I can say about Act III based on information from my inner colleagues and that is that death evolves as well. Although the organic death of the body is the same now as it was for our Cro-Magnon ancestors, what happens in the subtle worlds when someone dies and the nature of the post-mortem worlds is not. As human consciousness, both individually and collectively, has developed, changed and evolved, the complexity of the incarnational system has evolved as well. As I understand it, millennia ago the strength and complexity of individuality of the incarnate self was not what it is now. Individuality existed in the soul but was not projected that clearly or strongly into its incarnate field. Human consciousness was more collective in its nature, and as a consequence, when a person died, there wasn't a lot that survived and went on into the post-mortem realms, at least not compared to a modern person.

This is not to say that ancient person just disappeared at death, only that what remained and was retrieved wasn't as complex and filled with memory and awareness as is true today, speaking generally. There were always exceptions.

### ENDINGS AND THE FEAR OF DEATH

Now I want to say a couple of things about death itself and the fear of death. Years ago Woody Allen made a wonderful crack about not fearing death but just not wanting to be there when it happened! Ha! We probably all can relate to that.

Let me be personal for a moment. I am someone who by all rights should have no fear of death. My experiences with the subtle worlds, my inner journeys, my communications with non-physical beings and, more rarely, with those who are newly arrived in the post-mortem worlds, all give me an absolute sense of the continuity of life and the senselessness of fearing what is a natural portal back into the realms of spirit. And yet there are times when the fear of death arises unexpectedly but strongly within me, coming, it seems, out of nowhere and leaving me to ask why.

Exploring this, I've come up with several explanations. The first is that for some reason in the moment, I've touched into and am experiencing the fear of death that exists in the human collective. I've certainly experienced other thought-forms and feelings that move through this collective field we all participate in, so there's nothing unusual in the fact that I might experience this particular emotion as well. However, while I know this explanation is true, it's not the whole picture.

So one day I sat down to go more deeply into this feeling, deliberately invoking this fear within me and then seeing what it was connected to within my incarnational system. What I experienced was quite enlightening and helpful. It gave me more insight into the complexity and wonder of the communion of beings and intelligences that we call our incarnation.

It was this exploration that led me to the insights that I wrote about earlier. Parts of me "went on," so to speak and continued in existence as a coherent system. What I normally think of as "myself" or my personality does so, for instance, moving on into the spiritual realms. But there are parts of me that do not and that in fact come to an end. There is no continuation for them, at least not in the form in which they have existed as part of my incarnational system.

My cells certainly come to an end, though in some ways it may not really be an ending but a transmigration into other forms. I don't know. My body elemental comes to a kind of an end, but on the other hand, it doesn't die in the way I do as a body and is essential immortal, though it does change as it becomes the body elemental of someone else's new incarnation. However, my body mind and brain mind do come to an end. No body, no body-mind, no brain, no brain-mind. I suppose you could say that's a no brainer! I discovered in exploring this that my body-mind does identify itself as "me," or at least a part of me, but it will not continue on into the post-mortem and spiritual worlds as I do. It ends. Death for the body is an ending. I found much of my fear of death rooted in this deep body place.

On the other hand, there is a profound mystery here. Part of the body-mind does go on because it contributes to and becomes part of the "amalgam" I've written about, the blending of soul and matter and body. There is a long tradition in esoteric and spiritual thought that our destiny is to learn to "translate" our bodies so that they don't die but are transfigured into spiritual substance. The model for this in the West is, of course, Jesus and his Ascension. I think a lot of nonsense is written about this, much of it privileging the transcendental and diminishing the physicality of the body, as if the only way a body can be spiritual and "right" is to turn into Light. But there is also a mystery here, a deep truth that incarnation is about the transubstantiation of matter and spirit. (The problem comes when we privilege the spirit part and think only that its matter that has to be transubstantiated and transformed into a "higher state," when it would be more accurate to say that both matter and spirit in partnership are being alchemized into a combined and emergent state which has yet to fully appear on this planet; in this, spirit is undergoing change and must undergo change as much as matter.) I do not fully understand all this yet, but at the least it means that we learn to carry into the spiritual realm some of the attributes of matter in the form of some of the qualities and attributes of being physically a human being, creating a change in the texture of spirit and of the soul, if I may call it that.

We like to say that death is not an ending but just a transition, a passage into another phase of life, a beginning of something new. That is right, but death is also an ending, certainly for some parts of us. The incarnational system ceases to be in the way it has been throughout the physical life; the "team" splits up, so to speak. The relational field I create comes to an end. The relationships don't end, necessarily, but the form of them does. If I died at this instance, I would still be in a deep and loving relationship with Julie and with my children. That doesn't change. But I wouldn't be in a physical relationship with them any more, and what is possible in a physical relationship isn't possible or is expressed in a different way in a non-physical one. So something ends.

This idea of ending is really very important. It's one of the vital experiences that incarnational life offers. One of the characteristics of the subtle worlds is that there are no endings, at least not in the way we experience them. Shapes change, patterns change, there is fluidity, there is growth and evolution, but there is also continuity. To say, "I sacrifice my life for you" has virtually no meaning in the subtle worlds because life can't be sacrificed in the sense of being brought to an end, especially with no hope of continuity. But it can be sacrificed here. Things can be lost, things can come to an end. The experience of this is immensely important, I think, to soul consciousness and is one reason incarnation in a physical body is valued. The experience of ending adds something to the soul in the way of texture and depth. If and when we learn to simply transfigure and translate our physical bodies, turning their matter into Light, this may change. Perhaps by then we won't need the experience of endings, or perhaps it will take different forms. I don't know. That understanding is above my pay grade. But for now, knowing and experiencing that some things end is important. It is challenging, it carries a sense of loss with it, it undoubtedly is a root for the fear that surrounds death. But it is part of the richness of what incarnation offers.

There is one other aspect to this fear of death that I discovered. This, however, is not a natural thing but something created and perpetuated as a thought form by human beings over a very long period of time and continuing today. I sometimes think of it as the "karma of death."

Because death is an ending AND a portal out of this world for that which endures and continues, it has the effect of removing something from this world. If I die, I'm no longer here, at least not as I was.

Removal can be a good thing as it can make room for something else. But removal can also be seen as a strategy for what I don't like whether it should be removed or not. In this way, death becomes like a waste can or a disposal unit. If I don't like it, kill it! Then it won't be around to bother me anymore.

One of the blind alleys that humanity has stumbled into, in my opinion, is that of viewing death as a solution to what we don't like or want around. In terms of relationships, this represents a lack of imagination and willingness to do the extra work required to create wholeness out of conflict. Why try to understand you, work out our differences, even love you and appreciate you when I can just kill you and get you out of my face, presumably forever? It's the lazy person's way of resolving differences.

By now in our checkered history, killing has become practically a science, an art form, and certainly an expectation. Nations prepare for war and go to war; warlords commit genocide; individuals murder each other; individuals murder themselves. All to get rid of what appears as an intolerable bother without having to think of or imagine alternate routes to harmony and wholeness.

Imagine, though, the effect of this on the thought-form and energy of death itself? This is what I discovered, much to my amazement when I went through this exercise of attunement. If I visualize death as a river, then around it is a wasteland of a garbage dump, the sense that this is where we send things when we don't want them. It's a toxic thought form, and there's no wonder that the intuition of it can cause fear.

This doesn't mean that everyone who dies will or must experience this. We can certainly have graceful, beautiful, mindful deaths. But what it means is that when we think of death and try to approach it energetically, chances are good we will run into this cloud of revulsion, especially if we already have some fear or trepidation around death. It's just another factor that makes death a fearsome thing that we'd like to deny as long as possible.

And frankly, though this may be projection (and certainly is speculation) on my part, I think the Angel of Death is not satisfied at being seen as a garbage disposal and not as a teacher and partner in the incarnational enterprise.

# CHAPTER 7: SUMMATION
# AND FINAL OBSERVATIONS

The material we've covered in this text only scratches the surface of the mystery and wonder of incarnation or of the capacities we have as incarnate beings. When I was presented when I was seventeen with the vision of the radiant incarnate self, it came with a sense that there was a shift of focus taking place in the subtle or spiritual worlds that sought to redefine spirituality in terms of our earthly life rather than in terms of a transcendent or transpersonal reality. The emphasis was on the value of both and on the partnership between them, though it was many years later before I fully realized the depths and implications of what I had been shown. And I'm quite sure that there's much more that I have yet to learn and understand.

My work for the past fifty years since that vision has largely been in service to it. For the past fifteen years in particular, through the instrumentality of Incarnational Spirituality, I've been trying to give form and substance to the promise that vision held. It was—and is—above all a vision of who and what we are and of what we can become as generative sources of blessing for ourselves, for each other, and for the world as a whole.

It is a vision of the Self as partner and ally: partnering with others, partnering with the world, partnering with spirit, and most importantly, partnering inwardly with the different components of this Self. It is a vision of the energy systems and fields that such partnerships co-create and the capacities of these fields for blessing as well.

Incarnational Spirituality and the study and exploration of incarnation itself is rich and filled with potential beyond the capacities of one person to explicate or articulate. That is why this text is really just a compilation of my initial "field notes" arising from this exploration. Nothing here is cast in concrete nor should anything I've said be taken as "revelation" from "on High."

The most important research and exploration is what you conduct in the uniqueness of your own life and circumstances. You are your own laboratory for investigating the principles of IS. You are the living incarnation; this text is just words on a page. If the words open up a pathway that you can follow into the richness and depth of your own self—a "mysticism of the ordinary, a mysticism of the self"—then they have served their rightful purpose to be a beginning and not an ending.

There is much we haven't discussed that is part of Incarnational Spirituality such as the nature of the subtle worlds and partnering with subtle allies, Energy Hygiene, the Sacred Interiority, "Home" and hospitality, Gaian Consciousness, and Gaian (or Subtle) Activism. There is more that could be said about the application of Incarnational Spirituality principles in the arts of manifestation and blessing, as well. All these and more are covered in the Lorian Association's Path of the Chalice program.

But the material in this text is the foundation for all that follows. It is the heart of Incarnational Spirituality. It is the core presentation of the idea that we incarnate not simply into a body but into a complex, interactive, relational incarnational system which supports our emergence as a new form of Soul. Everything else builds on this idea and the experience of our partnering, generative, sovereign, holopoietic Self, our incarnational "star" on earth.

Here's a final observation that perhaps should be inserted elsewhere in the text, but I'll put it here for now. It's something that occurred to me as I was resting this afternoon.

In the text, I refer to both the "incarnational system" and the "incarnational field," the latter being in effect the result of the former. Plus I talk about our personal energy field, or aura, and our various subtle bodies.

I got to thinking that all these fields and subtle energies could be confusing and that some final statement might be useful in helping distinguish them.

What I mean by the incarnational system is a set of connections and relationships—symbolized for most of the text by the for icons of Transpersonal, World, Personal, and Humanity. These are the collectives or the spheres of consciousness in the case of the soul and the body/personality of which we are a part. As I mentioned above, there are actually a great many connections and relationships with a variety of subtle beings and forces that help co-created and maintain our incarnation, but most of them would fall, I think, into one or another of these four iconographic categories.

At any rate, the Incarnational System is a dynamic process, an activity taking place between these various connections, like a wiring circuit along which electricity flows. And the product of its activity is a field which can sets up boundaries and can hold the identity and overall energy of the incarnation.

This field is what I call the incarnational field, and it includes a host of subsidiary fields such as our body and its etheric matrix, our personal energy field, our aura, our relational field, our subtle bodies, and so forth.

Incoherency in the incarnational system creates surges of energy or blockages of energy which then the incarnational field and its subsidiaries have to deal with in one way or another.

Really, these two things, the incarnational system and the incarnational field blend and mesh together in intimate ways so it's not always easy to differentiate them, but here's a metaphor from the world of electricity. If I connect a wire between two points, I've created a system. If I run electricity through that wire, a magnetic field will come into being around the wire. The flow of the electricity creates a field.

The flow of life, love, energy, soul, thoughts, feelings, etc. along the many connections that make up the incarnational system—the many "wires" and their connections—then generates the incarnational field which in turn becomes the chalice that holds the presence of soul, among other things. What's neat about this is that we as conscious, mindful individuals can give attention and love and intention to any of the connections that make up the system and thereby increase the flow which augments and enhances the field. One of the generative products of this field is what I call our Self-Light.

Blessings.


# Publications by David Spangler

*An Introduction to Incarnational Spirituality*
*Apprenticed to Spirit*
*Call of the World*
*Subtle Worlds: An Explorer's Field Notes*
*Facing the Future*
*Blessing: The Art and the Practice*
*World Work*
*Crafting Home: Generating the Sacred*
*Crafting Relationships: The Holding of Others*
*The Call*
*Parent as Mystic—Mystic as Parent*
*Everyday Miracles*
*The Laws of Manifestation*
*The Story Tree*
*The Flame of Incarnation*
*World Work*
*Crafting Home: Generating the Sacred*
*Crafting Relationships: The Holding of Others*
*Midsummer's Journey with the Sidhe*
*The Soul's Oracle* (Card Deck and Manual)
*Card Deck of the Sidhe* (Card Deck and Manual)
*Manifestation: Creating the life you love* (Card Deck and Manual)